HISTORIC LANDMARKS

OF THE

DECCAN

HISTORIC LANDMARKS

OF THE

DECCAN

MAJOR T. W. HAIG

GYAN

Published by

Gyan Publishing House
5, Ansari Road
Daryaganj, New Delhi-110002
Phone: 011-47034999, 9811692060
E-mail: books@gyanbooks.com

Distribution Network
gyanbooks.com
India, USA, Canada, UK, Australia, France

ISBN: 978-81-212-8878-1 (PB)
First Published, 1907

2nd Impression 2023

Printed at: Gyan Press, Delhi.

HISTORIC LANDMARKS OF THE DECCAN
AUTHOR: MAJOR T. W. HAIG

HISTORIC LANDMARKS

OF THE

DECCAN

BY

MAJOR T. W. HAIG

OF HIS MAJESTY'S INDIAN ARMY; A POLITICAL AGENT UNDER THE FOREIGN DEPARTMENT OF THE GOVERNMENT OF INDIA.

PRINTED AT THE PIONEER PRESS

ALLAHABAD

1907

PREFACE.

The chapters of this book are chiefly historical and descriptive accounts of places famous in the history of the Deccan. The list of places so described is by no means exhaustive, for I have not attempted to describe any locality which I have not visited. This limitation must be accepted as my excuse for not having devoted chapters to such places as Bijapur and Ahmadnagar.

It is unfortunate that no good history of the Deccan under its Muhammadan rulers exists in the English language. That history is not, as one writer* remarks, "useless and inexpressibly tedious," but is full of interest, romance, and practical utility to the student of Indian history. From its romantic side it has been treated, merely as romance, by the most widely-read of Anglo-Indian novelists. Briggs and others have attempted to treat it more seriously, but their writings are chiefly uncritical translations of a single author whose work contains many inaccuracies and unexplained discrepancies. The latest *réchauffé*† of these translations is even more misleading than the work upon which it is based. Great advances have now been made in epigraphy and numismatics and various manuscript histories of the dynasties of the Deccan are accessible to the student, and these furnish ample materials for a detailed and critical history of the Deccan.

One of the most repellent features of works on oriental history consists in the confusing and apparently uncouth names and titles of historical personages. To remove confusion I have added as an appendix to this book a table containing lists of the dynasties in any way connected with the Deccan. For the dynastic lists of Vijayanagar I am indebted to Mr. Sewell's most valuable work "A Forgotten Empire" and for one or two other lists to "The Chronology of India" by C. Mabel Duff, but most of the lists are from original sources.

---

* Mr. Talboys Wheeler.

† J. D. B. Gribble's "History of the Deccan."

Most of the chapters of this book have appeared from time to time in the *Pioneer*, to the proprietors of which journal my best thanks are due for their courteous permission to republish them The chapters on Daulatabad and the siege of Golconda appeared in *East and West*, and I am indebted to the courtesy of Mr. B. M. Malabari for permission to republish these.

T. W. H.

CONTENTS.

CHAPTER I.

INTRODUCTORY.

I PROPOSE to give in this introductory chapter an outline of the history of the Deccan, slight indeed, but sufficient to supply the links necessary to connect the following accounts of places famous in story. Incidents fully described in the following chapters will here receive but slight notice, while important crises or events without a knowledge of which the history of southern India cannot be fully understood, but which are not part of the local history of any of the places of which accounts appear hereafter, will be more fully described.

The period which this sketch will embrace begins in 1294, in which year the Muhammadans first appeared in the Deccan. Our knowledge of the Deccan before this period is chiefly confined to the dry bones of history and has been most admirably summarised by Dr. Bhandarkar in his scholarly work.* This knowledge is not likely to be expanded otherwise than by the labours of the epigraphist and the numismatist, who have still much to do in the Deccan, for the mediæval Hindu failed conspicuously as a historian.

An account of Ala-ud-din Khalji's daring raid into the Deccan will be found in the following chapter. At the time when he surprised Devagiri or Deogir, then the northernmost kingdom of that part of India which had not been either overrun or threatened by Muhammadan invaders, three kingdoms existed in the Deccan and the Peninsula. Immediately to the south of the Satpuras lay Deogir, which was probably bounded on the south-east by the line which divides the ethnographical divisions of Maharashtra and Telingana, that is to say, a line running in a south-westerly direction from a point near the south-eastern corner of Berar towards Gulbarga. The western limit of this kingdom has not been ascertained, but it may have extended at times to the sea, though it is probable that the petty chiefs of the Konkan and the Western Ghats maintained, as a rule, a rude independence. The kingdom of Warangal or Telingana adjoined Deogir on the south-east, extended

* *Early History of the Dekkan down to the Mahomedan Conquest,* Bombay 1895.

to the sea on the east, and on the west at least as far as Raichur. Its southern boundary was probably formed by the Tungabhadra and Krishna rivers to within about a hundred miles of the sea, when it took a south-easterly direction and met the coast at a point to the south of Motupalli. To the south of Warangal lay the kingdom of Dvaravatipura or Dhorasamudra, the ruins of which city still exist at Halebid in the Mysore State. This kingdom was governed by the Hoysala dynasty, a branch of which, the Yadavas of Deogir, governed the northernmost kingdom. Warangal was under the sway of a dynasty known as the Kạkatiyas.

Ala-ud-din, on his return from his raid into the Deccan, murdered his uncle, Jalal-ud-din Firuz Shah Khalji, and ascended the throne of Delhi on October 26th, 1296. The sequence of expeditions from Delhi against Deogir and Warangal is given in the accounts of those places. In 1318 the kingdom of Deogir was finally annexed to Delhi, and in 1325 Telingana was annexed, and the whole of the Deccan was thus brought under the sway of the Muhammadans.

The empire had now reached dimensions which rendered efficient administration by one central controlling authority difficult, if not impossible; and disintegrating influences were at work. The ferocious tyranny of Muhammad bin Tughlaq, the second emperor of the house of Tughlaq, drove his subjects to rebellion in all quarters of the empire. In 1346 the *amirs* of the Deccan, who had for some time been disaffected, were summoned by the emperor to aid him in suppressing a rebellion in Gujarat. They set out on their journey in obedience to the summons, but had hardly left Daulatabad * when they began to suspect that the summons was a mere pretext, and that Muhammad's real object in sending for them was to mete out to them, for their past delinquencies, the cruel punishment which he was wont to inflict on the disaffected and the disobedient. They slew the officers who had been sent to summon them and returned to Daulatabad, where they imprisoned the imperial governor and elected one of their own members, Ismail Fath † the Afghan, king of the Deccan under the title of Nasir-ud-din Shah. The emperor immediately marched into the Deccan and laid siege

* Deogir had been renamed Daulatabad by Muhammad bin Tughlaq.

† Another reading is *Mugh*.

to Daulatabad, but before he could reduce the place he was recalled to Gujarat by the turn which affairs had taken in that province. The rebellious *amirs* had little difficulty in overpowering the force which he left to carry on the siege of Daulatabad, and the Deccan was independent of Delhi. Ismail the Afghan, an aged man, had little taste for the cares of government and voluntarily resigned the crown which had been placed on his head. In his place the *amirs* elected as their king Hasan Gangu, entitled Zafar Khan, an energetic soldier who had taken a prominent part in the rebellion. Hasan claimed descent from the hero Bahman, the son of Isfandiyar, and on ascending the throne of the Deccan on August 4th,* 1347, assumed the title of Ala-ud-din Bahman Shah,† and chose Gulbarga, where he had held a *jagir* from Muhammad bin Tughlaq, as the capital of the new kingdom.

The boundaries of Bahman Shah's dominions were the Tapti on the north and the Tungabhadra and the Krishna on the south. On the east and west the boundary varied with the power and warlike spirit of the petty Hindu chieftains of Urisa and Telingana on the one hand and of the Konkan and the Western Ghats on the other, but it was not until near the end of the fifteenth century, during the reign of Muhammad III, the thirteenth king of the dynasty, that the kingdom stretched from sea to sea.

The history of the Bahmani dynasty, so named from the title assumed by its founder, is largely the history of fierce warfare with the Hindu empire of Vijayanagar, which arose on the ruins of the kingdoms of Warangal and Dhorasamudra during the troubles of the later years of the reign of Muhammad bin Tughlaq. A detailed account of this warfare will be found in Chapter IV, which contains an account of the Raichur Duab, or the land lying between the Krishna and the Tungabhadra, always a fruitful source of strife.

The wars with Vijayanagar were varied by expeditions against the Hindu chiefs of Telingana and Urisa, and the petty rajas in the Western Ghats, and occasionally the Bahmanis found themselves at war with the Muhammadan Sultans of Gujarat, Khandesh and Malwa, or the Gond rulers of Kherla, but these hostilities were merely inter-

* December 4th according to another authority.

† Not, as is usually stated by historians, *Ala-ud-din Hasan Gangu Bahmani.* Vide *Journal of the Asiatic Society of Bengal*, Vol. LXXIII, Part I, extra number 1904.

ludes in the long period of warfare with the great Hindu empire which, though frequently defeated, was never entirely crushed by the Bahmanis. That task was reserved for a confederation of the rulers of the independent Muhammadan states which sprung into existence on the disintegration of the Bahmani Kingdom.

Ala-ud-din Bahman Shah divided his kingdom into four *tarafs* or provinces, Gulbarga, Daulatabad, Berar, and Bidar, appointing to each a governor whose powers were almost regal. Each maintained an army and made all civil and military appointments in his province, and it is strange that rebellion was not more frequent. This was checked by frequent royal tours in the provinces and by the regular employment of the provincial armies, under the king's command, in the campaigns against Vijayanagar.

In 1428 Ahmad Shah Wali, the ninth king of the Bahmani dynasty moved the capital of the kingdom from Gulbarga to Bidar.

One of the principal features of politics in the reigns of the later Bahmani kings was the perpetual strife between the Deccani and the "Foreign" nobles, which first became acute about the middle of the fifteenth century in the reign of Ala-ud-din Ahmad Shah II, the tenth king of the dynasty, and continued as long as any independent kingdom existed in the Deccan. It was the custom of the Bahmani kings to employ adventurers freely in their army. These strangers were chiefly fair-skinned foreigners from Persia, Arabia, and Central Asia, bold, energetic, and enterprising, who brought with them followers of their own race. They were employed as a rule, in preference to the less active and hardy Deccanis, in all difficult enterprises, and seldom failed to acquit themselves well. Many rose to the highest offices in the state, to the prejudice of the native Deccani, who found himself outstripped by the stranger at the council board as well as in the field. The success of the foreigners was, naturally enough, distasteful to the native-born Indians, and led to recriminations and quarrels, and at length to bloodshed; the Deccanis, as the aggrieved party, being the first aggressors. The ill-feeling between the parties was accentuated by religious differences, for large numbers of the foreigners were of the Shiah sect, while the Deccanis were generally orthodox Sunnis. It was probably for this reason that one class of foreigners ranged themselves on the side of the Deccanis. These were the Africans of whom large numbers were employed. They were, with few exceptions, Sunnis, and it may be surmised that the dark-skinned, unlettered, and unprepossessing African was at a disadvantage beside the fair, handsome, and cultured man of the north, and that this cause, as well as difference of religion, had the effect of throwing the Africans and the Deccanis together. When, therefore, the feuds between the Deccanis and the foreigners are mentioned, it must be understood that the parties consisted of the Deccanis and the Africans on the one side and the Turks, Arabs and Persians on the other. Ill-feeling between the two parties probably existed from the earliest days of the Bahmani kingdom, but it was not until a century had elapsed that it led to open violence.

When Berar was invaded in 1437-38 by Nasír Khan of Khandesh the foreigners under Khalaf Hasan Basri were employed in the field against the invader, the Deccanis being relegated to garrison duty. The foreigners drove Nasír Khan out of Berar, invaded Khandesh, and plundered its capital, and were received, on their return, with great honour. Khalaf Hasan received the title of Malik-ut-Tujjar, or "chief of the merchants" which was highly esteemed by the foreigners, whose first visit to the Deccan was usually in the capacity of merchants; another foreign noble, Shah Quli Sultan, received the king's daughter in marriage, and it was ordered that the foreigners should thenceforward ride on the King's right in royal progresses, and stand on his right in *Darbar*, the place on the left being assigned to the Deccanis and Africans. These orders caused grave discontent and the Deccanis sought occasion to overthrow the foreigners. Their opportunity came in 1546, when Khalaf Hasan was sent with an expeditionary force consisting of 7,000 Deccani and 3,000 Arab horse into the Konkan. There he trusted too readily to the promises of a petty chief named Sirka, who feigned submission and professed himself ready to accept Islam. Sirka then proffered his services as a guide in the difficult passes of the Western Ghats and offered to conduct the army in safety to the stronghold of the contumacious raja of Sangameshwar. The offer was accepted, and Sirka treacherously led the force into an ambush, where Khalaf Hasan and most of the foreign officers and troops with him were slain. The Deccani officers had held back, and thus escaped and fled to Chakan, near Junnar, which Khalaf Hasan had made his base. The few foreigners who escaped also returned to Chakan, and attempted to send thence a message to court, to inform Ala-ud-din Ahmad Shah that the disaster had been due to the pusillanimity of the Deccanis; but the Deccanis intercepted this message and sent another to the effect that the foreigners, having suffered defeat owing to their own rashness, had now retired in dudgeon to Chakan, where they had rebelled, and were prepared to hold the fort against any force that might be sent against them. Unfortunately the Deccanis were at this time all powerful at the capital, and persuaded the king to send an army against Chakan. The Deccanis and Africans besieged the place for some time with little prospect of success, and, fearing lest delay might bring the truth to light, changed their tactics, and informed the foreigners that they had interceded for them at court and that the king had been graciously pleased to pardon them. The unsuspecting foreigners came forth, and at a banquet to which they were invited by their enemies 1,200 Sayyids and 1,000 other foreigners were slain.

A few foreigners who, with great difficulty, effected their escape, succeeded in conveying to the king a true account of what had taken place, and inquiries were set on foot, with the result that the whole truth became known and the Deccanis and Africans were severely punished and the foreigners regained their ascendency.

These quarrels constantly broke out afresh, and the bitterness between the parties had lost none of its strength in the reign of Muhammad III, the thirteenth king of the Bahmani dynasty. His chief nobles were Khaja Mahmud Gawan Malik-ut-Tujjar, the prime minister, Yusuf Adil Khan, and Fakhr-ul-Mulk, all foreigners; Fathullah Imad-ul-Mulk, Malik Hasan Nizam-ul-Mulk, and his son Malik Ahmad, Deccanis; and Khudawand Khan and Dastur Dinar, Africans. Muhammad III, who was then encamped in Telingana, on the advice of Mahmud Gawan sub-divided into eight the four provinces into which the kingdom had originally been divided by his ancestor, Bahman Shah. Berar was divided into the two provinces of Gawil and Mahur; Daulatabad into Daulatabad and Junnar; Gulbarga into Gulbarga and Bijapur; and Telingana into Warangal and Rajamahendri; while the country around

Bidar remained under the administration of a selected noble at court. The result of this measure is described in Chapter IV. Malik Hasan Nizam-ul-Mulk, who had been governor of the whole of Telingana, was mortally offended by the division of his province, and, as will be seen, plotted with other Deccanis and Africans to bring about the downfall of Khaja Mahmud, and succeeded in compassing his death. The unjust execution of the greatest statesman who had ever served a Bahmani king excited distrust and unrest even among many of the Deccanis and Africans. The foreigners who had been in the service of the murdered minister fled for protection to Yusuf Adil Khan, and the foreign troops and officers in the other provincial armies followed their example. Yusuf thus became the most powerful *amir* in the kingdom. Fathullah Imad-ul-Mulk, the Deccani governor of Gawil, and Khudawand Khan, the African governor of Mahur, withdrew from the royal camp with the army of Berar, and, when ordered to return, excused themselves by saying that if the death of so great a man as Khaja Mahmud could be so easily compassed by slanderers they did not know what to expect. Muhammad Shah then tried persuasion, but to no purpose. They would return, they said, when Yusuf Adil Khan, who was then on service in southern Telingana, returned. Muhammad Shah therefore recalled Yusuf, who, on his return, at once joined Imad-ul-Mulk and Khudawand Khan, and these three *tarafdars* united to press their demands on the king. The first was that Yusuf should receive the late minister's province of Bijapur, to the government of which he was appointed. Here he was enabled to provide for all the foreign nobles and officers who had rallied round him on the death of Khaja Mahmud. A redistribution of appointments had become necessary and the Deccanis could not be entirely overlooked. Hasan Nizam-ul-mulk, who richly deserved death, was made minister, and another Deccani *amir* with the title of Nizam-ul-Mulk was appointed to the government of Daulatabad, rendered vacant by the transfer of Yusuf Adil Khan to Bijapur; Imad-ul-Mulk and Khudawand Khan retained the provinces of Gawil and Mahur, Dastur Dinar retained Gulbarga, and two Turki slaves who had joined the conspiracy of Hasan Nizam-ul-Mulk against Mahmud Gawan, Qivam-ul-Mulk, the elder and Qivam-ul-Mulk the younger, were appointed to the government of Warangal and

Rajamahendri respectively. Muhammad Shah then marched with his troops from Kondapalli to Bidar, but the *tarafdars*, who had lost all confidence in him since his appointment of Hasan Nizam-ul-Mulk to the post rendered vacant by the death of his victim, refused to enter the capital and encamped without the walls with their forces. The king was much humbled by this mark of mistrust, but dared not command them to enter the city and, with the best grace he could muster, dismissed Yusuf Adil Khan, Fathullah Imad-ul-Mulk, and Khudawand Khan to their provinces.

Meanwhile Hasan Nizam-ul-Mulk remained at the capital, doing his best to compass the ruin of the three refractory *tarafdars*. They were summoned to the capital with their armies in order to accompany the king on an expedition in the direction of Belgaum, but showed by their behaviour in camp and on the march that they were able to protect themselves, and that they had no intention of trusting either the king or his minister. They would not encamp in the neighbourhood of the royal troops nor march in their company, and invariably saluted the king from afar. After a short time Imad-ul-Mulk and Khudawand Khan returned to their provinces without leave, an act which would have been deemed open rebellion by any of the king's predecessors, and Muhammad Shah gave himself up to the delights of the wine-cup in Firuzabad.

On March 23rd, 1482, Muhammad III died, and was succeeded by his son Mahmud Shah, a lad of twelve years of age. We have already seen the condition of the kingdom in the closing years of Muhammad's reign. It was not such that it could be remedied by a youth, and it speedily went from bad to worse. The great nobles present in the capital at the time of Mahmud's accession were the minister, Hasan Nizam-ul-Mulk, Qivam-ul-Mulk the elder, and Qivam-ul-Mulk the younger who, though foreigners, believed that they had won the regard of the Deccanis, and Qasim Barid, a foreigner, who, for reasons of his own, one of which was probably hatred of Yusuf Adil Khan and another, probably, attachment to the Sunni faith, often identified himself with the Deccanis. The coronation was hurried on, and though there were some complaints that the greater *tarafdars* and the foreign nobles from Bijapur were not allowed time to attend, Hasan

Nizam-ul-Mulk allayed local irritation by explaining that it was impolitic to postpone the public recognition of Mahmud's accession, and that the *amirs* in the provinces could have another *darbar* assembled and arrange among themselves how they would divide the grants of titles and *jagirs* customary on the occasion of a coronation. Similarly all the Deccanis and African officials present in Bidar at the time endeavoured, by every means in their power, to conciliate the foreigners and to remove their apprehension.

Yusuf Adil Khan of Bijapur and Fakhr-ul-Mulk of Junnar were the first of the *tarafdars* to arrive at court. They encamped with their troops before Bidar more after the fashion of a hostile army intent on besieging the place than as vassals come to pay homage, for Hasan Nizam-ul-Mulk, who loved them not, was supreme in the city, and caution was necessary. When Yusuf Adil Khan entered Bidar to pay his respects to his sovereign he took with him his most trusted officers and a thousand picked troops, fully armed, two hundred of whom he took with him, in defiance of the etiquette of the court, inside the palace. He found that Hasan had five hundred of his men within the palace walls, but went on without fear. After making his obeisance Yusuf, as his custom was, took his place on the right of the throne, above all the other *amirs*, and carefully watched Hasan Nizam-ul-Mulk, at the same time setting Darya Khan, one of his officers, to watch Hasan's son, and to be in readiness to cut him down in case Hasan's Deccanis should make a movement. When the *darbar* was dismissed Yusuf took Hasan's hand and thus walked with him to the gate of the palace, as though in friendly converse, but in fact prepared to slay him at the first sign of any disturbance. On the following day Hasan Nizam-ul-Mulk waited on Yusuf Adil Khan and suggested that he and the other foreign *amirs* should lodge within the city walls. Yusuf, with expressions of friendship and a veiled threat, declined the invitation, but at the same time declared that he had no desire to interfere in the civil administration of the kingdom. It was agreed that Hasan Nizam-ul-Mulk should be regent, that Qivam-ul-Mulk the elder should be prime minister, as well as *tarafdar* of Warangal, that Qivam-ul-Mulk the younger, the *tarafdar* of Rajamahendri, should be associated with him, and that Dilawar Khan, the African, should command the royal forces. After this the Deccanis and the foreigners dwelt for some time in apparent amity, but the former had no intention of allowing the latter to have that share in the administration which they had promised to them and Hasan Nizam-ul-Mulk plotted with Qivam-ul-Mulk the elder to have Yusuf Adil Khan assassinated in order that Abdullah Adil Khan, the Deccani, Qivam-ul-Mulk's deputy in Warangal, might be appointed to the government of the province of Bijapur. In pursuance of this design Hasan Nizam-ul-Mulk issued *farmans* ordering the attendance of Adil Khan the Deccani and Fathullah Imad-ul-Mulk of Gawil at court. These two *amirs* came with their armies and Hasan felt himself strong enough to act, but as a measure of precaution persuaded his friend Qivam-ul-Mulk the elder to keep his foreign troops in their quarters on the day agreed upon for the massacre. Fathullah Imad-ul-Mulk was to lend a hand, and the arrangement was that his troops and those of Adil Khan, the Deccani, should defile past the Sultan, who would be seated on the battlements of his palace, and then fall on the foreigners. Qivam-ul-Mulk the elder, a simpleton who hated Yusuf Adil Khan and relied on the professed friendship of the crafty Brahman* Hasan Nizam-ul-Mulk, performed his part of the compact by preventing his troops from assisting their fellow foreigners, but though Hasan had thus thrown dust in the eyes of the Turk he had failed to conciliate a caste fellow†, and Fathullah Imad-ul-Mulk contrived that Yusuf Adil Khan, who had ever been his friend, should have sanctuary in the palace at the time when the plot was to be put into execution.

Hasan Nizam-ul-Mulk's plot was a failure. His miserable dupe, Qivam-ul-Mulk the elder and many of the foreign troops under his command were slain, but those of Yusuf's followers who were within the palace contrived to escape from the city, performing prodigies of valour, to give the alarm to the Turki troops encamped without the walls and to lead 10,000, or, according to another authority, 20,000 cavalry into the city. For no less than twenty days the city was a scene of conflict between Deccanis and foreigners, and at the end of this time a peace was patched up by the terms of which Yusuf Adil Khan

*Hasan Nizam-ul-Mulk was a Maratha Brahman of a family from Pathri domiciled in Vijayanagar who had been captured in boyhood and brought up as a Musalman.

†Fathullah Imad-ul-Mulk was a Brahman of Vijayanagar, whose history was similar to that of Hasan Nizam-ul-Mulk.

returned to his province while Hasan Nizam-ul-Mulk remained at Bidar, where he retained complete ascendance over the youthful king, and Imad-ul-Mulk was made prime minister, his son Ala-ud-din being sent to govern Gawil as his deputy. Imad-ul-Mulk was, however, no friend to the veteran intriguer Hasan, and soon returned to Berar with his troops.

In 1484 Hasan Nizam-ul-Mulk appointed himself to the government of the province of Junnar, and sent his son Malik Ahmad thither as his deputy. Ahmad appointed Vajih-ud-din and Sharaf-ud-din, two creatures of his own, to the government of Daulatabad, and Fakhr-ul-Mulk the Deccani, entitled Khaja-i-Jahan, to the government of Sholapur and Purenda. In 1486 Hasan Nizam-ul-Mulk was weakened by the death of Abdullah Adil Khan, the Deccani, at Warangal and Qivam-ul-Mulk the younger, of Rajamahendri, rose in rebellion and annexed Warangal to his own province. Hasan Nizam-ul-Mulk, taking Mahmud Shah with him marched on Warangal, and Qivam-ul-Mulk retreated to Rajamahendri whence he wrote a petition to Mahmud Shah complaining of the ascendency of Malik Hasan in the state. The petition fell, of course, into the hands of Hasan himself, and Qivam-ul-Mulk would have had little hope of redress had not a diversion been made in another corner of the kingdom. Hasan had no sooner arrived at Warangal than he received a report from his son Ahmad, then at Junnar, that affairs in the west of the kingdom were in a state of confusion. Bahadur Gilani, a servant of the lately deceased *jagirdar* of Goa, had possessed himself of his master's *jagir* and had extended his possessions to Dabhol on the north and Kolhapur on the east, and at the instigation of Yusuf Adil Khan was ravaging Chaul and other places in the province of Junnar. Malik Ahmad had called upon Zain-ud-din Ali, the *jagirdar* of Chakan, for assistance, but Zain-ud-din Ali had replied that the king was not his own master, but was in the hands of others, and that he would not obey commands until he was certain that they had been issued by the king himself of his own free will. Hasan Nizam-ul-Mulk ordered his son to deal first with Zain-ud-din Ali and sent orders to the governors of Parenda and Daulatabad to assist Malik Ahmad. Zain-ud-din Ali thereupon applied to Yusuf Adil Khan for help and Yusuf sent five or six thousand horse to Indapur with instructions to march against Malik

Ahmad should he advance on Chakan. When the news of Yusuf Adil Khan's action reached Warangal it caused a sudden fall of Hasan's prestige and Mahmud Shah appears to have realized that a minister whose order could be thus flouted by the provincial governors was but a broken reed. He turned to Qasim Barid and Dastur Dinar the African for advice, and finding them ready to profit by Hasan's downfall, ordered them to have him put to death. Hasan, on learning what had passed, fled from the royal camp at dead of night, but instead of joining his son at Junnar, entered Bidar with a view to securing the royal treasure. Here he persuaded the governor, Dilpasand Khan, a Deccani, to raise the standard of revolt and ordered Malik Ahmad to join him from Junnar. Mahmud Shah now made Sultan Quli Qutb-ul-Mulk, a Turk of a noble family of Hamadan, governor of Warangal, and marched with all speed on the capital. Hasan had no troops wherewith to withstand the royal army and, having secured the treasure, made preparations to flee to Junnar but Dilpasand Khan prevented him from carrying out this design and informed the king by a secret message that he was faithful and had merely feigned to fall in with Hasan's plans in order to detain him in Bidar and prevent him from joining his son. The king replied that he could readily prove his loyalty by sending him Hasan's head, and Dilpasand Khan after receiving this message, entered Hasan's chamber on pretence of taking counsel with him, strangled the hoary villain with his own hands, cut off his head, and sent it to the king. Mahmud Shah then returned to the capital, composed all disputes between the Deccanis and the foreigners, and gave promise of ruling well, but the temptations of the wine cup were too strong for him and he soon gave himself up to debauchery, leaving the affairs of the kingdom in the hands of the *amirs*. Disputes again arose between the two parties in the state, and in 1487 the Deccanis and the Africans entered into a plot against the king's life. A band of them entered the royal palace, and shutting the gates lest the foreign troops should come to the rescue, attempted to assassinate the king. The few foreign attendants with Mahmud Shah carried him to the *Shah Burj*, or royal bastion of the fort, and, all unarmed as they were, kept the traitors at bay. Thence they contrived to send a message to the foreign nobles in the city who brought up a few troops and rescued the king, but meanwhile the Deccanis and Africans plundered the houses of many foreigners in the city. In the morning Mahmud Shah gave orders for a general massacre of the Deccani and African troops. The slaughter lasted for three days, and was only checked at the instance of a holy man who was connected with the king by marriage.

After this escape Mahmud Shah gave himself up entirely to debauchery, leaving the management of affairs to Qasim Barid, the Turk. The great *tarafdars* grew weary of receiving orders which originated with this upstart, and from 1487 onwards were practically independent, while Qasim Barid himself, who had *jagirs* in the neighbourhood of Bidar, governed them without even the formality of using the king's name, which appeared only in *farmans* affecting unalienated lands in the province of Bidar, and in futile orders to the *tarafdars*.

It was not, however, till 1490 that the *tarafdars* openly declared themselves independent. In that year Malik Ahmad Nizam-ul-Mulk held the province of Daulatabad, Yusuf Adil Khan that of Bijapur, and Fathullah Imad-ul-Mulk that of Gawil, or northern Berar. Nizam-ul-Mulk was the first to propose that they should assume independence, and invited Yusuf Adil Khan, Fathullah Imad-ul-Mulk, and Sultan Quli Qutb-ul-Mulk of western Telingana to join him. The two first named agreed and, together with Nizam-ul-Mulk, assumed the insignia of royalty, but Qutb-ul-Mulk would not openly defy his master, and refused to declare himself independent. Twenty-two years later, in 1512, he found it impossible to maintain even the pretence of dependence, and followed the example of the other *tarafdars*.

The three new kings, in spite of their having openly thrown off their old master's yoke, remained well disposed towards him, and were exceedingly chary of using the royal title. They protested that they were as loyal as ever to the descendant of Bahman Shah, but that they would not take orders from Qasim Barid. They made several abortive attempts to rescue Mahmud Shah from Qasim's clutches, but the miserable debauchee could never summmon up courage to give adequate support to those who would have helped him, and invariably relapsed into his old condition of subservience.

Qasim Barid died in 1508 and his son Amir Barid took his place, Mahmud Shah died on December 8, 1518, and Amir Barid raised his young son to the throne as Ahmad Shah III, fearing openly to usurp the crown. lest the *tarafdars* should unite in defence of the scion of the Bahmani line. Ahmad Shah died early in 1521, poisoned, it is supposed. by Amir Barid, and his next brother was raised to the throne as Ala-ud-din Shah III. This prince showed a disposition to assert his authority, and was therefore deposed by Amir Barid in 1523, and shortly afterwards put to death, his next brother, Wali-ullah, being raised to the throne. After a reign of two years he, likewise, was put to death and Kalim-ullah, the youngest brother* of Ahmad III, was placed on the throne. This prince privately wrote a letter to Babar, who had recently invaded Hindustan, imploring him to deliver the writer from the tyranny of Amir Barid. On this fact becoming known Kalim-ullah fled to Bijapur, where Ismail Adil Shah made an attempt to seize and imprison him. The young king then fled, with no more than eighteen horsemen, to Ahmadnagar, where he was at first well received by Burhan Nizam Shah. Later however, he was regarded as a dangerous guest, and Burhan, fearing lest the heir of the Bahmanis should excite the pity and the loyalty of the nobles and the army, placed him under surveillance. He died at Ahmadnagar in 1526 or 1527, poisoned, it is supposed, by order of Burhan Nizam Shah, and with him ended the Bahmani dynasty.

On the extinction of the Bahmanis Amir Barid assumed the royal title in Bidar. Sultan Quli Qutb-ul-Mulk had already, as we have seen, assumed it in Golconda in 1512. There were now, therefore, five independent Muhammadan kingdoms in the Deccan, Bijapur, the kingdom of the Adil Shahi kings; Ahmadnagar, that of the Nizam Shahis; Golconda, where the Qutb Shahi kings bore sway; Berar, ruled by the Imad Shahi kings; and Bidar, by the Barid Shahi kings. Of these the first three were large and powerful kingdoms, while the other two were comparatively insignificant. The story of the wars of these states is extremely complicated and has never been adequately described in English, though materials for the task are not wanting. Bijapur and Ahmadnagar were frequently at war, the frontier fortress of Sholapur being a fruitful source of strife between them. Golconda as a rule endeavoured to hold itself aloof from these quarrels, being engaged in the early days of the

* According to another account Kalim-ullah was the son of Ahmad III.

Qutb Shahi dynasty in reducing to obedience the Hindus of eastern Telingana, but was, nevertheless, sometimes drawn into the quarrel, and on such occasions pursued a policy of apparently purposeless vacillation. This line of conduct was, however, dictated by prudence. Having become involved in the quarrel the king of Golconda would support his ally up to a certain point, but, when it appeared probable that the assistance rendered would enable one belligerent utterly to crush the other, he either withdrew or changed sides, for the mainspring of the foreign policy of the Qutb Shahi dynasty was the maintenance of the balance of power, and the kings of that line were astute enough to perceive that if, by any mischance, the kingdoms of Bijapur and Ahmadnagar should be welded into one, the independence of Golconda, which was a slightly weaker state than either, was doomed.

Berar in these quarrels sided sometimes with Ahmadnagar and sometimes with Bijapur, until a particularly acrimonious dispute between Burhan Nizam Shah and Ala-ud-din Imad Shah concerning the possession of the town and district of Pathri, which were included in Berar but were the patrimony of Burhan's Brahman ancestors, threw the smaller kingdom into the arms of Bijapur. This dispute, which led to frequent wars between Berar and Ahmadnagar, went near to imperilling the existence of both kingdoms when Ala-ud-din Imad Shah in 1529 was so ill-advised as to invoke the aid of the ambitious Bahadur Shah of Gujarat, whose intervention gave him a foothold in the Deccan which seemed at one time likely to become permanent.

Throughout all this wrangling the little kingdom of Bidar fought for its own hand, allying itself now with one power or combination of powers and now with another. The craft and political acumen of its rulers preserved the little state intact for a longer period than might have been expected, though its preservation is partly to be attributed to the jealousy existing between the three kingdoms of Bijapur, Ahmadnagar and Golconda which was for a long time sufficiently strong to ensure the combination of two of the three against an attempt by any one of them to absorb Bidar. Amir Barid not only intrigued incessantly with all three, but also coquetted with the Hindu empire of Vijayanagar.

About the year 1550 Burhan Nizam Shah of Ahmadnagar, in the course of his disputes with Ibrahim Adil Shah I of Bijapur, set the evil example of entering into an alliance with Vijayanagar against a brother Muslim. The strength which he thus acquired enabled him to capture the fortress of Sholapur, and Ibrahim was compelled to make peace. The death of Burhan Nizam Shah, who was succeeded by his son Husain, gave Ibrahim an opportunity of detaching Vijayanagar from Ahmadnagar and of following Burhan's example by entering into an alliance with the Hindus. On Ibrahim's death his son Ali Adil Shah I maintained the alliance, and in 1564 he invaded the dominions of Husain Nizam Shah in company with Sadashivaraya of Vijayanagar. The Hindus committed great excesses in the Ahmadnagar state and Husain Nizam Shah, in order to prevent the further desecration of mosques, was compelled to make peace on his enemy's terms. Almost immediately afterwards, Ali Adil Shah again declared war and invaded the kingdom of Ahmadnagar with his Hindu ally. The Hindus again took the opportunity of insulting the Musalmans by destroying copies of the *Quran* and desecrating mosques, until heavy rain compelled the allies to retire on Sholapur. Ali Adil Shah's position was now one of considerable difficulty. The conduct of his Hindu allies had exasperated not only the enemy, but all Musalmans in the Deccan, including his own troops, and Sadashivaraya, having been virtually the arbiter between the two most powerful Musalman kingdoms in the Deccan, now began to assume the position of their overlord, and openly treated Ali Adil Shah as his vassal, and demanded and received from him and from Ibrahim Qutb Shah, who had pursued a vacillating policy throughout the war, important cessions of territory. Sadashivaraya's next act was to issue a notice to the Muhammadan Sultans informing them that in future they would not be allowed to sit in his presence. This was more than could be borne, and Ali Adil Shah, who was primarily responsible for the indignity offered to himself and his co-religionists, exerted himself to form a confederacy against his late ally, and had no difficulty in persuading Ibrahim Qutb Shah of Golconda, Husain Nizam Shah of Ahmadnagar, and Ali Barid Shah of Bidar to join him. The confederates marched from Bijapur at the end of 1564 and met the army of Vijayanagar on January 24, 1565, at Talikota, where Sadashivaraya was slain and the mighty empire of Vijayanagar was overthrown.

Berar had not joined the confederacy which overthrew the Hindu power at Talikota, and the Sultans of Bijapur and Ahmadnagar now invaded that kingdom to punish Tufal Khan, its ruler, for his defection. After ravaging the whole of south-western Berar the invaders retired in consideration of a heavy indemnity.

Tufal Khan was the minister of Burhan Imad Shah, the last king of the Imad Shahi dynasty, whom he treated as the Barids had treated the later kings of the Bahmani dynasty in Bidar. Burhan was imprisoned in the fortress of Narnala and Tufal Khan governed the kingdom with scarcely a pretence of subordination to his nominal king.

In 1572 Murtaza Nizam Shah I of Ahmadnagar invaded Berar, nominally for the purpose of restoring Burhan Imad Shah and freeing him from the influence of Tufal Khan, but really with the object of annexing the kingdom. Tufal Khan and his son Shamshir-ul-Mulk were defeated in the field and pursued until the former took refuge in Narnala and the latter in Gawilgarh. Both fortresses fell, and Tufal Khan with Burhan Imad Shah, who had been taken in Narnala, and Shamshir-ul-Mulk, who had surrendered at Gawilgarh on receiving an assurance that his life would be spared, were sent to a fortress in the Ahmadnagar kingdom where, in a short time, all were put to death Berar now became a part of the kingdom of Ahmadnagar and the number of the independent kingdoms of the Deccan was thus reduced to four.

Very soon after the annexation of Berar by Ahmadnagar the Mughals began to appear in the Deccan, and in 1596 Chand Bibi, the queen regent of Ahmadnagar, was forced to cede the province to Sultan Murad, the fourth son of the Emperor Akbar, in order to induce him to retire from the siege of Ahmadnagar. The hold of the Mughals on the province was, for a long time, precarious, and they were harrassed for many years by the famous Malik Ambar, who, posing as the champion of the decadent Nizam Shahi dynasty, succeeded in keeping the Mughals at bay until near the end of the reign of Jahangir. The northern invaders did not succeed in establishing themselves firmly in Berar and the Ahmadnagar kingdom until early in the reign of

Shahjahan, when, in 1633, Daulatabad was captured,' and Husain II, the last titular king of the Nizam Shahi dynasty, and Fath Khan, the son of Malik Ambar, were made prisoners. The latter entered the imperial service, but the former was sent, as a state prisoner, to Gwalior, where his companion in captivity was his cousin Bahadur Nizam Shah, who had been captured some thirty years before this time, on the fall of Ahmadnagar.

Meanwhile Ibrahim Adil Shah II of Bijapur had, in 1619, annexed the small kingdom of Bidar; and when Shahjahan, later in his reign, appointed his third son, Aurangzib, viceroy of the imperial province of the Deccan with his head-quarters at Malik Ambar's capital of Khirki now renamed Aurangabad, there remained, of the five original kingdoms of the Deccan, only two, Bijapur and Golconda. In 1656 Aurangzib wrested Bidar from Bijapur and well nigh succeeded in taking Golconda, whence he was recalled by peremptory orders from Delhi. Two years later he was called northwards by the sickness of his father, and the evident intention of his brothers to maintain by force of arms their claims to the throne.

Some years later Aurangzib, now emperor of India, returned to the Deccan. His first objective was Bijapur, and that city fell in 1686, its young king, Sikandar Adil Shah, being sent into captivity at Daulatabad. Golconda fell, after a siege of eight months, in the following year, and Abul Hasan Qutb Shah, the last king of the Qutb Shahi dynasty, was sent to bear Sikandar company in Daulatabad.

The Mughal empire, now at its greatest extent, soon began to show signs of decay. The power of the Marathas was rising and their activity and influence increased during the fratricidal wars which followed the death of Aurangzib in 1707, and during the confusion which for the next twenty years prevailed at Delhi.

In 1724 a faction in Delhi incited Mubariz Khan, *subahdar* of Haidarabad, to attack Asaf Jah Nizam-ul-Mulk, *subahdar* of Malwa, promising him, as a reward in the event of success, the viceroyalty of the whole of the Deccan. Mubariz Khan, though a personal friend of Asaf Jah, was unable to withstand this temptation, and marched northwards to meet him. Asaf Jah, though he marched southwards into the Deccan and occupied Daulatabad, did his best to dissuade Mubariz Khan from breaking the peace, but Mubariz Khan refused to listen to his counsels and pressed onwards. His plan was to turn Asaf Jah's flank and thus interpose his army between Delhi and Asaf Jah. This movement nearly succeeded, but not quite, and though Mubariz Khan passed Asaf Jah the latter turned and overtook him at Shakarkhelda in the present Buldana district of Berar, where, in October 1724, a battle was fought in which Mubariz Khan was defeated and slain. Asaf Jah renamed the village Fathkhelda, to commemorate his victory, and took possession of the prize of the war, the viceroyalty of the Deccan. The present representative of his line is Mir Sir Mahbub Ali Khan Bahadur, Nizam of Haidarabad

The Nizams of Haidarabad never paid more than a nominal allegiance to Delhi, and the progress of the Maratha power, which drove a wedge between Hindustan and the Deccan, separated them entirely from northern India. Their wars with the Marathas, the part which they took in the struggle between the British and the French for supremacy in India, and later, in the wars against Haidar Ali of Mysore and his son Tipu Sultan, and their loyalty to the British Government in the dark days of 1857 are passages of history too well known to call for detailed treatment here.

CHAPTER II.

A FORMER CAPITAL OF INDIA.

TOWARDS the end of the twelfth century of the Christian era the Chalukyan dynasty of southern India, once overthrown and again restored, only to totter gradually to its fall, was blotted out, and its dominions, after being the prey of various petty chieftains, were united under the Yadavas, a dynasty of which the elder branch, the Hoysala Yadavas, ruled for many years at Dvaravatipura or Dhorasamudra, the ruins of which are to be found at Halebid, in the Hassan district of the Mysore State. The Yadava race was represented in the northern Deccan by Bhillama, a famous warrior who, after a severe struggle with his kinsmen in the south, established his rule throughout Maharashtra and extended his dominions southwards to the Krishna. In 1187 Bhillama founded Devagiri or Deogir and made it his capital. Here he and his descendants reigned, not ingloriously, for a century, in the course of which period they succeeded in adding Malwa to their dominions. In 1271 Ramachandra, styled Ramdeo by Muhammadan historians, the fifth in descent from Bhillama, ascended the throne in Deogir, and early in 1290, while Ramdeo was ruling at Deogir Jalal-ud-din Firuz founded the Khalji dynasty at Delhi. The Deccan was at this time no more than a name to the Musalmans of Northern India. The Arabs had long been engaged in maritime trade with the inhabitants of the Malabar coast, and Muhammadan emperors had for a century held sway over the Punjab and Hindustan, and had overrun Bengal, but no Muhammadan from the north had yet crossed the Vindhyan range or penetrated the forests of Gondwana.

Jalal-ud-din Firuz, who was an aged man when he was raised to the throne of Delhi, had a nephew, Ala-ud-din Muhammad, who was also his son-in-law, and whom the old emperor treated rather as a son than as nephew, slighting the advice of his counsellors who descried in the younger man's restless and ambitious disposition danger to the prospect of the peaceful descent of the crown to the natural heir. Ala-ud-din's ambition was stimulated by an unhappy marriage. The cousin whom he had married was a termagant, and his domestic troubles were accentuated by the interference of his mother-in-law, the Malika-i-Jahan, who espoused her daughter's cause and supported her in her opposition to her husband. Relations became so strained that the prince feared that his mother-in-law, who had great influence over her husband, the emperor, would contrive to compass his death. Ala-ud-din was at this time governor of the province of which Karra, on the Ganges, 42 miles north-west of Allahabad, was the capital. There he consulted with friends as to how he could best raise an army sufficiently strong to enable him to found a kingdom for himself in some strange land beyond the emperor's dominions, where he could forget his domestic troubles and be secure from the designs of the Malika-i-Jahan. To assemble a large army without the emperor's knowledge was impossible, and as a large army was necessary to the execution of his design, Ala-ud-din had recourse to artifice. He represented to the emperor that the safety of the empire required that Chanderi should be subdued, and asked for and obtained permission to undertake the task. He marched from Karra in 1294, keeping the real object of his expedition a secret even from his own troops. He had already heard, during an expedition to Bhilsa, vague rumours of the great wealth of the Rajas of Deogir, and resolved to attack that place. Passing through Chanderi he advanced southwards and arrived, after a march of two months' duration, at Ellichpur. Here he halted for a short time to rest his troops, and explained his presence by saying that he was one of the nobles of Delhi who was leaving the imperial service and wished to enter that of the Raja of Rajamahendri in Telingana. He then left Ellichpur by night and pressed on by forced marches towards Deogir. Fortune favoured his enterprise, and it so happened that Deogir was at this time almost denuded of troops, the army having accompanied the Raja's eldest son, Shankar Deo, who had gone on a pilgrimage. Ala-ud-din advanced as far as Lasura, about twelve miles from Deogir, without meeting with any opposition. Meanwhile Ramdeo, who had heard of the approach of the invader, had contrived to collect two or three thousand men and to despatch them to Lasura to stay his progress. This small force was easily defeated by the Muhammadan army and was pursued to the gates of Deogir. The Raja took refuge in the citadel, then a place of no strength and undefended even by a ditch. The small garrison was hastily provisioned with some merchandise in sacks, which had been brought by merchants from the Konkan, and abandoned where it lay when they fled on hearing of the approach of the stranger; but the sacks contained salt, not grain. Ala-ud-din meanwhile captured the Brahmans and principal merchants of Deogir and plundered the city, giving out that his troops were no more than the advance-guard of an army of 20,000 Musalmans, which was following him. Ramdeo was now seriously alarmed and opened negotiations with Ala-ud-din. He pointed out to him that the army of Deogir would soon return to the capital and would annihilate the invaders, and that if any escaped they would certainly be cut off by the Rajas of Malwa, Khandesh and Gondwana. Ala-ud-din, who was well aware of the perilous nature of his enterprise, agreed to depart within a fortnight, holding his captives meanwhile as a guarantee for a ransom of 50 maunds of gold, several maunds of pearls, and some valuable stuffs, in addition to 40 elephants, some thousands of horses, and the plunder which he had already collected from the city. In the meantime, Shankar Deo had heard of his father's plight and was returning to the city by forced marches. The treaty had just been concluded when news arrived that he was within six miles of Deogir. Ramdeo sent a message to his son, ordering him not to attack the "Turks," who were terrible men, as he had just concluded a treaty with them. Shankar Deo, whose army outnumbered that of the invaders by two to one, disregarded his father's orders and sent a message to Ala-ud-din ordering him to restore all the plunder that he had taken and leave the kingdom. Ala-ud-din disgraced the messengers by parading them through his camp with their faces blackened, and then, leaving Malik Nusrat with a thousand men to watch Deogir, marched against Shankar Deo. The fight was fiercely contested, and the Musalmans were on the point of retiring, when Malik Nusrat left Deogir without orders and came to his leader's assistance. The Hindus, seeing a fresh force of Musalmans, believed it to be the army of 20,000 horse of which Ala-ud-din had spoken, and broke and fled. Ala-ud-din then returned to the siege of the citadel, put his captives to death, and paraded a number of Ram Deo's relatives, who had been captured in the battle, in chains before the fortress. Ram Deo was on the point of applying for assistance to the neighbouring Hindu chieftains when the sacks of salt were opened and it was discovered that the garrison was absolutely without provisions. The Raja was thus forced to re-open negotiations on terms much less favourable than those which he had first obtained. Ala-ud-din inferred from his anxiety for peace that the garrison was hard pressed, and resolved to make the Hindus suffer for their breach of faith. He now insisted on a ransom of 600 maunds of gold, 7 maunds of pearls, 2 maunds of other jewels, 1,000 maunds of silver, 4,000 pieces of silk, and a yearly tribute of the revenues of the Ellichpur province, to be despatched annually to Karra. On his part, he agreed to release all his remaining captives and to turn back the mythical army of 20,000 horse. On these terms the Raja of Deogir rid himself of Ala-ud-din for a time, and thus ended one of the most impudent and daring raids known to history. The refugee had paved the way for Muhammadan rule in the Deccan, and with the wealth which he had collected he returned to Hindustan. On his return he murdered his uncle and benefactor, and after a brief conflict which was decided in his favour by means of a lavish but judicious expenditure of Deccan gold, ascended the throne of Delhi. He was not the last Musalman ruler to profit by the truth contained in the Hindu proverb that the legs of Lakshmi were broken after she had crossed the Narbada.

For some time the Ellichpur tribute was regularly remitted, but Ala-ud-din was too much occupied to attend to the affairs of the Deccan, and after an interval of a few years Ram Deo thought that he might safely discontinue the payment of the heavy toll imposed upon him by the adventurer; but he reckoned without his host. Not only did Ala-ud-din the emperor miss the tribute which had been demanded by Ala-ud-din the fugitive, but he soon had other grounds for invading Deogir territory. In an expedition to Gujarat he had captured Kamala Devi, the wife of Raja Rai Karan of that country, and had taken her into his harem. Kamala Devi seems to have been contented with her change of partners, but missed the companionship of her daughters. One had died, but the younger, Deval Devi, a beautiful girl, was sought in marriage by Shankar Deo, the eldest son of Ram Deo. Rai Karan had long refused his consent to the alliance on the score that a Rajputni princess could not degrade herself by marrying a Maratha. When, however, Ala-ud-din, at the instance of Kamala Devi, sent an army to Gujarat in order to compel Rai Karan to despatch his daughter to Delhi. Shankar Deo, without his father's permission, sent to Rai Karan a mission, at the head of which was his younger brother Bhim Deo, and represented that it was better that Deval Devi, should be married to a Hindu prince than that she should fall into the hand of the Turks. Rai Karan saw the force of the argument and made haste to despatch his daughter to Deogir. Ulugh Khan, commander of the imperial troops, hearing of this, attacked Rai Karan with all his force and defeated him, but was too late to prevent the despatch of Deval Devi to Deogir. Rai Karan fled towards Deogir closely pursued by Ulugh Khan. One day, when Ulugh Khan was halted by the bank of a river, probably the Girja, three or four hundred of his men asked for leave to visit the caves of Ellora, near which the camp lay. While they were wandering among the caves a force of Hindus came into sight. The sight-seers, who had their arms with them, believed that this force was one sent against them from Deogir, and formed up to receive it. A fight ensued, in which the Hindus were worsted and fled. The horse of a lady who was with them was wounded by an arrow, and the Musalmans surrounded it and were about to seize her as a prize, when her attendant came forward and entreated them not to dishonour Deval Devi. The Musalmans then learnt that they had had the good fortune to encounter Bhim Deo's mission on its way back from Gujarat. The princess was sent with all honour to Ulugh Khan, who escorted her with his army to Gujarat and thence despatched her to Delhi, where she was married to Khizr Khan, the emperor's son, and became the heroine of one of the most famous love stories of the East.

Meanwhile, the emperor's favourite, Malik Naib Kafur, known as *Hazar Dinari*, from the price which he had fetched as a slave, had been sent to reduce the Raja of Deogir once more to obedience. Ram Deo was captured and sent to Delhi, where he was well received and highly honoured by Sultan Ala-ud-din. Deogir was restored to him and he received the title of *Rai Rayan*, with permission to use a white umbrella. For the rest of his life he remained a faithful vassal of Delhi.

There is a conflict of authorities regarding the date of these two expeditions to the south under the command of Ulugh Khan and Malik

Naib Kafur, and it cannot be determined whether they were despatched in 1302-03 or in 1306-07.

As the Musalmans carried their arms southwards, they made use of Deogir as a base and source of supplies. Thus when Malik Naib Kafur marched in 1309 against the Telinga kingdom of Warangal, Ram Deo assisted him with treasure, elephants and horses. In 1310, when the same general marched through Deogir on his way to Dhorasamudra, the capital of the Hoysala Yadavas of the south, Ram Deo had, according to the historian Barani, who disposes of the Hindu's fate in a Calvinistic spirit, "gone to hell" and Shankar Deo ruled in Deogir. Early in 1317 Ala-ud-din himself died, or, as was believed, was murdered by Malik Naib Kafur. Khizr Khan, the heir-apparent, had been thrown into prison, and Shahab-ud-din Umar, Ala-ud-din's youngest son, was raised to the throne, but was deposed and blinded in the following year by his brother Qutb-ud-din Mubarak, who ascended the throne. In 1318 Harpal Deo, son-in-law of Ram Deo, was ruling at Deogir, and in the course of the disturbances which followed on Ala-ud-din's death, had thrown off his allegiance to Delhi. In this year Qutb-ud-din Mubarak Shah set forth to chastise him and to recover Deogir. Harpal Deo fled on the emperor's approach but was pursued and captured and was then flayed alive. Thus ended the line of the Yadava Rajas of Deogir.

Qutb-ud-din Mubarak Shah remained during the rainy season at Deogir, engaged in bringing the Maratha country for the first time under Muhammadan rule and in building the great mosque which still stands at Deogir. This structure is a monument of the establishment of Islam in the south. The numerous pillars which support its roof are purely Hindu in design and were evidently taken from some temple which stood on or near the spot where the mosque now stands. The effect of the Hindu carvings in the temple of monotheism is most incongruous, perhaps designedly so, for Qutb-ud-din Mubarak, who was three parts debauchee and one part theologian, evidently intended them to bear witness to future ages of the downfall of Hinduism and the establishment of Islam. The emperor, during his stay in Deogir, established military posts throughout the Gulbarga, Sagar, and Dhorasamudra country, and parcelled out Maharashtra among Muhammadan *jagirdars.*

Then, after having appointed Malik Yaklaki commander-in-chief of the army of the Deccan, he returned to Delhi and plunged into the grossest debauchery. His neglect of public business was naturally followed by a loosening of the bonds of authority, and in the Deccan Malik Yaklaki broke out into open rebellion. An army was sent against him and he was taken captive and sent with his principal followers to Delhi, where all were put to death, Malik Yaklaki himself, as the leader of the rebellion, being mutilated before he was executed. Ain-ul-Mulk of Multan was then appointed governor of Deogir, with Malik Taj-ud-din as his assistant. In 1320 Qutb-ud-din Mubarak Shah was murdered by his unworthy favourite Hasan, by birth a low caste Hindu, who had received the title of Khusrav Khan and had been appointed *Vazir* of the empire by his infatuated master. This infamous wretch now ascended the throne of Delhi under the title of Nasir-ud-din Shah, but the great nobles of the empire could not long endure the domination of the upstart, and later in the same year he was overthrown and executed, Malik Fakhr-ud-din Jauna, a Turki noble, being raised to the throne under the title of Ghiyas-ud-din Tughlaq Shah.

While these events were happening in Delhi, the affairs of the Deccan fell once more into confusion, and in 1321 the new emperor's eldest son, Ulugh Khan, who afterwards ascended the throne as Muhammad bin Tughlaq, was sent to restore order in Deogir and to annex Warangal. The first expedition to Warangal was a failure, and Ulugh Khan was forced to fall back on Deogir, where he halted to restore order in his mutinous army. The Hindus captured the leader of the mutiny, flayed him, and sent his skin to Ulugh Khan. Other officers captured by them were sent alive to the prince, who despatched them to Delhi, where they were either impaled or crushed to death by elephants Ulugh Khan remained in Deogir until 1323, when he received reinforcements and set out once more for Warangal, capturing Bidar on his way. Warangal fell on this occasion and received the new name of Sultanpur on its annexation to the empire.

Early in 1325 Ghiyas-ud-din Tughlaq Shah died, and was succeeded by his son Muhammad. It was in this emperor's reign that Deogir, now renamed Daulatabad, reached the zenith of its fame. In 1337 the new emperor came to the conclusion that since the Deccan had been added to his dominions, Delhi was no longer sufficiently central to be a suitable capital for the whole empire, and orders were issued declaring that Daulatabad would henceforth be the capital This order did not signify only a transfer of the imperial residence, which would naturally have been followed by a transfer of trade and population. A moderate measure of this nature would have accorded ill with Muhammad bin Tughlaq's fiery and impetuous disposition. It was his intention that all that made Delhi what it was, save only its stones, bricks, and mortar, should be bodily transferred to Daulatabad. The emperor made all possible arrangements for the comfort of travellers on the road between the two cities, but no arrangements that could be made were sufficient to prevent unspeakable suffering. The inhabitants of Delhi evinced a natural disinclination to leave their homes, and Muhammad bin Tughlaq expelled them by armed force, and drove the wretched and homeless citizens across India to make new homes for themselves in the capital of his choice. One historian says that Delhi was so completely deserted that no sound was heard in it save the cries of wild beasts; and others tell us that most of the old, the widowed, the weak, and the poor died on the toilsome journey, and that of those who reached their journey's end all were sick at heart and many sick even to death. The most graphic description is that of Ibn Batutah, who thus describes the rigour with which the tyrant's orders were executed: "The Sultan ordered all the inhabitants to quit the place; and upon some delay being evinced, he made a proclamation stating that what person so ever, being an inhabitant of that city, should be found in any of its houses or streets, should receive condign punishment. Upon this they all went out; but his servants finding a blind man in one of the houses and a bed-ridden one in another, the emperor commanded the bed-ridden man to be projected from a *balista* and the blind one to be dragged by his feet to Daulatabad, which is at the distance of ten days,* and he was so dragged; but, his limbs dropping off by the way, only one of his legs was brought to the place intended, and was then thrown into it, for the orders had been that they should go to this place. When I entered Delhi it was almost a desert. . . . Its buildings were very few; in other respects it was quite empty."

*Daulatabad is 610 miles distant from Delhi as the crow flies.

It was certainly during the period of Daulatabad's importance as the new capital of the Indian empire that the works which are its most marvellous feature were undertaken and executed. What these works were, and what labour was expended on them, may best be indicated by a quotation from a later historian, the official chronicler of the reign of Shahjahan, the fifth of the great Mughals. He writes as follows: "This lofty fortress, the ancient names of which were Deogir, and Dharagir, and which is now known as Daulatabad, is a mass of rock which raises its head towards heaven. The rock has been scarped throughout its circumference, which measures 5,000 legal yards, to a depth which ensures the retention of water in the ditch at the foot of the escarpment. The escarpment is so smooth and even that neither an ant nor a snake could scale it. Its height is 140 cubits, and around its base a ditch 40 cubits in width and 30 in depth has been dug in the solid rock. Through the centre of the hill a dark spiral passage, like the ascent of a *minar*, which it is impossible to traverse, even in daylight, without a lamp, has been cut, and the steps in this passage are cut out of the rock. This passage is closed at the foot of the hill by an iron gate, and after passing through this gate and ascending the passage one enters the citadel. At the head of the passage is a large grating of iron which is shut down in case of necessity, and when a fire is lighted upon it the ascent of the spiral passage becomes impossible owing to the intense heat. The ordinary means of reducing fortresses, such as mines, covered ways, batteries, etc., are useless against this strong fortress."

This accurate description of the works at Daulatabad conveys some idea of the enormous amount of labour expended on them, and from what we know of the methods of Muhammad bin Tughlaq we may assume that exile was not the only, nor perhaps the greatest, hardship which its alien population had to bear. It can have mattered little to them that they dwelt in a city of which the courtly poet laureate sang that the heavens were the anvil of the knocker of its door, that its gates were the eight gates of Paradise, and much more in the same strain of bombastic hyperbole. We know at least that a very large majority of the forced settlers never regarded their new home otherwise than with loathing.

The eccentric tyranny of Muhammad bin Tughlaq produced its inevitable result in the form of rebellions in almost every quarter of the empire save that in which the presence of the ferocious despot cowed all opposition. In 1341, when a rebellion broke out in the southern peninsula, the emperor set out in person to punish the rebels, but his army had marched no further than Warangal when it was attacked by a pestilence, possibly cholera or small-pox, and was unable to proceed. Muhammad himself was smitten, but made his way back to Daulatabad. At Bid, on his way thither, he suffered from toothache and lost a tooth, which he buried in that town, erecting a domed tomb over it. In Daulatabad he rested until he had recovered from the effects of his illness, and in 1343-44 returned to Delhi, leaving his brother Qutlugh Khan as governor of Daulatabad. Before his departure he issued a proclamation to the effect that those who had been driven from Delhi to Daulatabad might now, if they wished, return. The result of this order was that Daulatabad, after being the capital of the empire for seventeen years, ceased to be so, for even this period had been insufficient to reconcile the wretched exiles to their new abode, and most of them elected to return, despite the prevalence of famine in the country between the two cities, the probability that a large number of those who set out would never reach their destination, and the certainty that those who succeeded would arrive at Delhi empty-handed and destitute.

The history of the troubles of the empire during the period which followed the return to Delhi, and of Muhammad's tyranny in other parts of the empire, forms no part of the history of Daulatabad, which, though largely depopulated and probably far from prosperous, was relieved of the immediate presence of the tyrant.

Shortly afterwards the emperor divided the Maratha country into four provinces under provincial governors, all worthless men. Imad-ul-Mulk, of whom more will be heard, was appointed *Vazir* at Daulatabad and Commander-in-Chief of the Deccan, Qutlugh Khan being removed from his post in 1346. Later in the same year a lowbred adventurer, Aziz Himar ("the ass") was appointed viceroy of Daulatabad, Malwa, and Dhar with instructions to watch closely the centurions of Daulatabad and other cities, who were the originators of all the insurrections which, from time to time, broke out in the Deccan. A rebellion broke out in Gujarat, Baroda, and Bahroch, and Aziz marched against the rebels, but was defeated and slain. The emperor then marched against the rebels in person and defeated and dispersed them. After tranquillity had been restored he remained in Gujarat and supervised the collection of the revenues of that province and of Bahroch and Cambay. Thence in 1346 he despatched two nobles to Daulatabad to summon to his presence the centurions of that province. Some of these centurions had been concerned in the disorders of the Deccan, and although it does not appear that the emperor had any motive in summoning them other than that of employing them in Gujarat, the officers were apprehensive of evil, and, after moving one march out of Daulatabad, took counsel together, slew the two nobles who had been sent to summon them, and marched back to the fort. On their arrival they imprisoned Maulana Nizam-ud-din, slew other imperial officers, and broke out into open rebellion. They opened the imperial treasury in the citadel and divided its contents, and then, after being joined by some of the rebel centurions from Gujarat, proclaimed one of their number, Ismail Fath the Afghan, king, under the title of Nasir-ud-din. The emperor, who was in Bahroch, at once marched on Daulatabad, met the rebels in the field, and defeated them after a hotly contested battle. Ismail Fath and his immediate followers took refuge in the citadel of Daulatabad, while the other rebel officers among whom was Hasan Gangu, dispersed to their *jagirs*. Muhammad bin Tughlaq laid siege to the citadel and gave the town of Daulatabad up to plunder, while he despatched Imad-ul-Mulk, now governor of Ellichpur, in pursuit of Hasan Gangu and the other fugitive centurions. After besieging Ismail Fath in the citadel for three months, the emperor received news that rebellion had broken out afresh in Gujarat and at once marched northwards to quell the rebellion taking with him all the unfortunate inhabitants of Daulatabad. Malik Jauhar, Shaikh Burhan-ud-din Bilgrami, and other nobles were left behind to carry on the siege of the citadel, but they were unable to prevent the Deccani *amirs* from pursuing the imperial army and attacking it with considerable success, and immediately after the emperor's departure the centurions who had dispersed reassembled their troops under the leadership of Hasan Gangu, attacked and slew Imad-ul-Mulk and then marched on Daulatabad. Here they defeated and put to flight the imperial forces which had been left to besiege the citadel and were joined by the titular king of the Deccan, Ismail Fath. The brief nominal reign of Ismail Fath had been far from auspicious, and he had the sense to see that Hasan Gangu was the man of the hour. He wisely determined to take time by the forelock and resigned the royal dignity on the plea that he was too old and too fond of his ease to undertake the onerous task of ruling The *amirs* agreed to abide by his nomination in the selection of a king, and he proposed Hasan Gangu, "entitled Zafar Khan, of the race of Bahman." The proposal was accepted without a dissentient voice, and Hasan ascended the throne in Daulatabad in 1347 under the title of Ala-ud-din Bahman Shah.*

The death of Muhammad bin Tughlaq in 1351 freed the new king of the Deccan from all apprehensions, for Firuz Shah, Muhammad's successor on the throne of Delhi, was so busily employed in restoring order in the provinces near to his capital that he had no leisure to turn his attention to the south.

It is strange that Ala-ud-din Bahman did not choose as his capital Daulatabad, which had for forty years been the centre of Muhammadan influence and power in Southern India, but whether from attachment to his own *jagir* or from a notion that Daulatabad. the importance of which had declined owing to its recent depopulation, was too near the northern border of the Deccan and had been too closely connected with Delhi to be desirable as the capital of his kingdom, he passed over its claims and made Gulbarga the capital of the Deccan.

As soon as Ala-ud-din Bahman had consolidated his power he divided his kingdom into four *tarafs* or provinces, Gulbarga, Daulatabad, Berar, and Bidar. He died on February 11th, 1358, and was succeeded by his eldest son, Muhammad I, who completed the organisation of the army. Daulatabad still remained an important city, for each of the four great provincial governors maintained his own army at his capital, besides appointing all the commandants of forts within his province. Each, too, had his distinctive title, the governor of Daulatabad being known as Masnad-i-Ali. Whenever the Sultan declared war against his Hindu neighbours on the south or east, or against his Muhammadan neighbours on the north, the provincial governors were

* *Journal of the Asiatic Society of Bengal*, Vol. LXXIII, Part I, Extra No 1904.

summoned to join him with their armies. In 1365-66 Muhammad I was engaged in a war with Krishna Raya of Vijayanagar. The Hindu was defeated, but the Sultan fell ill during the campaign and reports of his death obtained credence in various parts of the kingdom. In the absence of the provincial governors with their armies, the government of the provinces had been left in the hands of inferiors, and one Bahram Khan Mazandarani, who had been a favourite of Bahman Shah, seems to have been left in authority at Daulatabad. At the insigation of a Maratha officer named Kondba Deo, he raised the standard of rebellion, and was joined by some of the nobles of Berar. He retained in Daulatabad several years' revenue from Berar and the Maratha country, which was due to the royal treasury, obtained promises of assistance from a petty Hindu chief, and collected a force of 12,000 horse and foot. Muhammad Shah, hearing of these proceedings, sent a letter to Bahram Khan promising him forgiveness if he would repent of his fault, but Bahram Khan, acting on the advice of his evil genius Kondba Deo, paid no attention to the warning and redoubled his efforts to strengthen himself against attack. The messengers returned to the king and informed him of the failure of their mission, and he, on his return to Gulbarga, sent Masnad-i-Ali Khan Muhammad to restore order in his province, and followed him leisurely. The rebels advanced to Paithan on the Godavari to meet Masnad-i-Ali, who advanced without opposition as far as Shivagaon, about 15 miles from Paithan, where the rebels made an inffectual night attack upon his camp. He then prepared to attack them, but first sent a message to Muhammad Shah, who was then hunting in the neighbourhood of Bid, with no more than three hundred troops, apprizing him of his intention. The king, without waiting for his army to join him, pressed on with the small force which he had with him and joined Masnad-i-Ali just as he was about to attack the rebels. The latter, hearing of the Sultan's approach, dispersed, and the leaders fled to Daulatabad, where they prepared to stand a siege; but, being closely followed by the Sultan and Masnad-i-Ali, they could not persuade their troops to resist the royal army. Finding themselves deserted by their followers, they fled towards Gujarat, closely pursued by Masnad-i-Ali. They succeeded, however, in eluding him and crossed the frontier, and ultimately ended their days in exile.

Firuz Shah, the eighth king of the Bahmani dynasty, assembled the armies of Daulatabad and Berar in 1398-99, to assist in the expulsion of Deva Raya of Vijayanagar from the Raichur Duab, but no sooner had they joined the Sultan than news arrived that Berar had been overrun from north to south by the Gonds of Kherla, and they were despatched northwards to repel the invaders, but were unequal to the task. The Gonds remained in possession of Berar until Firuz Shah had driven the Hindus from the Duab, and was left at liberty to march to the support of his northern army. In the following year Firuz Shah not only succeeded in driving the Gonds beyond his northern frontier, but sent in pursuit of them an army which defeated Narsingh, the Gond Raja, at the gates of his capital of Kherla.

During the reign of Ahmad Shah Wali, the brother and successor of Firuz Shah, Daulatabad became the base of military operations against the turbulent Rajas of the Konkan, whose depredations called for punishment, and in 1429 the Sultan appointed Khalaf Hasan Basri, the ablest of his servants, to the command of the province. Khalaf Hasan, in the course of an arduous campaign, reduced the refractory chiefs to obedience and enriched his master's treasury with the spoils which he captured from them. Unfortunately, the lust of conquest led him to attack the island of Bombay, within the territories of Ahmad Shah of Gujarat. His conquest of the island involved the Bahmani kingdom in an unprofitable war with Gujarat, peace being ultimately concluded on the condition that each of the belligerents should retain the possessions which it had held before the capture of Bombay. Meanwhile, Hushang Shah of Malwa had taken advantage of the quarrel between his powerful neighbours, and had seized Kherla, then a recognised fief of the Bahmani kingdom, and put to death the Raja Narsingh. Ahmed Shah Wali was too exhausted by the campaign in the Konkan and the war against Gujarat to punish this act of aggression, and was compelled to leave Kherla in the hands of Hushang on the condition that he refrained from molesting Berar.

In the reigns of the tenth and twelfth kings of the Bahmani dynasty, Daulatabad was again disturbed by war's alarms. Ala-ud-din Ahmad II, the son of Ahmad I, had married Agha Zainab, entitled Malika-i-Jahan, the daughter of Nasír Khan Faruqi, Sultan of Khandesh, but afterwards took into his harem the daughter of the petty Raja of Sangameshvar in the Konkan, giving her the name of *Ziba Chihra*, or "Beautiful face." Agha Zainab, who was neglected for the Hindu girl, wrote to her father and complained of her husband's behaviour. Nasír Khan espoused his daughter's cause and resolved to punish his son-in-law, but, well aware that he was not strong enough to attack the Bahmani kingdom single-handed with any hope of success, he prepared his way by corrupting the officers serving in Berar, and as soon as his machinations had met with some measure of success, he followed them up by invading Berar in 1437. The officers who had been won over by Nasír Khan were besieging their governor, the Khan-i-Jahan, in the hill fort of Narnala, and the invaders were left free to advance unmolested in the direction of Daulatabad. Here Khalaf Hasan Basri, who had once more been selected for the command of an expedition, was assembling his forces. He was joined by the Khan-i-Jahan, who managed to effect his escape from Narnala, and marched northwards through Berar, inflicting a crushing defeat on the invaders at Rohankhed. Nasír Khan was pursued to his capital, which was sacked, and the troops of Daulatabad returned with much booty.

In 1461, during the reign of the young king Nizam Shah Bahmani, Mahmud Shah Khalji of Malwa invaded the Deccan and took the capital, Bidar, but was unable to reduce its citadel. The province of Daulatabad was overrun by the invaders, but the old fort held out and once again was a base of military operations against the invaders. Mahmud Shah of Gujarat came to the assistance of the Bahmani king, and in the neighbourhood of Daulatabad joined forces with the soldier-statesman of the Bahmani kingdom, Mahmud Gawan, thus threatening the communications of the invaders, who retreated hastily through the jungles of the Satpuras closely pursued by Mahmud Gawan. In the following year Mahmud Shah Khalji again invaded the Daulatabad province, but before he could attack its capital he received news that Nizam Shah was advancing against him from the south-east and would probably be joined by Mahmud Shah of Gujarat from the north-west. He had no hope of resisting successfully such a combination, and hastily retreated to Malwa. In 1471 Yusuf Adil Khan, who afterwards founded the Adil Shahi dynasty of Bijapur, was appointed governor of Daulatabad, "than which post there was none higher in the service of the Bahmanis." This appointment was made in the reign of Muhammad III, the thirteenth king of the Bahmani dynasty, and later in the reign a reform which had already been too long delayed was effected. The four original provinces of the kingdom were sub-divided into eight, Daulatabad being divided into the new provinces of Daulatabad and Junnar. The almost regal powers of the *tarafdars* were also curtailed in other directions. Formerly, all the forts in the provinces had been in the hands of the *tarafdars*, who appointed and removed the commandants. It was now ordered that only the fort at the capital of each of the provinces should be in the hands of the *tarafdar*, and that the commandants of all other forts should hold their appointments directly from the Sultan. The nature and effect of this policy have been misapprehended by a modern historian,* who, referring to the dissolution of the Bahmani kingdom, says, "A recent division into large provincial governments hastened the dissolution." This statement is misleading. The kingdom had originally been divided into large provincial governments and the "recent division" referred to was the sub-division of those large governments into smaller ones. This step, though not taken in sufficient time to prevent, did not itself accelerate the dissolution of the kingdom, though an act of injustice committed by Muhammad III, who had the innocent author of the reform put to death, disgusted the more powerful provincial governors. The disruption of the kingdom, however, was due solely to the degeneracy of the later Bahmanis and to their subserviency to ministers whom the provincial governors would not accept as masters.

After the subdivision Malik Hasan Nizam-ul-Mulk was transferred from the government of Telingana to that of Daulatabad, and Yusuf Adil Khan from that of Daulatabad to the new province of Bijapur which had formed part of the old *taraf* of Gulbarga.

Early in the reign of Mahmud Shah, the son and successor of Muhammad, Hasan Nizam-ul-Mulk, profiting by the absence of Yusuf Adil Khan in Bijapur, acquired a predominance of influence in the capital, and sent his son, Malik Ahmad, to carry on the government of

---

* See *Mediæval India under Muhammadan Rule* ("Story of the Nations" series), by Stanley Lane-Poole, p. 184.

Daulatabad as his deputy. Shortly afterwards, Malik Hasan, who was also known as Malik Naib, died, and his son Ahmad inherited his dignities.

The dynasty founded by Malik Ahmad was connected, as long as it lasted, with Daulatabad. Malik Hasan, or Naib, the father of Ahmad, is said to have been by birth a Brahman, of a family which had its home in Pathri, in southern Berar, a village which afterwards became, on this account, a bone of contention between the Sultans of Berar and the Sultans of Ahmadnagar; but the family migrated to Vijayanagar, and Malik Hasan, whose original name was Tima Bhat, was captured as a child in Ahmad Shah Wali's expedition against the Carnatic empire, and was brought up as a Musalman. After his death, when the complete ascendency of Malik Barid at Bidar compelled the provincial governors to assert their independence, Malik Ahmad proclaimed himself king in 1490. At this time Daulatabad was held by two brothers, Malik Vajih-ud-din and Malik Sharaf-ud-din, of whom one was *faujdar* and the other *qal'ahdar*. They had been brought up by Ahmad's father, but remained, for a time, faithful to the Bahmani king, and ignored Ahmad's pretensions to royalty. But the elder brother, Vajih-ud-din, had married Bibi Zainab, the sister of Ahmad Nizam Shah, and had a son by her. The favour shown by Ahmad Nizam Shah to his brother-in-law and nephew excited the jealousy of Sharaf-ud-din, who, fearing that the boy would ultimately oust him from his appointment, began to plot against the life of Vajih-ud-din and his son. At length, with the help of his followers, he put Vajih-ud-din to death and poisoned his son, and, having thus offended Ahmad Nizam Shah beyond hope of forgiveness, was forced to look for support He entered into correspondence with Fathullah Imad-ul-Mulk of Berar, and Adil Khan Faruqi and Daud Khan Faruqi of Khandesh, and also tendered his homage to Muhammad Shah of Gujarat. Bibi Zainab fled to her brother, then in Junnar, and demanded vengeance on her husband's murderer. Ahmad Nizam Shah set out in 1494 to punish Sharaf-ud-din, but was met on his way by messengers from Qasim Barid, now the *maire du palais* of the Bahmani king, who reported that their master was besieged in Bidar by Yusuf Adil Shah of Bijapur and implored Ahmad to march to his assistance, promising that Qasim Barid would capture Daulatabad for Ahmad as soon as he was relieved. Ahmad Nizam Shah relieved Qasim Barid and returned by way of Daulatabad. He laid siege to the fort for two months, and then, finding that he had no prospect of success, returned towards Junnar. On his way thither he was attracted by the situation now occupied by Ahmadnagar, and conceived that with his headquarters in this place he would be able to carry off the crops of the Daulatabad country twice every year, as harvest seasons approached, and starve out the garrison of the fortress. He therefore founded, in 1495, the city of Ahmadnagar, and, when it was completed, began his depredations in the neighbourhood of Daulatabad, carrying off as much of the harvest as he could, and burning the rest. He then formed an alliance with Fathullah Imad-ul-Mulk of Berar and Adil Khan Faruqi of Khandesh, and obtained a promise of 2,000 horse from the latter to assist in the reduction of Daulatabad. Adil Khan Faruqi, trusting to the power of his new ally, now withheld the tribute which he had been accustomed to send to his powerful neighbour, Mahmud Shah of Gujarat. Mahmud Shah, annoyed by the defection of his vassal, marched towards the Deccan under pretence of making a tour in the southern district of his kingdom, and Sharaf-ud-din contrived to communicate with him from Daulatabad, and complained bitterly of the persecution to which he was subjected by Ahmad Nizam Shah. Mahmud continued his march southwards with the avowed object of bringing the Sultan of Khandesh to his senses, but with the secret intention of obtaining possession of Daulatabad. The Sultans of Berar, Khandesh, and Ahmadnagar combined to resist the invader, and Ahmad Nizam Shah, by bribing Mahmud Shah's *mahout* to let his master's elephant loose at night and by simultaneously attacking the camp of the Gujaratis, routed Mahmud's army and forced Mahmud himself to flee. Peace was then concluded and Ahmad returned to Daulatabad. He encamped in the hills above the town and in the neighbourhood of Ellora, leaving his troops in the plains below to invest the fort. Sharaf-ud-din, now seriously alarmed by Ahmad's persistence, contrived to send another message to Mahmud Shah, promising, if the fortress were relieved, to send tribute yearly to Gujarat and to have the *khutba* read in Mahmud's name in Daulatabad. Mahmud, anxious to retrieve the disgrace of his flight as well as to gain possession of Daulatabad, marched southwards through Khandesh, where he collected arrears of tribute, into Ahmadnagar territory. Ahmad Nizam Shah, hearing of Mahmud's approach, left Daulatabad and returned to Ahmadnagar, and Sharaf-ud-din, relieved from his apprehensions, had the *khutba* read in Mahmud Shah's name in the mosque of Qutb-ud-din Mubarak Shah at Daulatabad, and then hastened to join the invader, taking with him valuable presents. Mahmud Shah accepted the presents and returned to his own country, leaving only 3,000 Gujarati horse with Sharaf-ud-din, who returned with his reinforcement to Daulatabad, whither he was immediately followed by Ahmad Nizam Shah. The reading of the *khutba* in the name of Mahmud Shah of Gujarat had greatly offended the Daulatabad garrison, which now secretly proffered its allegiance to Ahmad Nizam Shah. Ahmad received the message while he was halting on the Godavari and at once pressed on with two or three thousand light horse to Daulatabad. Sharaf-ud-din at length realised that resistance was hopeless, aud turned his face to the wall. According to one account he died of chagrin and vexation, and according to others he took poison.* Thus in 1500 Ahmad Nizam Shah took possession of the fortress, which formed part of the Ahmadnagar kingdom as long as the Nizam Shahi dynasty lasted. Ahmad then had the fort put into a state of thorough repair and returned in triumph to Ahmadnagar.

In 1540 Burhan Nizam Shah, the son and successor of Ahmad, taking advantage of the confusion prevailing in Bijapur, entered into an alliance with Amir Ali Barid of Bidar, with whom he invaded the territories of Bijapur. The invaders were at first successful, but Ibrahim Adil Shah sought help from Ala-ud-din Imad Shah of Berar who, following the almost invariable policy of the lesser Sultans of the Deccan, the object of which was the preservation of the balance of power, responded to the call. Ibrahim was at the same time joined by his nobles and ventured to take the offensive. Burhan and Amir Ali Barid were defeated and driven northwards through the Bidar dominions, and as far as Ahmadnagar. Not venturing to halt even here, they fled to Daulatabad. Here Amir Ali Barid died in 1542, and Burhan, being reduced to extremities, was forced to make peace and to restore

* Khafi Khan in the *Munta hab-ul-Lubab* (Vol. III.) transposes the names of the brothers making Sharaf-ud-din the elder and Vajih-ud-din the younger, and the fratricide

all the Bijapur territory which he had conquered in the early days of the war.

For some time after this the history of Daulatabad is uneventful. Murtaza Nizam Shah used the fortress as a prison for his son, Miran Husain, of whom he was jealous. The young prince had been for some time in prison when he was sent for by his father, who pretended that he could no longer endure separation from his son. Murtaza, having, as he thought, got his son into his power, made an attempt to murder him by setting fire to his bedclothes, but the prince escaped with a few bad burns and shortly afterwards retaliated by suffocating his father in the baths.

Towards the end of the sixteenth century the Nizam Shahi kingdom was hard pressed by the Emperor Akbar. Berar was ceded to Delhi in 1595 and peace was concluded, but the imperial troops found a pretext for renewing the conflict in the following year. At length, in July 1599, Bahadur Nizam Shah being then the nominal king and Chand Bibi the actual ruler of Ahmadnagar, prince Daniyal, Akbar's youngest son, and the Khan-i-Khanan laid siege to Ahmadnagar, which fell about the middle of 1603 after an intermittent siege of four years. The "noble queen" Chand Bibi was put to death by the *amirs* of Ahmadnagar, and after the fall of the capital Bahadur Nizam Shah was carried off to Gwalior, where, after a long captivity, he ended his days.

The dynasty, however, still remained. After the fall of Ahmadnagar those nobles who remained faithful to the Nizam Shahi house raised to the throne Murtaza, the son of Shah Ali, one of the sons of Burhan Nizam Shah I, the second king of the dynasty. Shah Ali, whose mother was Mariyam Bibi, a Bijapur princess, had retired to Bijapur, and his son was brought thence and enthroned at Purenda, which became for a short time the capital of the Nizam Shahi kingdom. The new king was accompanied from Bijapur by one of the most remarkable characters in Indian history, Malik Ambar the Abyssinian. Murtaza was a king in name only and Malik Ambar soon possessed himself of the southern and eastern districts of the Nizam Shahi kingdom, while Raju, the Deccani, held the northern districts, including Daulatabad. It is not necessary to recount the circumstances of the inevitable quarrel between Ambar and Raju, or their intrigues with the

Khan-i-Khanan and the imperial troops. In 1607 Murtaza Nizam Shah marched against Raju, who held Daulatabad. Raju was defeated and captured and Daulatabad became the capital of the Nizam Shahi kingdom. Malik Ambar soon acquired the supreme power in the state. It is difficult to say how far he was a faithful servant to his master and how far he fought for his own hand. His position was, in fact, very similar to that of the Barids during the reigns of the later Bahmanis. Despite his intrigues with the Mughals, there is no doubt that the maintenance of the independence of the Muhammadan kingdoms of the Deccan was the object of his life.

Leaving Murtaza II in barren state at Daulatabad, Malik Ambar established himself in his city of Khirki, afterwards named Aurangabad, about eight miles from the old fort. "Ambar the black-faced" is frequently mentioned in Jahangir's memoirs as a dangerous enemy. In 1612 confusion reigned in the imperial army of the Deccan. The Khan-i-A'zam, who held the chief command, was slothful and the principal officers were quarrelling among themselves. In this year an expedition was despatched against Daulatabad. Abdullah Khan was ordered to advance by way of Nasik with an army of 14,000 men from Gujarat, while Raja Man Singh, with another large army, was to march southwards through Berar. The two armies were directed to maintain constant intercommunication and to attack the enemy at Daulatabad from opposite sides on the same day. The plan was sound, but it failed owing to the jealousy and selfish ambition of Abdullah Khan, who, unwilling to divide with Man Singh the glory of a victory, deliberately neglected to maintain communications with the Berar army, and with his own 14,000 men fell upon Malik Ambar at Daulatabad. He was defeated with great slaughter and driven back to Gujarat, and Man Singh, who had halted to wait for news of his movements, did not know where Abdullah Khan was until he received news of his defeat, upon which he promptly retreated to the neighbourhood of Burhanpur, leaving the whole of Berar in the hands of Malik Ambar. The Deccanis were now in a position to offer terms of peace. Ibrahim Adil Shah II guaranteed the restoration of some of the districts from which the imperial troops had been driven, and early in 1613 peace was concluded on these terms, Malik Ambar retaining Ahmadnagar.

Early in 1616 there was disaffection in Malik Ambar's camp. Some of his principal officers, including the leaders of the Maratha irregulars, betook themselves to Shahnavaz Khan, who was then commanding the imperial troops stationed at Balapur in Berar, and offered their services to him. He welcomed them effusively and bestowed on each a horse, an elephant, a robe of honour, and a sum of money, and then, taking the deserters with him, marched against Malik Ambar. Shahnavaz Khan dispersed a small force which opposed him and advanced to within about a day's march of Khirki. Here Malik Ambar, whose troops had been reinforced by contingents from Bijapur and Golconda, made a stand, but was defeated, and on the following day the imperial troops entered Khirki, which they first laid waste and then renamed Fathabad, "the town of victory." Shahnavaz Khan found it impossible to hold a position so advanced as Khirki, and after a short stay in the town retreated to Rohankhed in Berar.

In 1617 Sultan Khurram, afterwards the emperor Shahjahan, recovered Ahmadnagar and many other forts which had been recaptured by the Deccanis from the imperial troops, but Daulatabad remained the capital of the tottering Nizam Shahi dynasty. Later in this year Malik Ambar set himself to deal with those who had deserted him and joined the imperial army. He succeeded in detaching Adam Khan, the Abyssinian, from his allegiance to the emperor and imprisoned him in Daulatabad until he found it convenient to put him to death; but his troops sustained a defeat while they were attempting to capture Uda Ram, another of the renegades.

In 1620, during Jahangir's absence in Kashmir, Malik Ambar once more embarked on a war against the imperial troops, and besieged Khanjar Khan in Ahmadnagar. Darab Khan inflicted a defeat on Ambar's troops, but the imperial army was so beset by the Maratha horse, which cut off all supplies, that it retreated to Balapur, pursued by Malik Ambar. He was worsted in a skirmish in the neighbourhood of Balapur, but by this time the Deccanis had overrun so much of the imperial dominions that Shahjahan was once more appointed to the army of the Deccan. Although Malik Ambar had collected an army of 60,000 horse, the imperial army had advanced, before the arrival of Shahjahan, as far as Mehkar, which now became the prince's headquarters. The Deccanis were three times defeated in the open field, but the imperialists could not profit by their victories, for they were continually harassed by the Maratha horse and were again compelled to retreat to Balapur. Hither the Marathas followed them and reduced them to such a plight by cutting off their supplies that many were fain to desert to Malik Ambar and the rest were compelled to retreat to Burhanpur, leaving Berar and Khandesh once more in the hands of Malik Ambar. At the end of the year, Shahjahan was again despatched with large reinforcements to the Deccan, and, after defeating the Deccanis, who hemmed in the imperial army at Burhanpur, pursued them as far as Khirki. Malik Ambar had barely time to remove Murtaza Nizam Shah for safety to Daulatabad before Shahjahan arrived. Khirki was captured and so laid waste that "the city which had taken twenty years in the building would not be restored for twenty years to come." Shahjahan then raised the siege of Ahmadnagar, and, after receiving promises of submission from Malik Ambar, who agreed to restore all the country captured from the Mughals, together with other districts yielding a revenue of fourteen crores of rupees, and to pay an indemnity of fifty lakhs of rupees, withdrew to Berar. Soon after this Shahjahan rebelled against his father, but was defeated and forced to flee to the Deccan, where he took refuge, in the Qutb Shahi dominions. In 1624 Mahabat Khan, Jahangir's general, sent a force to the Balaghat to receive the envoy of Ibrahim Adil Shah II, and Malik Ambar, hearing of its approach, placed his family in Daulatabad and fled with Murtaza Nizam Shah to Kandhar in the Qutb Shahi dominions, leaving Khirki undefended. He then entered into correspondence with Muhammad Qutb Shah, and demanded from him two years' arrears of the annual contribution which he had formerly agreed to pay towards the expenses of the army maintained to oppose the imperial forces. The money was paid and the treaty was renewed, and Malik Ambar then turned his attention to Ibrahim Adil Shah, who had entered into a treaty with Jahangir and had in return been nominated by him governor of the whole of the Deccan. Bidar, which had since the fall of the Barid Shahi dynasty been included in the Adil Shahi dominions, was plundered, and Malik Ambar then advanced and besieged Ibrahim in his capital of Bijapur. Ibrahim appealed to the imperial governor at

Burhanpur for help, which was sent, and Malik Ambar had the effrontery to send a message deprecating interference and alleging that the quarrel between him and Ibrahim Adil Shah was a private matter which the parties should be left to settle between themselves. The reinforcements, however, continued to advance, and Malik Ambar withdrew from Bijapur. When the Bijapuris and their allies approached his position and demanded that he should retreat, he put them off with excuses, at the same time expressing contrition and humbling himself, thereby inducing his enemies to believe that he would not fight. Having thus misled them, he fell upon them and utterly defeated them, slaying their commander and capturing several imperial officers. He then laid siege to Ahmadnagar, but abandoned the siege almost immediately and invested Bijapur and Sholapur, at the same time ravaging the Bijapur territories. Sholapur fell and Malik Ambar despatched Yaqut Khan, his fellow-countryman, with a large army to besiege Burhanpur, Yaqut Khan received assistance from Shahjahan, who was still in rebellion, and captured the city of Burhanpur, but was unable to reduce the citadel, which held out until news of the approach of Sultan Parviz and the Khan-i-Khanan arrived, when the Deccanis retired.

In 1626 Malik Ambar died in the eightieth year of his age. Jahangir, who never mentioned him when living without undignified abuse, did justice to his memory thus :—" Ambar, whether as a commander or as a strategist, was without an equal in the military art. He kept the bad characters of that country (*scil.* the Deccan) in perfect order, and to the end of his days lived in honour. There is no record elsewhere in history of an Abyssinian slave attaining to such a position as was held by him."

In the same year Yaqut Khan, who had been deputed by Malik Ambar to besiege Burhanpur, and Fath Khan, Malik Ambar's son submitted in Jalna to the imperial governor, Sarbuland Rai. Their accession to the imperial cause was welcomed and they were well received. Yaqut soon rose to be a commander of 5,000, but after a time returned to his old allegiance. Fath Khan's submission was even shorter lived than that of Yaqut, for in the same year he was despatched by Murtaza Nizam Shah, who still retained in Daulatabad the semblance of sovereignty, on an expedition towards Berar, and the

Khan-i-Jahan had to be sent by the emperor to the defence of Burhanpur. Murtaza Nizam Shah now appointed as his minister Hamid Khan, another Abyssinian, and fell completely under his influence. Hamid Khan, well aware of the venality of the imperial officers, utilised to some purpose such revenue as could be collected. A present of twelve lakhs of rupees was sufficient to induce the Khan-i-Jahan not only to refrain from attacking Daulatabad, but also to surrender to Murtaza Ahmadnagar and the Balaghat of Berar. The treachery of "that faithless Afghan," as his master termed him, was partly neutralised by the refusal of the faithful commandant, Sipahdar Khan, to surrender Ahmadnagar without an imperial *farman*; and he held out successfully against the Deccanis, but the officers in the Balaghat surrendered their commands and retired to Burhanpur. The Khan-i-Jahan, henceforward known as Pira the Afghan, deserted to Murtaza Nizam Shah, and was soon afterwards captured and executed. Hamid Khan's wife, the daughter of a "foreigner," was a woman of great ability and unbounded energy. She obtained access to the harem of Murtaza Nizam Shah and soon became the recognised means of communication between the effeminate and luxurious king and his subjects. Ibrahim Adl Shah II, conceiving that he might now with impunity take vengeance for the past on the kingdom of Ahmadnagar, prepared to invade it. When the news of his approach reached Daulatabad, Hamid Khan's wife solicited for herself the command of the Nizam Shahi army, supporting her strange request by an ingenious argument. If she were victorious, she said, the Bijapuris would henceforth hide their heads for shame; while if they were victorious they could only boast that they had triumphed over a woman. The lady's request was granted, and she justified the unusual appointment. She cajoled the officers and distributed largesse to the soldiers, and in the end she utterly defeated the Bijapuris, capturing all their elephants and artillery.

In 1627 Jahangir died, and the sick man at Daulatabad had rest for a while, but all the garrisons in the Balaghat were surrendered to the imperial troops. In 1629 Shahjahan resolved to put an end to the Nizam Shahi dynasty, and at the end of that year, by which time many of the Nizam Shahi officers had deserted to the imperial army, set out for Burhanpur, and early in 1630 sent an army to invade the Nizam

Shahi dominions. Fath Khan, the son of Malik Ambar, now murdered Murtaza Nizam Shah, and placed his son Husain on the throne. At the same time he sent a message to the imperial camp and assured Shahjahan that he had carried out this measure solely in his interests. The truth, however, seems to have been that Fath Khan was not satisfied with the extent of his influence over Murtaza, and caused him to be murdered with the object of governing Daulatabad in the name of Husain. At all events the imperial army was not withdrawn, and ultimately drove Husain Nizam Shah and his followers into Daulatabad. Once again, however, the Mughals were compelled by scarcity of supplies to retreat. In February 1632 Vazir Khan, commander of five thousand, was sent from Court to reduce the fortress of Daulatabad, but immediately after his departure Sayyid Abu-l-Fath, the agent of Fath Khan, arrived at Court and reported that Abd-ur-Rasul, Fath Khan's eldest son, was following him with a large quantity of jewels and elephants. Vazir Khan was accordingly recalled, and Abd-ur-Rasul arrived at Court and presented thirty elephants, nine horses, and jewels to the value of eight lakhs of rupees Meanwhile the Mughal army of the Deccan was engaged against Bijapur in operations which ended in the conclusion of a treaty of peace. Shahjahan, in return for the offering which Fath Khan had sent by his son, transferred to him some *jagirs* which had formerly been included in the Nizam Shahi dominions but had since been assigned by the Mughals to Shahji, the father of Shivaji. Shahji, as soon as he heard of the transfer of his *jagirs*, entered the service of Ibrahim Adil Shah II, of Bijapur, and late in 1632 persuaded that ruler to let him lead the army of Bijapur against Fath Khan in order that he might recover his lost lands and capture Daulatabad. Fath Khan, on hearing of the approach of the Bijapuris, sent a message to Mahabat Khan, the Khan-i-Khanan, who was then in Burhanpur, imploring him to assist him and promising that if the fort were saved by the imperial troops, he would surrender it to the Khan-i-Khanan and personally make his submission at the imperial court. The Khan-i-Khanan was not the man to miss the opportunity of obliterating the last traces of Nizam Shahi independence, and at once sent Sayyid Khan-i-Jahan, who had succeeded Pira Lodi in that title, to Daulatabad, and followed him in January, 1633. The Khan-i-Jahan found the army of Bijapur in the neighbourhood of Khirki, fell upon it and utterly defeated it, pursuing the fugitives for ten or twelve miles, and then returned to his camp near Khirki.

Affairs now took a turn which entirely changed the aspect of the operations. The officers of the army of Bijapur approached Fath Khan with a proposal that he should join them against the Mughals, promising on their part to victual Daulatabad, where supplies were much needed. Fath Khan, with almost incredible treachery and ingratitude, accepted the offer, and the Bijapuris occupied Nizampur, a mile or two from Daulatabad, and attempted to convey food and forage into the fort. The Khan-i-Zaman, acting under the orders of the Khan-i-Khanan, now made an attempt to induce Fath Khan to adhere to his original compact, but without success. Meanwhile, the main body of the Bijapuris again advanced, and were defeated and pursued for some miles, and the force which was attempting to victual Daulatabad was driven out of Nizampur. In this village the Khan-i-Zaman now took up his quarters and began the investment of the fortress, which was completed by the Khan-i-Khanan, who advanced from Zafarnagar and occupied the Nizam Shahi palace in Nizampur. The Khan-i-Zaman was then placed in command of a flying column of 5,000 horse with instructions to prevent any communications between the garrison and the Bijapuris. Yaqut Khan the Abyssinian, who, as has been said, had deserted from the Nizam Shahi service and now held a command in the imperial army, attempted more than once to convey supplies to the besieged, but these were intercepted on each occasion, and when at length his treachery was discovered, he fled from the camp and joined the army of Bijapur. Three attempts were then made by the Bijapuris to convey grain into Daulatabad, but the convoy was attacked on each occasion and the grain fell into the hands of the victors. On the other hand the army of Bijapur, now encamped at Khirki, did its utmost to cut off supplies from the besiegers, and Turkman Khan, the *thanadar* of Zafarnagar, was unable to push supplies through to the army before Daulatabad. The Bijapuris took the field and would have captured the convoy had not the Khan-i-Zaman been despatched with a small force to its rescue. He attacked and defeated the Bijapuris who, in the course of their flight towards Khirki, fell in with a small force which had been sent to the assistance of the Khan-i-Zaman, on seeing which they concluded that the whole of the Khan-i-Khanan's army was scattered and that its camp might be destroyed. They therefore turned towards Daulatabad, only to be met by the force which they had seen near Khirki and which had withdrawn towards the main body. The Bijapuris then retired discomfited to Khirki and the Khan-i-Zaman escorted the Zafarnagar convoy to the Khan-i-Khanan's camp. After the failure of this attempt to cut off the besiegers' supplies, the Bijapuris made another determined effort to convey grain to the defenders, but the grain, as well as a quantity of other booty, was captured by the Khan-i-Zaman, who then fell upon and plundered the camp of the Bijapuris. During his absence Fath Khan made a sortie from the fort, but was repulsed. The imperial army now suffered from want of grass and firewood, and the Khan-i-Zaman was sent out with a force to collect supplies of both. During his absence the Bijapuris attacked the camp at Nizampur, but were repulsed with loss, and the Khan-i-Zaman returned with the grass and fuel.

The next episode of the siege was the explosion of a mine which destroyed 28 yards of the curtain and 12 yards of the bastion in the *enceinte* of Ambarkot, the outer fort, beneath which it was exploded. The explosion was mistimed by some hours, and when it occurred the storming party was not ready. The Bijapuris attacked the besiegers and fully occupied the attention of the Khan-i-Zaman's flying column, so adding to the confusion that before the storming party could assemble the breach was partly repaired, and the defenders, who rapidly concentrated at the vulnerable point in their defences, were able to pour upon the storming party, when it at length advanced to the assault, a fire so galling that the assailants fled to their trenches and steadfastly refused to move from them. The Khan-i-Khanan, smarting with chagrin, was with difficulty dissuaded by Nasiri Khan from leading a second assault in person, a duty which was ultimately assigned to Nasiri Khan himself at his urgent request. The Deccanis at first offered a most stubborn resistance and the carnage was great, but gradually the determination of the picked men led by Nasiri Khan prevailed, and the Deccanis withdrew behind the walls of Mahakot, their second line of defence, leaving Ambarkot in the hands of the besiegers. Meanwhile, the Khan-i-Zaman had been engaged with the Bijapuris without the walls, and the fight had lasted until the latter heard of the fall of Ambarkot, when they broke and fled. On the following day the Khan-i-Khanan transferred his headquarters from the Nizam Shahi palace in Nizampur to Yaqut Khan's house within the walls of Ambarkot, and henceforth personally directed all the operations of the siege, leaving the Khan-i-Zaman and his flying column to deal with the Bijapuris beyond the walls. This was no light task, for Rindula Khan, who was now commanding the army of Bijapur, had arranged to send troops into Berar and Telingana to prevent the despatch of supplies to the besiegers, and the flying column was charged with the duty of acting against such detachments wherever they might be found.

Three days after the fall of Ambarkot, Rindula Khan and Shahji with 3,000 horse and a large force of foot, escorting a convoy, came into sight. Their object was to convey grain as far as the ditch of Ambarkot and to deposit it there for the besieged Deccanis, who were by this time reduced to feeding upon the hides of dead horses and cattle. The Khan-i-Khanan, on receiving information of this design, placed two forces in ambush, one within and one without the gate near which the grain was to be left. When the attempt to deliver the grain was made the troops in ambush attacked simultaneously those who had brought the grain and those who expected to receive it, putting both parties to flight and capturing the supply. The besiegers were now approaching the defences of Mahakot, and Fath Khan sent his family to the citadel, Balakot, above the escarpment. Hitherto he had been assisted in the defence by about two hundred Bijapuris among whom was the uncle of Rindula Khan.

This small force, which had hitherto shared the privations of the garrison and now foresaw that the fall of Daulatabad was inevitable, secretly made terms with the Khan-i-Khanan, who agreed to allow them to depart to Bijapur. Precautions were taken to conceal their defection from Fath Khan and they left the fortress by night, descending a rope made fast to one of the battlements. All were kindly received by the Khan-i-Khanan, who found a use for them. They were made the bearers of a message to Ibrahim Adil Shah II, who was warned to desist from further opposition to the imperial army in its operations against

Daulatabad. The Khan-i-Khanan added that he was expecting reinforcements which would enable him to bring the siege of Daulatabad to an early conclusion, and that unless the alliance between Bijapur and Fath Khan terminated immediately, the imperial troops would invade Bijapur territory as soon as the cessation of the rains rendered the movement of troops possible.

After the despatch of these deserters to Bijapur, the siege was resumed with vigour. Rindula Khan and Shahji were now with the army of Bijapur on the hills above Ellora, and the Khan-i-Khanan found it necessary to post a large force at Kaghazipura to prevent any attempt to victual the fortress. The Khan-i-Zaman was in Zafarnagar ready to move in any direction to the assistance of convoys for the imperial army. He received information that a quantity of treasure and supplies had been despatched from Burhanpur by way of Rohankhed, and that the Bijapuris were preparing to make a descent on the convoy. He therefore marched towards Rohankhed to escort the convoy to its destination, leaving in Zafarnagar only a small force under Ahmad Khan Niyazi. Ahmad Khan was at once attacked by the Bijapuris but held his ground until reinforcements arrived and finally defeated his assailants with great slaughter. The Khan-i-Zaman now brought the convoy safely into Zafarnagar, and the Bijapuris, notwithstanding their defeat, resolved to make a final effort to prevent it from reaching the besieging army. The Khan-i-Khanan sent large reinforcements under Nasiri Khan and Jagraj to the Khan-i-Zaman, and when the latter, advancing from Zafarnagar, reached Khirki and was attacked by Rindula Khan, Yaqut Khan, and Shahji, he routed the Bijapuris and escorted the supplies and treasure, consisting of 20,000 ox-loads of corn, six lakhs of rupees, and 100 maunds of powder, to the army besieging Daulatabad.

On May 25, 1633, Morari Pant arrived with a fresh force from Bijapur and joined Rindula Khan and Shahji at Ellora, inspiring their army with fresh confidence. The Khan-i-Zaman, who was sent to Kaghazipura to prevent a descent on the besieging force, was attacked by night and was unable to repulse his assailants until the morning, when, having received reinforcements, he fell upon the Bijapuris and pursued them for many miles. On the same day Khudawand Khan and Sidi Salim, two of Husain Nizam Shah's principal officers, deserted from

Daulatabad and were well received by the Khan-i-Khanan. On June 3 the Bijapuris made their most determined attempt to raise the siege. Morari Pant, leaving Rindula Khan and Shahji to hold the Khan-i-Zaman in check, marched against the Khan-i-Khanan. The latter, believing that he had the whole of the army of Bijapur arrayed against him, ordered the Khan-i-Zaman to join him, but that officer was engaged with Rindula Khan and Shahji and could not at once assist his chief, and the Khan-i-Khanan, keeping a small force to guard the trenches in Ambarkot, despatched the greater part of his troops to meet Morari Pant and Yaqut Khan. Meanwhile, these two generals marched down from the hills and interposed their army between the troops which had been sent to attack them and the small force which the Khan-i-Khanan had kept with himself. The Khan-i-Khanan, being reinforced by a detachment which was sent to his aid by the Khan-i-Zaman, fell upon the enemy and was joined at the same time by some of the troops which he had detached. The Bijapuris were defeated and put to flight, while fresh corps of the imperial troops continued to arrive on the field, and were desptached to report on the movements of the retreating enemy. They reported that the Bijapuris had rallied and were preparing to attack Luhrasp, who had been the first to be sent against them and had marched far from the imperial camp. A small body of the imperial troops was cut up by a force of Bijapuris which was lingering near the scene of its defeat, but this episode had no effect on the general result of the day's fighting. The Khan-i-Khanan was pressing on to the assistance of Luhrasp, when he came suddenly on a large force of Bijapuris under Yaqut Khan, Ambar, and Kheloji. This force was lying in ambush in a *nala* while Morari Pant with another force was attempting to entice Luhrasp within striking distance of the ambuscade. The Khan-i-Khanan at once fell upon this force and defeated it. The flight of the Bijapuris was interrupted by another *nala* which threw them into great confusion. The pursuers cut their way through the seething mass to where Yaqut Khan was. He was valiantly defended by his Habashis, but their valour was fruitless, for they were gradually beaten back, and their master, the doubly-dyed traitor, was slain. The Habashis again returned to the charge, intent on recovering his body, but were again beaten back, and the body was carried off by the imperial troops. The pursuit of the flying Bijapuris was then continued for two miles with great slaughter, until Nasiri Khan, who had been with the Khan-i-Jahan, arrived on the scene and reported the enemy had been every where vanquished, thus relieving the Khan-i-Khanan of his anxiety for the Khan-i-Jahan and Luhrasp.

On the following day (June 4) the Khan-i-Zaman was ordered to withdraw from Kaghazipura, where his presence was no longer necessary since Morari Pant had retreated to Khirki, and to occupy Nizampur, in order that the imperial troops might not again be attacked in detail. Rindula Khan and Shahji, finding the plateau deserted, returned and encamped there and threw rockets among the besiegers at night. A force was despatched to hold them in check for the night, and on the morning of June 5 they were attacked and defeated with much slaughter and the loss of many prisoners and horses. On this day the Khan-i-Khanan ordered that a mine which had been run under the *enceinte* of Mahakot should be fired. Fath Khan, hearing of this, sent a message to the Khan-i-Khanan saying that he could not surrender without consulting the Bijapuris, and begging that the firing of the mine might be delayed one day in order that he might inform them that his supplies had failed and that he could hold out no longer. The Khan-i-Khanan refused to countermand his original order unless Fath Khan sent his son as a hostage, and as this condition was not accepted the mine was fired. On this occasion the storming party was ready, and as soon as the charge exploded, destroying a bastion and fifteen yards of the curtain, rushed forward, undeterred by the deadly fire poured upon them by the defenders. The imperial troops made good their position in Mahakot and opened trenches against Balakot, to which the defenders were now confined. Morari Pant, hearing of the fall of Mahakot, made a demonstration against the besiegers, but the Khan-i-Zaman and Nasiri Khan attacked him and put him to flight.

At this time a Nizam Shahi noble, Mahaldar Khan, sent a message to the Khan-i-Khanan offering to submit to the emperor and to surrender his fort of Trimbak to any officer who might be appointed to command it. He was informed that he could better serve the imperial cause and earn the imperial favour by making a descent on Baizapur, where the treasure of Rindula Khan and Shahji was stored, and where the latter's family was lodged. Mahaldar Khan reached Baizapur without opposition and captured the wife and daughter of Shahji and a large quantity of supplies and treasure, including 400 horses, 100,000 *huns* and much personal property belonging to Shahji, and property valued at 12,000 *huns* belonging to Rindula Khan. The Khan-i-Khanan complimented Mahaldar Khan on his success and ordered him to place Shahji's wife and family in safety with the commandant of the fort of Kalna, recently captured by the imperial troops, and to join the imperial army.

Fath Khan now realised that he could hold out no longer and sent his eldest son, Abdur Rasul Khan, to the Khan-i-Khanan, praying for a week's time in which to convey his and his sovereign's families to a place of safety and for the means of conveying them and the expenses of their journey. Abdur Rasul Khan was to remain meanwhile as a hostage with the imperial army. The Khan-i-Khanan generously placed his own elephants and *palkis* at the disposal of Fath Khan and Husain Nizam Shah and supplied them with more than a million rupees for expenses. Fath Khan then sent the keys of the fort to the Khan-i-Khanan and made preparations for the journey of his family, while the gates were guarded by the imperial troops. On Monday, June 28, 1633, Fath Khan and Husain Nizam Shah came forth and the imperial army occupied the citadel of Daulatabad. Thus, after a siege of more than four months, " the nine forts of Daulatabad, whereof five are on the plain and four on the slopes of the hill, with many guns and other material of war, lead, powder, grenades, and rockets, fell into the hands of the leaders of the host of the glorious empire." The drums of victory were beaten and the *khutba* was read in the mosque of Qutb-ud-din Mubarak Shah in the name of the emperor Shahjahan. Abdul Hamid Khan Lahori, whose description of the fort has already been quoted, records that no conqueror had hitherto been able " to cast the noose of contrivance over the battlement of subjection " at Daulatabad, and explains the Khan-i-Khanan's success. In the year before that in which the siege was undertaken the failure of the rains caused a famine in the Deccan, and when the siege began, Daulatabad, as we have seen, was scantily victualled. Had supplies been sufficient the imperial army could never have effected an entry into Balakot, the upper fort. The failure of the rains and the consequent famine are of course attributed to the intervention of Heaven on behalf of Shahjahan.

After the fall of Daulatabad the Khan-i-Khanan, leaving the Khan-i-Dauran with a small force to hold the fortress, set out for Zafarnagar on his way to Burhanpur, taking Husain Nizam Shah and Fath Khan with him. Morari Pant and Rindula Khan not only harassed the army on its march to Zafarnagar, but invested Daulatabad, where very little grain had been left, and occupied the siege-works of the imperial army. During the Khan-i-Khanan's halt at Zafarnagar they attempted to obtain favourable terms of peace and sent Farhad, the father of Rindula Khan, as an envoy to the Khan-i-Khanan. The latter, however, refused to treat, and Farhad returned mortified to his son's camp. As soon as the Khan-i-Khanan continued his march northward the Bijapuris invested Daulatabad more closely, but the Khan-i-Dauran made several sorties, in each of which he inflicted severe loss on them, and his distress was relieved by the cultivators whom he had wisely conciliated, and who now supplied him with grain to the best of their ability. The Khan-i-Khanan, conceiving that this second siege of Daulatabad was likely to become a serious affair, turned back, but the Bijapuris would not await his return, and fled by way of Nasik and Trimbak to the Adil Shahi territories. The Khan-i-Khanan, after provisioning Daulatabad, resumed his journey to Burhanpur. Husain Nizam Shah and Fath Khan were sent to court, whence the former was sent as a state prisoner to Gwalior, where his cousin Bahadur Nizam Shah had been immured since the fall of Ahmadnagar thirty years before. Fath Khan was given an appointment in the imperial service and received a present of two lakhs of rupees, but did not live long enough to requite this generous treatment. An old wound in the head affected his brain and shortly afterwards caused his death.

On February 3, 1636, Shahjahan visited Daulatabad and spent the following *Naurus* festival there, while his generals were engaged in consolidating his rule in the country which had formerly owned allegiance to the Nizam Shahi kings. During his sojourn in Daulatabad he built the fine *baradari* which is still a conspicuous object near the summit of the hill, and early in the following year he marched to Mando and thence returned to Burhanpur. As soon as he had left the Deccan the Bijapuris overran the whole of the Nizam Shahi country and even Berar, as far as Burhanpur, but Daulatabad stood fast and Muhammad Adil Shah of Bijapur was ultimately compelled to make peace with the Khan-i-Dauran.

When Aurangzib resided in the Deccan as viceroy he made Khirki, which had been renamed Fathabad, his capital, and again renamed it Aurangabad; but Daulatabad still remained the principal fortress in his viceroyalty, and when he marched northward, in 1658, to seize the throne of Delhi, he left his second son, Muhammad Mu'azzam, to defend Aurangabad, but placed his wives and his youngest son Akbar in Daulatabad for safety.

After the fall of Bijapur and Golconda Aurangzib used Daulatabad as a state prison for Sikandar Adil Shah and Abul Hasan Qutb Shah. The remains of the prison house of the latter, known as the *Chini Mahal*, are still to be seen. After the cruel execution of Shivaji's son Sambhaji in 1689, his mother and daughter were imprisoned in Daulatabad. Since that time the history of Daulatabad has been uneventful. Since 1724, the year in which the battle of Shakarkhelda or Fathkhelda was fought, it has been included in the dominions of the Nizams of Hyderabad, though it passed for a time into the hands of the Marathas, and the old fort is now garrisoned by a small guard, while the once populous capital of India has dwindled down to one or two hamlets within the walls. At the village of Kaghazipura in the hills above the fort the paper for which Daulatabad was once famous is still made.

The principal mosque in the fort, that constructed by Qutb-ud-din Mubarak Shah from the remains of Hindu temples has already been described. Apart from the citadel itself, the most striking building at Daulatabad is a high column known as the Chand Minar, at the base of which is a small mosque containing a long and bombastic inscription in the most contemptible Persian doggerel. This inscription records the fact that the column and the mosque were built by one Malik Parviz, the son of Qaranfal, who apparently held a *jagir* in Daulatabad, in the year 1445, in the reign of Ala-ud-din Ahmad II, of the Bahmani dynasty. The builder is not mentioned in history, but from his title and his father's name it may be presumed that he was an Abyssinian slave, a supposition which coincides with his evident ignorance of Persian.

Aurangzib lies buried, surrounded by the tombs of saints, in the small town of Khuldabad or Rauza in the hills above Daulatabad, and at the outskirts of the same town is the humble grave of his victim Abul Hasan Qutb Shah, the last king of Golconda.

CHAPTER III.

AMONG THE TOMBS.

I.—RAUZA.

THE small town of Khuldabad, better known as Rauza or "the garden," is situated about seven miles from the old fort of Daulatabad, in the Nizam's dominions, on an undulating plateau overtopped again by higher hills, and is probably best known to Europeon travellers as the halting place whence the caves of Ellora may most conveniently be visited. The tombs of saints sent forth as missionaries in the days when the Deccan was a land little known by the followers of Islam, earned for the town its original name of Rauza which has special reference to the garden of Paradise, and its selection as the last resting place of the greatest save one of the Mughal emperors of Hindustan, known after his death by the title of *khuld makan* ("he whose abode is heaven") gained for it the title of Khuldabad, or the heavenly abode. Most visitors, probably, include in their round of sight-seeing the tomb of the great emperor, though not a few perhaps, omit it, as being destitute of architectural grandeur or beauty. It is, indeed, mean in the extreme as compared with the tombs of his predecessors or with those of the kings of Bijapur and Golconda, but its very meanness and obscurity invest it with a melancholy interest. The great conqueror would have no splendid mausoleum. "The rich," he said "build lofty domes to cover their remains, for the poor the blue vault of heaven, suffices." A sneer at "the pride which apes humility" may be allowed, but if Aurangzib was a hypocrite he was at least a consistent hypocrite, and purchased by a long life of unremitting labour and austerity the power which he loved to acquire and to wield. His reign of fifty years was one long period of warfare, principally in the Deccan. He left his capital in 1679, never to return, and died at Ahmadnagar at the age of ninety. From Ahmadnagar his body was carried, in accordance with his will, to Rauza, there to be buried in a humble grave on which the grass should always grow, surrounded by the tombs of saints of whose company he professed to be unworthy, and whose holiness is now overshadowed by his greatness.

The first of the missionaries of Islam to be buried at Rauza was the saint Muntajab-ud-din, known as *Zar Bakhsh* or "the bestower of gold," in consequence of a supposed miraculous gift which enabled him to supply from day to day, the wants of his seven hundred followers. He was sent from Delhi in 1309 by the famous saint Nizam-ud-din Auliya, but did not long survive his journey to the Deccan. He was succeeded by his younger brother Burhan-ud-din Auliya, who died in 1343 and was buried near the spot afterwards selected as the site of Aurangzib's tomb. He was succeeded by his disciple Zain-ud-din, who also has a fine tomb, at Rauza. With this saint the succession of authorized leaders of missionary enterprise in the Deccan, which was one of the immediate consequences of the southern conquests of Ala-ud-din Khalji, came to an end.

A later sojourner at Rauza was the saint known as Sayyid Raju Qattal, ("the slayer"), so called from the gift of the evil eye, which he is said to have possessed to such a remarkable degree that he could kill by a glance. His powers have not, it is said, died with him. The inhabitants believe that no bird can settle on the dome of his tomb without bursting asunder. Near this saint's tomb is a small mosque known as the mosque of the fourteen hundred saints. who are supposed to have accompanied Muntajab-ud-din to the Deccan. The number of these worthies seems to have doubled by some mysterious process, for the most authentic information which we have is that Muntajab-ud-din was accompanied by seven hundred disciples. The tombs of the saints who have been mentioned are still objects of veneration, and Burhan-ud-din Auliya is further commemorated by a cenotaph in the fort of Narnala, in Berar, a visit to which is said to be a prophylactic against hydrophobia.

Near the tomb of Sayyid Raju Qattal is a large empty tomb, now used as a rest-house, which formerly held the remains of Ahmad Shah, who died in 1508, and Burhan Shah, who died in 1554, the two first kings of the Nizam Shahi dynasty of Ahmadnagar. Their bones, after resting here for some time, were removed and taken to the shrine of Karbala, where they were re-interred. In an enclosure near this tomb stands the fine tomb of Malik Ambar the African, the able solder and administrator who long stemmed the tide of Mughal conquest in the Deccan and fitly finds a resting place near the tomb of the earlier kings of the dynasty which he served so well in the years of its decay. He died in

I

626, in the eightieth year of his age, and the emperor Jahangir, who during the African's life could not mention his name without vituperation, recorded after his death, that he had no equal in his time, either in the art of war or in administrative ability.

To the east of these tombs and nearer to the town of Rauza are a few smaller and less pretentious domes. These are the tombs of the later kings of the Ahmadnagar dynasty, but the several tombs cannot be identified, as they bear no inscriptions Nearly all are ruinous. Only one building in this neighbourhood bears an inscription. This is the tomb of Khundamir Ankas Khan Sakhi, son of Ankas Khan. This *amir* was the brother of Tahir Khan and foster brother of Miran Husain Shah, the fifth king of the Nizam Shahi dynasty, notorious on account of his having suffocated his father, Murtaza Shah, in a hot bath. The date of the death of Ankas Khan is not given, but he was much concerned in Ahmadnagar politics in 1588. He was probably the son of that Ankas Khan of Bijapur who quarrelled with the Portuguese commandant of Goa in 1516.

Asaf Jah, Nizam-ul-Mulk, the founder of the line of the present ruler of Haidarabad, lies buried near the tomb of Burhan-ud-din Auliya, and near him lies his son Nasir Jung. Here also is buried the poet Azad of Bilgram, that nursery of learned men, the secretary of Asaf Jah and the tutor of his son. The fame of the poet's learning is such that parents take their children to his shrine in order that they may, by picking up with their lips a piece of sugar from the tomb, obtain both a taste for knowledge and the ability to acquire it.

The most pathetic of all the monuments at Khuldabad is a simple stone *taviz* or *tumulus* in the enclosure of Sayyid Raju Qattal's tomb. Here lie the remains of Abul Hasan Qutb Shah, commonly known as Tana Shah—"the dainty king,"—the last independent king of Golconda, and a victim to Aurangzib's lust of conquest. His fortress capital was wrested from him by treachery in 1687 after a gallant defence of eight months' duration, and he was sent by his conqueror to end his days in captivity at Daulatabad, where he lingered for twelve years, and was buried, in accordance with his last wishes, at Rauza. The environs of the small town contain the tombs of greater men, but of none more unfortunate.

II.—Golconda.

To the north of the old fort of Golconda stands a large group of domed buildings, some large and imposing and others of meaner design, interspersed with many mosques of various sizes, some of which are very ornate. These are the tombs of the kings of the Qutb Shahi dynasty, who ruled Telingana from 1512 to 1687, and of their dependants. Of these tombs the historian of architecture* says:—"The tombs of the kings of this dynasty and of their nobles and families do form as extensive and as picturesque a group as is to be found anywhere, but individually they are in singularly bad taste. Their bases are poor and weak, their domes tall and exaggerated, showing all the faults of the age in which they were executed, but still not unworthy of a place in history if the materials existed for illustrating them properly."

These remarks, if it be not presumptuous to differ from so great an authority on architecture, do the tombs scant justice. Their domes are large but not unduly tall, and though the bases of some of the smaller tombs may be poor those of the larger tombs are not overpowered by the domes which they carry. Each of the three latest of the larger tombs is surrounded by a massive arcade, forming a verandah which gives an appearance of bulk to the base of the building. The mosques, which are not mentioned by Mr. Fergusson, are far more open to criticism than the tombs. The profusion of ornament in stucco is not always in the best taste, and the characteristic galleries round the minarets, not perhaps out of place in large buildings like the Char Minar in Haidarabad, become ridiculous when in a small mosque they are necessarily so much reduced in size as to be palpable imitations, added for no purpose other than ornament. It may also be remarked that materials for illustrating these buildings in the light of history do exist, though they have unfortunately not been extensively utilized as yet.

The Qutb Shahi dynasty, to which these tombs belong, was founded by Sultan Quli Qutb-ul-Mulk, governor of Telingana, in 1512. Sultan Quli reigned at Golconda for thirty-one years after 1512, during which period he expelled Qivam-ul-Mulk the Turk, who had been appointed by the Bahmani king governor of eastern Telingana, and was engaged in almost ceaseless warfare against the Hindus of Telingana, in the

* Fergusson, *History of Indian and Eastern Architecture*, 1899, p. 567.

course of which he overcame and expelled a renegade Musalman named Shitab Khan, who had made common cause with the infidels. He also engaged in a campaign against Ismail Adil Shah of Bijapur. He was murdered on September 3, 1543, in the ninety-eighth year of his age, at the instigation of his second surviving son Jamshid.

Sultan Quli is buried in a small and unpretentious tomb near the south-western corner of the whole group of buildings, and beyond the garden in which the later tombs now stand. He is described in his epitaph as "the prince who has received pardon for his sins, the fortunate, the martyr, the warrior for the sake of God, the striver in the way of God, Malik Sultan Quli, entitled Qutb-ul-Mulk, known as Bare Malik," the last being evidently a familiar Indian nickname. The absence of the royal title distinguishes his epitaph from those of his successors, for the word Sultan is not here part of the royal title as some English historians have erroneously taken it to be. *Quli* is a Turki word meaning "servant" or "slave," and Sultan Quli ("servant of the king") was the personal name of the founder of the Qutb Shahi dynasty. Those who regard the word Sultan in this case as a royal title and call him as one historian does King Quli, do but call him King "Coolie."

Jamshid Qutb Shah, who ascended the throne on his father's death, was a warlike ruler who interfered far more than was the custom of the Qutb Shahi kings in the quarrels between the other independent Sultans of the Deccan. He was also a poet of respectable ability. Towards the end of his reign he sank into debauchery, possibly with the object of deadening the severe pain caused by a cancer from which he suffered, and which so inflamed a temper naturally fierce that he became a terror to all about him.

Jamshid Qutb Shah died early in 1550 and was buried in a high and narrow tomb, of no architectural merit near that of his father.

On the death of Jamshid his son, a boy of seven years of age, was raised to the throne as Subhan Quli Qutb Shah, but was not permitted to enjoy his kingdom long in peace. At the time of Jamshid Qutb Shah's accession his younger brother Ibrahim, alarmed for his safety, fled to Vijayanagar, where he lived for seven years under the protection of Sadashivaraya, the ruler of that kingdom. After Jamshid's death Saif Khan Ain-ul-Mulk, the prime minister of the kingdom, formed the design of seizing the royal power for himself, and in his capacity as regent carried himself so haughtily towards the nobles of the kingdom that a large number of them sent a message to Ibrahim in Vijayanagar, imploring him to come to Golconda and seize the crown and promising him their assistance. Ibrahim left Vijayanagar, declining assistance from Sadashivaraya, and invaded his nephew's dominions, where he was joined by many of the discontented nobles. Ain-ul-Mulk marched to meet him but had no sooner left the capital than his principal supporters were overthrown and imprisoned by Ibrahim's party, who had been encouraged by letters and message from Ibrahim. Ain-ul-Mulk, finding himself helpless before the invader, feigned submission to him in the hope of getting him into his power once the capital should be reached, but Ibrahim saw through the artifice and refused to receive the regent. Ain-ul-Mulk then fled from the kingdom by way of Kaulas and took refuge in Bidar, and Ibrahim, finding the way clear before him, marched to Golconda and ascended the throne on October 28, 1550.

Ibrahim Qutb Shah reigned for nearly thirty years, taking his part in the troubled politics of the Deccan during that period. The most notable event of his reign was his participation in the confederacy of the Sultans of the Deccan, which on January 24, 1565, destroyed the Hindu empire of Vijayanagar on the field of Talikota.

Ibrahim died on June 6, 1580, and lies buried in a fine and lofty domed tomb, surrounded by the graves of his dependants. On the south-eastern corner of the plinth of the tomb is a small building containing the tomb of his sixth son Mirza Muhammad Amin, who was nine years of age at the time of his father's death and died a natural death at the age of twenty-five on April 25, 1596, leaving a son, Muhammad, who eventually came to the throne.

In an enclosure on the north-east corner of the plinth of Ibrahim's tomb stands the grave of Niknam Khan, who died on March 30, 1673. At the head of this grave is a stone bearing an inscription of an unusual character. It is a grant in perpetuity of the revenues of the village of Mangalwaram, twelve miles to the west of Golconda, for the distribution of alms and the maintenance of lights at the grave, and for the support of attendants and reciters of the *Quran*. The grant, according to the inscription, is to last until the coming of the Mahdi.

Ibrahim Qutb Shah was succeeded by his third son, Muhammad Quli Qutb Shah. This king was the founder of Haidarabad. In 1591 he found that the air of Golconda, which was now very densely populated, did not agree with him, and therefore founded, on the banks of the Musi, his new city which he first named Bhagnagar, changing its name later to Haidarabad.

Muhammad Quli Qutb Shah died on January 24, 1612, and was buried in the large domed tomb without but nearest to the wall of the garden in which stand the tombs of his son-in-law and daughter and those of numerous members of the royal family and of their dependants. Muhammad Quli's grave is in the crypt of this tomb and is covered by a plain *tumulus* of black stone. In the chamber above the crypt and immediately over the grave, is another *tumulus* of black stone, bearing an elaborately carved epitaph.

Within the garden already mentioned are two large and numerous smaller tombs. Of the two large tombs that to the south-west is the tomb of Muhammad Qutb Shah, the nephew and son-in-law of Muhammad Quli Qutb Shah, who left no male issue. Muhammad Qutb Shah was, as has been said, the son of Mirza Muhammad Amin, already mentioned as having died in 1596.

Another error into which English historians have fallen calls for notice here. Confused by the similarity between the titles of the uncle and nephew they have regarded them as the same person, styled indifferently Muhammad Quli or simply Muhammad.* One writer makes Muhammad the elder brother of Muhammad Quli.† The epitaphs of Golconda and the Persian histories of the Qutb Shahi dynasty which have come down to us clear up this matter Muhammad Quli Qutb Shah reigned, as has been said, from 1580 to 1612, and was succeeded by his nephew and son-in-law, Muhammad Qutb Shah, who reigned from 1612 to 1626.

In the north-eastern corner of the garden is a large tomb very similar to that of Muhammad Qutb Shah. This is the tomb of his queen, Hayat Bakhsh Begam, daughter of Muhammad Quli Qutb Shah. Its peculiarity is that it is equal in size and grandeur to the tombs of

---

* *Vide Chronology of India*, by C. Mabel Duff, p. 318.

† Mr. J. D. B. Gribble, on p. 285 of Vol. I of *A History of the Deccan*, an extremely inaccurate work.

any of the kings of the dynasty who actually reigned, Hayat Bakhsh Begam being the only lady so honoured. The explanation of this is that Hayat Bakhsh was something more than an oriental queen-consort. She was the daughter of a king, the wife of a king, and the mother of a king, and seems to have been a lady of strong character who held the view that Muhammad Qutb Shah owed his elevation to the throne to his alliance with the daughter of Muhammad Quli rather than to his own descent from Ibrahim. She certainly had great influence over her husband during his comparatively short reign, and after his death practically governed the kingdom till her death, which occurred on February 24, 1667, as appears from her epitaph.

Muhammad Qutb Shah died on February 11, 1626, and was succeeded by his son Abdullah Qutb Shah, then a boy of eleven. Abdullah had a long and eventful reign of forty-six years, during which period his chief anxiety was to hold the Mughals, now advanced well into the Deccan, at bay. In 1656 Aurangzib, then viceroy of the Deccan, advanced to Haidarabad and besieged Abdullah in Golconda. He was bought off by a heavy subsidy and promise of future tribute, but the principal condition of the treaty was the marriage of the second daughter of Abdullah, who had no son, to Muhammad Sultan, the eldest son of Aurangzib, and the formal recognition of Muhammad Sultan as heir apparent to the throne of Golconda. The marriage was duly celebrated but the prince predeceased Abdullah Qutb Shah, and the question of his ascending the throne thus never arose.

Abdullah Qutb Shah died on May 1, 1672, and was buried in the large tomb beyond the garden to the north-east, which is almost a replica of his mother's tomb. Food is still distributed once a year at his tomb on the anniversary of his death, according to the lunar reckoning.

Abdullah left no son, and his son-in-law Muhammad Sultan, the formally recognized heir apparent, had predeceased him. He was succeeded by another son-in-law, Abul Hasan, who had married his third daughter. Abul Hasan Qutb Shah commonly known as Tana Shah, besides being married to the daughter of Abdullah, was descended, either in the male or the female line, from the Qutb Shahi family, and it was this descent that ensured his elevation to the throne.

The story of Abul Hasan is told elsewhere. Notwithstanding the premature death of Muhammad Sultan Aurangzib affected to regard the succession of Abul Hasan as an act of usurpation, the absurdity of this pretension is manifest, seeing that it was only in his wife's right that Muhammad had been recognized as heir apparent, but any excuse was sufficient for Aurangzib, and Abul Hasan, throughout his short reign, lived in constant dread of the emperor's aggressive ambition.

The blow fell at last in 1686, when Aurangzib, having taken Bijapur and sent its young king into captivity, marched on Golconda, which fell in October 1687, after a siege of eight months. Abul Hasan was sent into captivity at Daulatabad where he died some twelve years later and was buried in a humbl egrave at Rauza, in the hills above his prison house.

By the gate of the garden already mentioned stands an unfinished tomb with rough-cast walls and an incomplete dome, considerably meaner in design than the tombs of the more fortunate kings of the dynasty. This building, though it is now occupied by other graves, is believed to be the tomb which Abul Hasan was building for himself when he was so rudely interrupted by Aurangzib's invasion.

CHAPTER IV.

WARANGAL.

NEAR the south-eastern corner of the Haidarabad State stand the remains of an old town, once the capital of a kingdom and for a time one of the strongholds of Hinduism in southern India against the Muhammadan invaders from the north, but now so decayed as to be little more than an appanage of a town which, though older than itself, was for a long period no more than one of its suburbs. Warangal is a station on the Haidarabad-Bezwada branch of the Nizam's State Railway, but the traveller who alights there will be borne, unless he clearly explains his destination, to Hanamkonda, which is itself a delight to the antiquary and now overshadows the former Hindu capital.

Warangal was for many years the capital of the Kakatiya dynasty of Telingana, which, according to the Muhammadan historian Badaoni, reigned for 700 years before the capture of the city by Muhammad bin Tughlaq of Delhi in 1321, and therefore, if Badaoni is to be trusted, rose to power early in the seventh century of the Christian era. According to Hindu legend a Chalukya king, possibly one of the Chalukya feudatories of the Rashtrakutas, reigned at Nandagiri (Nander) in the Deccan, and before his death divided his dominions between his two sons, one of whom reigned at Hanamkonda and the other at Kandhar, now in the Nander district of the Haidarabad State. Ballahundu, king of Cuttack, warring against Kandhar, slew king Somadeva, whose widow, Siriyal Devi, fled to Hanamkonda and there gave birth to a posthumous son, who founded the Kakatiya dynasty. There may be a substratum of truth in the legend, but at present it is of little or no historical value, for no dates are given; much remains to be done by the epigraphist in Telingana, and it is possible that inscriptions exist which would verify or contradict both the Hindu legend and Badaoni's chronology. The first known king of the Kakatiya dynasty is Tribhuvanamalla Betmaraja, whose exact date cannot be ascertained. His grandson built the temple of the thousand pillars in Hanamkonda in 1163 and, allowing about thirty years as the average length of a reign, it may be surmised that

Tribhuvanamalla ascended the throne in 1100. He was succeeded by his son Prolaraja or Prodaraja whose accession may be roughly fixed by the same method of computation in 1130. In any case he was reigning about 1150. He married a lady named Muppaladevi and seems to have been both warlike and powerful. He captured but released Nurmadi-Tailapadeva III, the Chalukya Raja of Kaliani, who seems to have been his overlord, and defeated a king Govinda whose kingdom, which cannot be identified, he gave to one Udaya; conquered Gunda, ruler of the city of Mantrakuta, which has not been identified, and repulsed an attack made on Hanamkonda by Tribhuvanamalla-Jagaddeva, raja of Patti Pombuchchapura, now Humcha in the Nagar district of Mysore, who was, like his foe, a vassal of the Chalukya rajas of Kaliani. Tradition ascribes the foundation of Warangal to Prolaraja.

Prolaraja was succeeded, probably about 1162, by his son Prataparudradeva I, who built the temple of the thousand pillars at Hanamkonda and from whose long inscription therein all of this information concerning the Kakatiyas is gathered. He conquered Domma, who cannot be identified, and Mailigideva or Mallugi, the sixteenth king of the Yadava dynasty of Seunadesha, the district which lay between Nasik and Deogir, the modern Daulatabad. He also conquered the country of Polavasa, which has not been identified, and repulsed a king named Bhima, who had seized part of the Chola and Chalukya dominions after establishing himself by the murder of a king named Gokarna. Prataparudradeva I was succeeded by Mahadeva, who was probably his son, but neither the length of his reign nor of that of Prataparudradeva can be ascertained at present. Mahadeva was succeeded in 1223 by his son, Ganapati, who defeated the Yadava raja Singhana, who reigned in Seunadesha from 1210 to 1247. There is some difference of opinion regarding the date of Ganapati's death, which is variously placed in 1257 and 1261, by which time he had begun the building of the inner or stone wall of Warangal. No son survived him and he was succeeded by his widow Rudrammadevi, who completed the stone wall of Warangal and surrounded the city by an outer wall of earth. She is said to have reigned for 38 years and was reigning when Marco Polo*

* Marco Polo extols her as a wise and well beloved queen, who remained a widow for her husband's sake and ruled his kingdom well.

visited southern India. In 1294, a date which does not coincide with the date given for her husband's death and the length of her reign, she is said to have abdicated in favour of his grandson Prataparudradeva II, who was evidently the son of a son of Ganapati who had predeceased his father. In the year given as that of the accession of Prataparudradeva II the dominions of the Kakatiyas extended as far westward as Raichur, for in that year the fort of Raichur was founded by Gore Gangayya Ruddivaru, a servant of the family. Prataparudradeva II was reigning when Telingana was first invaded by Malik Kafur Hazardinari, entitled Malik Naib, the general of Sultan Ala-ud-din Khalji of Delhi, and was still reigning, though nominally as a tributary of the emperor of Delhi, when Muhammad bin Tughlaq invaded Telingana in 1321 and was forced to retire to Deogir. Later in the same year or, according to another account, in 1323, Muhammad bin Tughlaq returned to Warangal, on which occasion the city was captured and Prataparudradeva II was sent as a prisoner to Delhi, whence, however, he was allowed to return to Warangal where he reigned, as a vassal of Delhi until his death in 1325, when he was succeeded by his son Virabhadra or Krishna, who retired immediately after his accession to Kondavir, after which event the Kakatiya dynasty is believed to have disappeared from history; but, as will be seen, the Hindus of Telingana rebelled in 1343-44, towards the end of Muhammad bin Tughlaq's reign, and one Kanya or Kanhayya Naik, who may possibly have been identical with Krishna the Kakatiya, recaptured Warangal while one of his relatives, who had accepted Islam and held Kasupala for the emperor of Delhi, recanted and declared himself independent.

Some of the monuments of the Kakatiyas are still to be seen at Warangal, and at Hanamkonda, their earlier capital. The earliest of these, so far as legend helps us, is the magnificent temple of the thousand pillars at Hanamkonda. This temple, which, as has been said, was built by Prataparndradeva I, is probably one of the finest examples of Chalukyan architecture now extant, and exhibits the best characteristics of that style. It is dedicated to the god Rudra, the thunderer, who seems to have been the tutelary deity of the Kakatiyas, and contains, carved on a square pillar in what is now an outlying portion of the temple, a long Sanskrit inscription in the old Kanarese character with an exordium of eight lines in old Telugu commemorating *Mahamandaleshwara* ("the great Lord") Rudradeva, son of Prolaraja, Jagatikesarin Kakatiya, son and successor of Tribhuvana Betmaraja of Warangal. To this inscription, which is dated in *Shaka* 1084 (A. D. 1162-63) we are indebted for most of the knowledge of this dynasty which we at present possess. The temple also contains another inscription of much later date, in Telugu, which commemorates the heroism of a Muhammadan general named Shitab Khan. The existence in a Hindu temple of an inscription written in a Hindu language in praise of a Muhammadan general calls for some explanation, and we shall see later how it happened that this general was deemed by Hindus worthy of the honour accorded to him.

The next monument in chronological order is the inner or stone wall of Warangal. This, we have seen, was begun by Ganapati and completed by his widow Rudrammadevi, who also built the outer wall of the city. The circumference of the stone wall is 4 miles and 630 yards, and though it is evidently of Hindu workmanship, as appears from the architecture of the gateways, it must frequently have been repaired by Musalmans, for countless stones carved with figures of Hindu gods and their attendants which have been removed from the large temple which stood in the centre of the inner fort, have been built at random into the wall, their carved surfaces being sometimes turned inwards for the better concealment of objects of idolatrous worship. Of the large temple just mentioned nothing remains but four magnificent gates, even the enclosing wall having been removed, but from the large area which this wall enclosed and the exquisite carving of the stones which have been used for the repair of the fort wall there can be no doubt that the Warangal temple far excelled in magnificence the temple of the thousand pillars at Hanamkonda. The Muslims in their iconoclastic zeal unfortunately destroyed not only the temple, but also any inscription that it may have contained, thus rendering it impossible to say by whom it was built, but it may be conjectured that its builder was one of those who followed Prataparudradeva I on the throne, anxious to surpass his ancestor. The diameter of the area enclosed by the earthen wall built by Rudrammadevi is about two miles, and this space was occupied by the city of Warangal, while that within the stone wall seems to have contained, besides temples, the palaces of the Raja and his nobles. There is yet another outer wall, also of earth, the remains of which are distinctly visible, enclosing an almost circular area, the diameter of which varies between 8½ and 9 miles. The use of this outer rampart can only be conjectured, for it is obvious that it cannot have been the wall of a fenced city. The defence of more than 29 miles of wall would have been a task beyond the capacity even of those vast armies which the Hindu rulers of the south were able in old times to gather round themselves, and an urban area of more than 127 square miles would have been an extravagant allowance for the population of the greatest cities of antiquity. It may be conjectured that this outermost wall enclosed all the suburban villages and was no more than an unnecessarily costly suburban boundary; but its existence has stimulated lovers of the marvellous to flights of fancy, and the modern inhabitant of Warangal will inform the visitor that the old city had no less than seven walls, of which three have already been mentioned. The remainder are said to have disappeared, but it is gravely asserted that the rock fortress of Bhongir was merely a bastion on the outermost wall, from which it may be roughly calculated that this mythical wall had a circumference of 373 miles and enclosed an urban area of 20,240 square miles; but the retailers of the legend have evidently not made this calculation.

One of the most interesting facts revealed by the Hanamkonda inscription is that the Kakatiya dynasty did not lay claim to independent kingship, for Prataparudradeva I refrains from styling himself by any title higher than that of *Mahamandaleshwara*, or "great lord," a style used by rajas who were admittedly vassals. Prola Raja, who was reigning in 1150 and was the father of the author of the inscription, was a feudatory of the western Chalukyas of Kaliani, of whom nothing is known after the year 1183. It is evident that Prataparudradeva I acknowledged the supremacy of this dynasty, but the position of the Kakatiyas after its subversion is not clear. They probably assumed complete independence, but may have been beset by claims of overlordship put forward by the northern Yadavas of Deogir, the Hoysala Ballalas of Dwarasamudra, or both, but there is not sufficient evidence to show that such claims were ever admitted. The attitude of the Yadavas towards the

Kakatiyas when the Musalmans appeared on the scene affords little indication of the relations between the two dynasties, for it was probably dictated by unavoidable subservience to the hand which held the sword.

It is now necessary to notice very briefly the first invasion of southern India by the Musalmans. In 1294, twenty years before the battle of Bannockburn. Ala-ud-din Khalji, nephew and son-in-law of Jalal-ud-din Firuz Shah Khalji, the reigning emperor of Delhi, descended like a thunderbolt on the Deccan, hitherto an unknown land to the Muhammadans of northern India, and in the course of a brief campaign succeeded, by the mere force of almost incredible rashness and effrontery, in reducing the Yadavas of Deogir to the condition of vassals of the empire of Delhi. Ala-ud-din, on his return from Deogir, murdered his uncle and usurped his throne, and having learnt during his raid the position and power of the Hindu kingdoms of the south despatched an expedition in 1309 under the African Kafur Hazardinari, who bore the title of Malik Naib, to Warangal. The invading army was assisted by Ramchandra of Deogir with men, money, and supplies, and on passing Indur,* the frontier post between Deogir and Warangal, began to plunder and devastate the country. The wretched inhabitants fled headlong to the capital, where they took refuge in the outer fort surrounded by Rudramma Devi's earthen wall, while the Raja Prataparudradeva II and his nobles remained in the stone fort which was the inner line of defence. The Hindus, hemmed in by the invader, had little chance of obtaining relief from without, as any convoys destined for Warangal would have been compelled to run the gauntlet of the Muhammadan army; but Malik Naib had instructions to content himself with a substantial acknowledgment of suzerainty, and the scion of the Kakatiyas preferred submission to extinction. He sent his Brahmans and Bhats to Malik Naib and offered to deliver to him all the treasures, jewels, elephants, and horses then in Warangal and thenceforward to send annually to Delhi a fixed tribute of treasure and elephants: Malik Naib accepted without hesitation terms which accorded so well with his instructions, and, after receiving 100 elephants, 7,000 horses and a large quantity of jewels and precious stuffs, returned to Delhi in 1310.

* Lately renamed Nizamabad. It is the headquarters of the district of the same name in the Nizam's dominions and is a station on the Haidarabad-Godavari Valley Railway.

Between that period and the date of the next invasion of the Warangal kingdom the Khalji dynasty was overthrown and one of the principal Turki nobles of the empire, Malik Jauna, better known as Ghiyas-ud-din Tughlaq, was raised to the throne. In 1321 he sent his eldest son, Muhammad, against Warangal. Prataparudradeva feared to meet the Musalmans in the open field and shut himself up, with his nobles, in the fort of Warangal. Muhammad bin Tughlaq ravaged all the neighbouring country and collected large quantities of supplies, but the besieged were reinforced by troops from districts and some fierce fighting ensued, in which the Muhammadans were victorious. Prataparudradeva then offered to surrender all his treasure and to pay tribute, in the hope of ridding himself of the invaders, but Muhammad's instructions from his father differed from those which Malik Naib had received from his master and precluded him from acceding to any offer save that of an unconditional surrender. The besiegers were unable to effect an immediate entry into the fort and the siege continued, but communications with Delhi were now interrupted, and the prince, who had hitherto received periodical messages from his father, became alarmed at the absence of news from headquarters, where, for all that he knew, a revolution might have placed an usurper on the throne. Some self-seekers in his army who were tired of their sojourn in the south, and, jealous of the confidence placed in the old *amirs* of Ala-ud-din Khalji, deliberately gave currency to a rumour that Ghiyas-ud-din Tughlaq had died and that a usurper had ascended the throne, and then falsely assured the older officers of the army that Muhammad suspected them of disloyalty and was seeking occasion to slay them. Ala-ud-din's *amirs*, alarmed for their safety, assembled their troops and withdrew from the prince's camp, leaving him no alternative but to retire with the force under his immediate command. As he retraced his steps to Deogir he was pursued by the men of Telingana, who, without venturing to bring him to battle, harassed him during his retreat and plundered his baggage train. When Muhammad reached Deogir with his following he found the Raja of that place still loyal, and succeeded in collecting some of the scattered remnants of the army, but the leader of the *amirs* of the old *régime*, Malik Tamar, who either still believed the false report that Muhammad was seeking his life or deemed that he had sinned beyond forgiveness, fled with a small following of horsemen into Gondwana, where he perished. Another of the old *amirs* of Ala-ud-din was slain by the Hindus and flayed, his skin being sent to the prince at Deogir. Other fugitives were seized by the Hindus and were by them bound and sent to the prince, who sent them on to his father at Delhi. These wretches, with their wives and families, were brought forth in the presence of multitudes and executed in oriental fashion by being impaled alive or by being trampled or dragged to death by elephants, so that as the historian says, "Such fear and terror were implanted in the bosoms of the spectators that the whole city fell a-trembling."

Muhammad remained in Deogir, having no intention of presenting himself before his father *re infecta,* and four months later he received reinforcements from Delhi, and written instructions from the emperor to march at once on Warangal. Nothing daunted by his previous failure, which had been due rather to treachery and lack of self-confidence than to actual mismanagement, he set forth, and captured Bidar on his way. On reaching Warangal he resolutely besieged the place and in a very short time succeeded in taking both the outer and the inner forts by storm. Prataparudradeva, his wives and children, and all his principal nobles were made captives, and were sent to Delhi together with much treasure. Warangal was then formally annexed to the empire and was renamed Sultanpur.

This second expedition of Muhammad bin Tughlaq to Warangal, which according to most accounts was undertaken in 1321, is placed by Badaoni in 1323. Prataparudradeva II, as we have seen, returned to Warangal from Delhi and reigned as a vassal until his death in 1325. His son Virabhadra, or Krishna, retired to Kondavir and, so far as is generally known, ended his days there in peace; but when the Deccan was in rebellion against Muhammad bin Tughlaq in 1334-35, the Hindus of Telingana seized the opportunity of shaking off the Muslim yoke and rebelled under the leadership of Kanya or Kanhayya Naik, who may be conjecturally identified with Krishna the Kakatiya Kanhayya recaptured Warangal and a relative of his who, as has been mentioned, had accepted Islam and held Kampula for the emperor of Delhi, recanted and proclaimed himself independent.

In 1347 the Bahmani dynasty was founded by Ala-ud-din Bahman Shah, who wrested the Deccan from the emperors of Delhi. Kanhayya Naik profited by the campaigns of Bahman Shah, which rendered impossible the transmission of tribute to Delhi, to assume an unobtrusive independence, but, when the new Sultan had established himself on his throne and reduced the minor Hindu pretenders to obedience, he turned his attention to Telingana and captured the picturesque rock fortress of Bhongir, a structure surmounting one of the largest of those strange mammiform masses of solid rock which occur in Telingana. The ruler of Warangal wisely refrained from provoking the Muslim king to advance on his capital, and agreed to remit to Gulbarga, the capital of the new kingdom of the Deccan, the tribute which Prataparudradeva II had been accustomed to remit to Delhi, thus safeguarding his semi-independent kingdom against the interference of the Musalmans. Bhongir became the frontier post of the Bahmani kingdom and eastern Telingana was left undisturbed. Later in his reign Bahman Shah divided his kingdom into four *tarafs* or provinces, the capitals of which were Gulbarga, Daulatabad, Ellichpur, and Bidar. The last named town was regarded as the capital of western Telingana, which formed part of the Bahmani kingdom. The extent of the province may be estimated with some approximation to correctness by the names of the principal towns, Bidar, Kandhar, Indur, and Kaulas, which it contained. Bhongir is not mentioned, and it would appear that this fortress had been allowed to fall quietly into the hands of the Hindus and that a line running due north and south through a point a little to the east of Indur formed at this time the eastern boundary of the Bahmani dominions. Bhongir was perhaps exchanged for Kaulas, which is mentioned as a place which was specially ceded by the Raja of Telingana to Bahman Shah.

In 1358 Ala-ud-din Bahman Shah died and was succeeded by his eldest son, Muhammad I. This king became involved in a dispute with Bukka I, Raya of Vijayanagar, who claimed the Raichur Duab as part of his kingdom and demanded that it should be restored to him. The Raja of Telingana, who seems to have been the Kanhayya Naik already mentioned, seized this opportunity and preferred a request for the retrocession of the fort of Kaulas. He explained that his son

Vinayaka Deva, called Nag Deo by Firishta, was in rebellion and demanded the government of the fort and district of Kaulas, and hinted that Muhammad Shah would be wise to surrender the fort and thus gain a friend and ally, for if he refused he would find Warangal leagued with Vijayanagar against him. Muhammad Shah received the envoys from Warangal and Vijayanagar with courtesy, and in return sent envoys with temporizing messages, for he was doubtful of his ability to cope with the allies at once. Having thus gained time he set his house in order, dismissing all officers who did not merit his confidence and replacing them by others more active and trustworthy. When his preparations were complete he summoned the Hindu envoys to an audience and in the presence of his whole court reproached the rajas of Vijayanagar and Warangal for not having sent him the complimentary tribute which fell due on his accession, and demanded all the elephants and valuables which they could collect. The envoys, dismayed at the turn which affairs had taken, communicated the Sultan's demands to their masters. The raja of Warangal at once sent his son Vinayaka Deva with a large army against Kaulas, and Bukka of Vijayanagar sent an army of 20,000 horse and foot in the same direction. The armies of the provinces of Bidar and Berar were sent against the invaders, defeated them, and pursued them as far as Warangal, where a heavy indemnity was levied from Kanhayya. The Muhammadan army then retired to Gulbarga, but further trouble was to be brought on Warangal by the head-strong Vinayaka Deva.

In 1361 a caravan of horse dealers visited Gulbarga, and Muhammad Shah, who was a lover of horses, sent for them and inspected their stock. He found no horse fit for the royal stable and upbraided the dealers for bringing sorry nags to the court of the king of the Deccan. They replied that they had brought to India a number of fine horses, but that Vinayaka Deva, who was then governor of Vailampallam,* had compelled them to sell the best of their horses to him at a low price. The king then asked them why they had not told Vinayaka Deva that the horses were intended for Muhammad Shah Bahmani, who had the

*The identification of this place is not certain. Firishta calls it Vailampattan, and the authors of the *Burhani Maasir* and the *Tabaqat-i-Akbari* call it Filampattan and Balampattan. The place was probably Vailampallam, north of the Godavari and near its mouth, and it is likely that the horses were landed near this spot.

first refusal of them. The dealers replied that they had done so, but Vinayaka Deva had paid no heed to what they said. It needed but this to inflame the wrath of Muhammad Shah, who was already incensed by the thought that Vinayaka Deva had once escaped him, and he took the field without delay, leaving his minister as his deputy at Gulbarga. He marched by way of Kaliani to Bidar, where he left the main body of his army to follow at leisure while he pressed on with no more than a thousand horsemen to Vailampallam, travelling at such speed that he covered a month's march in a week. On arriving at Vailampallam with his small force he found that success was not to be attained without stratagem. A small body of Afghans was sent on in advance of the army and gained admittance to the city on the pretence that they were peaceful merchants who had been robbed of their goods and were fleeing from the robbers. While the guards at the gates were employed in questioning the pretended fugitives Muhammad Shah arrived with his thousand horsemen, and the guards made for the gates in order to shut them on the newcomers, who were believed to be the robbers. This belief throws some light on the administration of criminal justice and the nature of the government of a Hindu state in the fourteenth century. That a band of robbers who had already secured their booty should pursue their victims into a fenced city with murderous intent was apparently regarded us nothing unusual. The Afghans meanwhile played the part assigned to them. They attacked and overpowered the guards and Muhammad Shah entered the city with his small force and massacred all who were found in the streets. Vinayaka Deva was enjoying himself in a garden, and with difficulty escaped to the citadel, to which Muhammad Shah laid siege, impressing all the citizens into his service for the manufacture of scaling ladders. The Hindu prince lost heart on observing the determination of the besiegers and considering the impossibility of the arrival of aid, and at nightfall a wicket in rear of the citadel was opened and Vinayaka Deva with a few faithful attendants took to flight. Muhammad Shah had received information of the prince's intention, and the fugitives were pursued and overtaken almost immediately, and meanwhile the Muhammadan force entered the citadel and took possession of all the treasure. On the following morning Vinayaka Deva was summoned to the royal presence and was asked how he had dared to appropriate horses reserved for the Bahmani King. Ignorant of the fact that Muhammad Shah was inclined to be merciful, and deeming that death would in any case be his meed, he gave rein to his tongue, and indulged himself after the fashion of the Deccan, with foul and scathing abuse of his conqueror. His offence met with its fitting reward. His tongue was torn out by the roots, and a large pyre of wood just without the city wall having been made ready for his reception he was projected into it from a *balista*. Muhammad Shah remained for a fortnight in Vailampallam, enjoying his conquest, and from time to time detachments from the army at Bidar joined him, but were not allowed to participate in the revels of the conquering force. He then set out on his homeward way, but by this time the Hindus had recovered somewhat from their surprise and beset the retreating Musalmans, who were obliged to abandon the heavier articles of plunder and to content themselves with the gold and jewels which had fallen into their hands. The troops had to leave even their tents behind them and collected supplies day by day from the villages through which they passed. At night they could not venture to unsaddle their horses, and the Hindus hung on their flanks and rear until the frontier of the Bahmani dominions was reached, occasionally even venturing to attack the retreating army. In these combats the Musalmans were invariably victorious, but were unable to shake off their pursuers, and in one of them the Sultan himself was wounded. The Muhammadan troops at Vailampallam had been reinforced, before the Sultan's departure, by 3,000 horse, and numbered 4,000 when the retreat began, but of these no more than 1,500 reached their homes. After crossing the frontier Muhammad Shah halted at Kaulas, and the minister at Gulbarga, on hearing of his losses, sent a fresh force from the capital. Muhammad Shah despatched these troops into the territories of Warangal, where they laid waste village after village and slaughtered the inhabitants. When they returned, glutted with carnage, Muhammad Shah took them back with him to Gulbarga.

The insignificant successes of the Hindu troops during Muhammad Shah's retreat did not console the Raja of Warangal for the loss of his son and the sufferings inflicted on his people by the Musalmans, and in 1363 he sent a petition to Firuz Shah of Delhi beseeching him to order the *amirs* of Malwa and Gujarat to march against Muhammad, and promised, with the aid of Bukka of Vijayanagar, to invade the Bahman dominions simultaneously from the south and south-east, and to submit himself to the emperor and pay tribute regularly as a vassal of Delhi. Firuz Shah, however, was not disposed to meddle with the affairs of the Deccan, and Muhammad Shah, hearing of the letter to Delhi, resolved to crush the Raja of Warangal. He sent orders to his cousin, Khan Muhammad, governor of Daulatabad, to assemble his troops in the hills above Daulatabad and to protect the northern provinces against invasion from the north or north-east; and summoned Saffdar Khan Sistani from Berar and Azam-i-Humayun from Bidar, with the troops of those provinces, to the capital. The minister was again appointed lieutenant of the kingdom and Muhammad Shah marched to Kaulas, which he made his base. Azam-i-Humayun was sent against Golconda and Saffdar Khan against Warangal, while the Sultan and Bahadur Khan, with the army of Gulbarga followed the two columns, ready to support either.

The Raja of Warangal was now reduced to serious straits. For some reason which is not clear he was disappointed of help from Vijayanagar. Firishta says that the Raya of Vijayanagar, that is to say, Bukka I, died at this time and was succeeded by his nephew and that the empire of the Peninsula was consequently unprepared to take the field, but according to Mr. Sewell, Bukka I did not die until 1379. Mr. Sewell adds, however, on the authority of inscriptions, that Kampa seems to have reigned in Vijayanagar from 1343 to 1379 and that he was succeeded by his son Sangama, who was reigning in 1356. It would appear, therefore, that the throne of Vijayanagar was in dispute, and that neither claimant was in a position to undertake a campaign beyond the frontier. The Raja of Warangal fled from his capital and took refuge in the jungles, at the same time sending many of his most trusty and able courtiers to Bahadur Khan to entreat him to use his influence to dissuade the Sultan from proceeding to extremities. The entreaties of these envoys were fruitless, and the Muhammadan armies devastated Telingana. The wretched raja then sent his younger son with a deputation of nobles to Muhammad Shah's camp, professing his entire submission to the Bahmani king and beseeching forgiveness for the contumacy of which he had been guilty. He basely urged that the guilt was less his own than that of the Raya of Vijayanagar, who, he said, had instigated him to oppose the Musalmans. Muhammad Shah at first turned a deaf ear to these entreaties, but at the instance of Bahadur Khan, who was probably actuated by motives other than an altruistic love of peace for its own sake, he agreed to negotiations for peace and appointed Bahadur Khan, the raja's intermediary, his plenipotentiary. Peace was concluded on the following terms:—Three hundred elephants, thirteen lakhs of *huns*, and two hundred horses were to be sent to Gulbarga, and the fortress of Golconda, with the district of which it was the capital, was to be ceded to Muhammad Shah. These terms were considered hard but Muhammad had already occupied Golconda and they were the best that could be obtained. Muhammad Shah retired to Bidar and left Azam-i-Humayun in Golconda and Bahadur Khan in Kaulas to see that the terms of peace were fulfilled. The latter received the envoys of Warangal at Kaulas and sent them on with the stipulated gifts to Muhammad Shah at Bidar, where they were courteously received. In a second audience the envoys presented to Muhammad Shah a magnificent jewelled throne which had originally been made by Prataparudradeva II for Muhammad bin Tughlaq. This throne, which was afterwards known as the *takht-i-firuza*, was made of ebony and was three yards in length and two and a half in breadth. It was overlaid with plates of gold heavily jewelled which were removable and could be packed in boxes for travelling. Successive kings of the Bahmani dynasty added more jewels until, in the reign of Mahmud Shah, the fourteenth king, the throne was valued at ten millions of *huns*, or about £400,000. Muhammad Shah, in consideration of this splendid gift, gave a solemn undertaking that he would regard Golconda as his frontier and would not seek to molest Warangal unless the raja should break the peace.

After this campaign the rajas of Warangal were left unmolested by the Bahmani Kings for many years. In 1417 their instalments of tribute had fallen into arrears and Firuz Shah, the eighth king of the Bahmani dynasty, sent messengers to demand payment, which was peaceably made. Ahmad Shah Wali, the brother and successor of Firuz Shah, made war on Devaraya II of Vijayanagar in 1422, and the latter summoned the Raja of Warangal to his assistance. Ahmad Shah halted on the north bank of the Tungabhadra for forty days while the allied

Hindu armies encamped on the south bank and harassed his army. At the end of the forty days Ahmad Shah resolved to cross the river, and the Raja of Warangal, on hearing of his intention, deserted his ally and fled with his army to Warangal. Devaraya II was ultimately defeated and compelled to pay tribute and Ahmad Shah then prepared to punish the Raja of Warangal for having entered into an alliance with Vijayanagar, and, late in 1424, marched on Golconda. Having reached that fortress he sent the Khan-i-Azam with a force against Warangal and, after halting for a month and twenty days at Golconda, followed him with the main body of the army. Before he could reach Warangal he heard that the Khan-i-Azam had captured the place. The raja, who had heard of the approach of Ahmad Shah, hastened to deal with the advanced guard of the Musalmans before their main body arrived, and attacked the Khan-i-Azam. He was defeated and slain, with seven thousand Tailanga horsemen, and Warangal, with all the treasure which the rajas of Warangal had with so much difficulty concealed from the invading hosts of Muhammad bin Tughlaq, fell into the hands of the Khan-i-Azam. Ahmad Shah bountifully rewarded his successful general and halted at Warangal while the Khan-i-Azam reduced the other fortresses of Telingana, a task which occupied him for four months, at the end of which time, having garrisoned the forts so captured, he rejoined his master in Warangal and received further rewards. Ahmad Shah then returned to Gulbarga, leaving the Khan-i-Azam in Warangal with instructions to extirpate all members of the raja's family. Thus eastern Telingana came, for the first time, directly under the sway of the Musalmans.

In 1459 Humayun Shah Bahmani set out to punish the *zamindar* of Devarkonda, who had assisted the rebel Sikandar Khan, and marched to Warangal, which he made his headquarters. Khaja-i-Jahan the Turk and Nizam-ul-Mulk Ghori were sent against Devarkonda and, after defeating the Hindus in the field, besieged them in the fortress. The defenders were hard pressed and sent to the Raja of Urisa for assistance. He sent to their aid a large force with several elephants and assured them that he would soon arrive on the scene in person. The Hindus were much encouraged by the news, and Nizam-ul-Mulk and Khaja-i-Jahan took counsel together as to what they should do. Nizam-ul-Mulk urged the necessity of withdrawing from the cramped position before the fortress and meeting the Hindus in the open plain, but the Khaja-i-Jahan opposed any change of position on the ground that the enemy would certainly attribute it to fear, and would pursue the army as it withdrew, and Nizam-ul-Mulk was forced, against his own better judgment, to acquiesce in his colleague's view. What he had foreseen happened. The allied Hindu army attacked the Musalmans in a position in which the cavalry of the latter could not act and completely routed them. The two generals, with the remnant of the army, fled to Warangal closely pursued by the Hindus. The Khaja-i-Jahan was the first to find his way to the presence of the tyrant Humayun, and when asked what had been the cause of the defeat, basely lied, and said that it had been due to the insistence of Nizam-ul-Mulk on awaiting the enemy in a bad position. Humayun soundly rated the Khaja and then, as his custom was, issued immediate orders that Nizam-ul-Mulk should be put to death without allowing him an opportunity of explaining matters. Whether Nizam-ul-Mulk actually suffered death or whether he succeeded in escaping, as his followers did, to the court of Mahmud Shah Khalji of Malwa is not quite certain, but it is probable that he was executed. The Khaja-i-Jahan was tortured and imprisoned. Humayun Shah was preparing to send a second army against Devarkonda when in April, 1460, he received information of a rebellion in the capital and returned to Bidar in haste, leaving Mahmud Gawan to settle affairs in Telingana. In September 1461, Humayun Shah died and was succeeded by his son Nizam Shah, a boy of eight. Khaja-i-Jahan the Turk was appointed governor of Telingana and the country appeared to be settled, but evil days were in store for the Bahmani kingdom. The raja of Urisa, elated by his victory at Devarkonda, summoned to his aid the *zamindars* of Telingana, now thoroughly disaffected and in no way cowed by the presence of a Muhammadan army in their midst, and invaded the Bahmani kingdom, laying waste the country as far as Kaulas. The young king's mother, with the help of the Khaja-i-Jahan and Mahmud Gawan, assembled an army of 40,000 horse at the capital and marched to meet the invaders, who had advanced to within twenty miles of Bidar. The raja of Urisa was utterly defeated and his army was pursued so vigorously that had he not purchased safety by a heavy indemnity the

Musalmans would certainly have made good their boast that not one Hindu should reach his home alive. But the Hindus had scarcely been driven from the kingdom when Mahmud Shah Khalji of Malwa invaded it. The details of this campaign need not be related. It is sufficient to say that Mahmud Shah, before he was driven back to his own country, captured the city of Bidar and that the raja of Urisa and the chiefs of Telingana again rose against Nizam Shah and were with difficulty held at bay by the local Muhammadan forces while the armies of the other provinces of the Bahmani kingdom dealt with the Sultan of Malwa.

After this outburst Telingana and Urisa gave no trouble to the Bahmani kings until the following reign, when the raja of Urisa died in 1471, leaving a nephew named Hambar and a supposititious son Mangal Raya, who ascended the throne. Hambar appealed for aid to Muhammad Shah Bahmani III, who responded to the call by despatching Malik Hasan Bahri, on whom the title of Nizam-ul-Mulk was at the same time conferred, to eastern Telingana, where he captured Rajamahendri and Kondavir and sent Hambar back to Urisa.

The reign of Muhammad III was a series of campaigns. In 1477 the inhabitants of Kondavir rose against their tyrannical Muhammadan governor, slew him, and raised the standard of revolt, calling upon Hambar the Uriya and the raja of Urisa for help. The appeal was answered and Hambar with a thousand horse and seven or eight thousand foot invaded Telingana and marched on Rajamahendri, of which place Nizam-ul-Mulk was governor. The governor was not strong enough to meet the enemy in the field and prepared to stand a siege in Rajamahendri, at the same time sending to the capital letters explaining his position. Muhammad Shah at once set out for Telingana and the Hindus were demoralised by the news of his approach. Hambar took refuge in Kondavir, where he was besieged, and the raja of Urisa retired across the river and encamped on its northern bank after seizing all the boats that could be found. The king joined forces with Nizam-ul-Mulk at Rajamahendri, but before they could cross the river to attack the Hindus the latter retreated northwards to Urisa. Muhammad Shah then left his son with Mahmud Gawan to hold Rajamahendri and in 1478 invaded Urisa with 20,000 horse, slaying the inhabitants and laying waste the country. The raja fled to the uttermost parts of his kingdom and Muhammad Shah was on the point of placing a Muhammadan governor in charge of the country when the raja sent costly gifts and many elephants to royal camp and undertook never again to help the rebels of Telingana if his country were left to him. Muhammad Shah, after demanding and receiving some more elephants from the raja, abandoned his design of annexing Urisa and set out on his return journey. On his way he was detained for a month and a half at a fortress the garrison of which had offended him. The raja caused the fortress to be surrendered to him and he continued his march to Kondavir, where he besieged Hambar for five or six months. At the end of that time Hambar surrendered on receiving a promise that his life should be spared. Here a large Hindu temple was demolished and some of the Brahmans and their attendants were slain as an act of religious merit. On the site of the temple a mosque was built and Muhammad Shah assumed the title of *ghazi*, as being the first of his line to slay a Brahman with his own hand. He remained for the next three years in eastern Telingana, consolidating his power and settling the country. At the end of this time he resolved on invading the eastern provinces of the kingdom of Vijayanagar, and before setting out he appointed Nizam-ul-Mulk, by the advice of Mahmud Gawan, governor of eastern Telingana. At the same time Azam Khan, the son of Sikandar Khan, the son of the rebel Jalal Khan, was appointed governor of western Telingana with his headquarters at Warangal. This appointment gave bitter offence to Nizam-ul-Mulk, who considered that he should have been entrusted with the government of the whole province, and laid the foundation of his quarrel with Mahmud Gawan which ended in the murder of that great man. Nizam-ul-Mulk could not openly object to the appointment of Azam Khan, but he endeavoured to escape from what he regarded as a humiliating position by suggesting that he might be allowed to place one of his sons in charge of the government of eastern Telingana while he himself accompanied the king on his expedition into the Vijayanagar country. The son indicated by him was Malik Ahmad, who had some years before been given a *jagir* in Mahur at the instance of Mahmud Gawan, who judged it unwise to employ both the father and his more able and ambitious son in the same province. Muhammad Shah, against the advice of Mahmud Gawan, granted this request and Malik Ahmad was recalled from Mahur and placed in charge of the government of eastern Telingana while Nizam-ul-Mulk accompanied the king in his extensive crescentade in the dominions of Raja Narsingha, a vassal of the raya of Vijayanagar. The details of this campaign are interesting, but have no immediate connection with the history of Warangal.

On Muhammad Shah's return from his campaign the reform which had been foreshadowed by the division of Telingana into two provincial governments was completed, and the four *tarafs* or great provinces of the Bahmani kingdom were divided into eight. Berar was divided into the provinces of Gawil and Mahur, Daulatabad into those of Daulatabad and Junnar, Gulbarga into those of Gulbarga and Bijapur, and Telingana was finally divided into the two provinces of Warangal and Rajamahendri, of which the former remained under the government of Azam Khan and the latter under that of Nizam-ul-Mulk. The powers of the *tarafdars* or provincial governors were at the same time curtailed. Each *tarafdar* had formerly had in his hands all the forts in his province, but under the new regulation only the fort at the headquarters of each province was to remain in the hands of the *tarafdar*, all other forts being commanded by *amirs* appointed by and directly responsible to the sovereign. The military regulations, too, were revised. By the regulation of Bahman Shah, the founder of the dynasty, commanding officers were allowed either in the form of the revenue of *jagirs* or by drafts on the treasury, or from both sources combined, a lakh of *huns* for every five hundred men whom they were expected to maintain, but their forces were not regularly mustered or minutely inspected. By the new regulation the allowance for every five hundred men was raised to a lakh and a quarter of *huns*, but at the same time a more rigorous system of supervision was introduced and deductions were made for each man short of the establishment. These excellent regulations made both for efficiency and for the well-being of the soldier, but were extremely unpopular among the great nobles, and caused widespread resentment against the reformer Mahmud Gawan, whose chief supporters were Yusuf Adil Khan and other Turki *Amirs*. The Deccanis and Africans to a man opposed the innovations, and set on foot schemes for the overthrow of their author. Zarif-ul-Mulk the Deccani and Miftah the African, two *protégés* of Mahmud Gawan, taking advantage of the absence of Yusuf Adil Khan in Narsingha's country, plotted with Nizam-ul-Mulk to bring about their master's downfall, and bribed an African who was the keeper of his seal to lend them the seal for a short time. Having obtained it they affixed an impression of it to a sheet of blank paper on which a treasonable letter to the raja of Urisa was afterwards written. Possessed of this forgery Zarif-ul-Mulk and Miftah awaited their opportunity until Nizam-ul-Mulk had an audience of the king, when they presented the paper. Muhammad Shah was astounded at what he deemed to be his minister's treachery and Nizam-ul-Mulk heaped fuel on the fire of his wrath. Mahmud Gawan was summoned. Though urged by his followers to fly he refused to admit that he had any reason for fear and presented himself before his sovereign. Muhammad Shah asked him what was the fitting punishment for one proved to be guilty of treason against his king, and the minister unflinchingly answered "Death." He was then shown the letter, which he at once declared to be a forgery. He protested his innocence and demanded an inquiry, but the king, whose wrath was inflamed with wine as well as with the false witness borne against his victim, gave orders for his immediate execution: and rose and left the hall. Jauhar, an African executioner, then drew his sword and raised it to strike. The great minister recited the short creed of Islam, and as the sword fell, cried, "Praise be to God for the blessing of martyrdom." This great crime, perpetrated on April 6, 1481, was the primary cause of the dissolution of the Bahmani kingdom. The foreign nobles refused to trust a king who could thus reward his most faithful servant, and returned to their provinces without leave. Muhammad Shah soon learnt that he had shed innocent blood, and, after vainly trying to drown remorse with wine, died within a year of his minister, crying with his last breath that Mahmud Gawan was tearing at his entrails.

In the following reign all save one of the greater *tarafdars* proclaimed themselves independent and in 1490 the governors of Berar, Daulatabad, and Bijapur assumed the royal title. In the meantime Sultan Quli Qutb-ul-Mulk had been appointed governor of western Telingana and had chosen as his head quarters Golconda, where he built a fort which he named Muhammadnagar. He refused to join the *tarafdars* who revolted in 1490 and remained steadfastly loyal until 1512, when it was no longer possible to maintain the fiction of a Bahmanid reigning as king at Bidar. He then followed the example of the other *tarafdars*, though it does not appear that he encouraged the use of the royal title. During the period of Sultan Quli's government of Telingana it is probable that Warangal fell into the hands of Hindus or other rebels, for in the most detailed history of his reign which has come down to us it is mentioned among his conquests. The most frequent aggressor was a mysterious Musalman entitled Shitab Khan. This warrior, regarding the reading of whose title there is no manner of doubt, is described in the *Tarikh-i-Muhammad Qutb Shahi* as "the Raja of Khammamet, a fearless infidel". This description has much puzzled Lieutenant-Colonel Briggs who, in volume III of his *History of the Rise of the Muhammadan Power in India*, makes Shitab Khan a Hindu, and confers on him the title of "Seetaputty." The historian of the Qutb Shahi kings is, however, corroborated by the Telugu inscription in the Hanamkonda temple, bearing the date 1503, which has already been mentioned. The truth seems to be that Shitab Khan was a renegade Musalman who, on the disruption of the Bahmani kingdom, allied himself with Hindus and by means of their aid established a small independent principality. From the inscription we may infer that he was in possesssion of Hanamkonda and Warangal in 1503, and he was still in possession of the same tract in 1515 after Sultan Quli Qutb Shah's war with the Sultan of Berar, at which period Khammamet, Warangal, and Nalgunda were included in Shitab Khan's dominions. On Sultan Quli's return to Golconda after his campaign against Ala-ud-din Imad Shah his nobles reported to him that Shitab Khan had ravaged the borders of the kingdom and was preparing for war. No attempt was made by Shitab Khan to hold Warangal, which passed without a struggle into Sultan Quli's hands while he marched on southwards to the siege of Belamkonda. After a protracted campaign, in the course of which Shitab Khan received much assistance from his Hindu allies, the whole of eastern Telingana, as far as the sea coast, was conquered and included in the Qutb Shahi dominions. Shitab Khan escaped and found a refuge with his Hindu friends and though he, or, as seems more probable, a son bearing his title, caused some trouble in the latter years of the reign of Ibrahim Qutb Shah, who reigned from 1550 to 1580. Warangal was never again annexed to a Hindu kingdom of Telingana, and remained part of the Qutb Shahi dominions until those dominions were annexed to the Mughal Empire by Aurangzib in 1687.

Aurangzib had small leisure for composing troubles in his extensive conquests in the south, and the administration of these provinces, between the incompetence of the Mughal officials and the turbulent rapacity of the Marathas, was in the most hopeless confusion. Before Aurangzib's death the inhabitants of the country around Haidarabad had implored him to take measures for the destruction of a freebooter named Papra, a toddy-drawer by caste, who had assembled a small army, built for himself a fort at Shahpur in the Bhongir *pargana*, and raided the country far and near. Aurangzib appointed Rustam Dil Khan *subahdar* of Haidarabad, and the new *subahdar*, after the defeat of detachments which he had sent out against the rebel, took the field in person, but, after besieging Shahpur unsuccessfully for two or three months, retired on receiving from Papra a gift which may be regarded either as tribute or as a bribe but which, whatever it might be called, was accompanied by no guarantee that the marauder would stay his hand, which fell with equal weight on the goods and the families of his victims. Prince Kam Bakhsh who, after his father's death, was governor of Bijapur and Haidarabad, did nothing to repress Papra, who was so much encouraged by the retirement of Rustam Dil Khan that he ventured to attack Warangal, from which his stronghold was about thirty miles distant.

On Muharram 10, A. D. 1120 (April 1, 1708) when all, Musalmans and Hindus alike, as the historian says were engaged in the procession of the *tabuts*, Papra arrived at the fort of Warangal with two or three thousand infantry and four or five hundred horse, and closed the roads in order to prevent news of his arrival from reaching the interior of the town. Before dawn the infantry set to work to scale the walls of the fortress while the cavalry sacked the town. The fort was captured and money and property to the value of lakhs of rupees and many of the famous carpets of Warangal fell into the hands of the plunderers, and about 12,000 men, women, and children were taken prisoners. Among the women the wife and daughter of the Qazl, Muhammad Sald, were captured. Papra kept the former for himself and placed the latter, who was eight or nine years of age, with a troupe of dancing girls, in order that she might learn their profession. After this exploit he continued his successful career until the inhabitants of Warangal sent a petition to the emperor Bahadur Shah, beseeching him to come in person and crush the rebel. The emperor replied that it would ill become his dignity to set forth in person, at the head of the imperial army, against a toddy-drawer; but he sent Yusuf Khan Ruzbihani, an active and resourceful officer, to suppress the rebellion. Shahpur was captured, but Papra contrived to escape to Tarikonda, which was garrisoned by some of his men. Here he stood a siege of nine months, at the end of which time many of his men having deserted him, he contrived to flee alone and without the knowledge of any to Hasanabad, two stages distant from Tarikonda. Here he was recognized, and was surrounded, wounded, and brought as a prisoner before Yusuf Khan. The captured bandit poured foul abuse on his conqueror and was suffered to live for a few days only, until his hoards were discovered. He was then severed into pieces, joint by joint. His head was sent to the emperor and his limbs were set above the gates of Haidarabad.

In 1767, during the war between the East India Company on the one side and Nizam Ali of Haidarabad and Haidar Ali of Mysore on the other, the Government of Bengal created a very successful diversion by despatching a force from Calcutta under Colonel Peach. This force landed in the northern Sarkars and occupied Khammamet and Warangal, thus immediately threatening Haidarabad. The movement induced Nizam Ali to treat with the Company's officers and the result of the negotiations was the treaty of 1768, which, though its terms have been adversely criticised by the historian of Mysore, finally detached Nizam Ali from his alliance with Haidar Ali.

Since 1768 the history of Warangal has been uneventful. It was for some time a cantonment of the Haidarabad Contingent, but was abandoned many years ago.

CHAPTER V.

TWO OLD CAPITALS OF THE DECCAN.

I.—Gulbarga.

GULBARGA, though easily accessible, is not a resort of sight-seers, and is, if the truth must be spoken, an uninviting spot. It lies in an undulating plain of black cotton soil, fertile enough, but in the hot weather, dismal, dusty, and scorched. Yet the town was selected as the capital of a famous dynasty and held its place as the chief city of an important kingdom through the reigns of eight kings, and it still contains some buildings which might entice even the amateur antiquary to the decayed and otherwise unpicturesque town, as well as one building which is, in its design, unique in India. Towards the end of the reign of Muhammad bin Tughlaq of Dehli the *amirs* in the Deccan, disgusted with his fantastic tyranny, revolted, and proclaimed Ismail Fath, the Afghan, king of the Deccan, under the style of Nasir-ud-din Shah. The new king was besieged in Daulatabad by the emperor, who, though he laid waste the city, was unable to capture the citadel, in which Nasir-ud-din maintained a pretence of regal state, while the surrounding districts were seething with discontent. Suddenly a rebellion broke out in Gujarat and Muhammad bin Tughlaq hastened to repress it, leaving Nasir-ud-din unconquered, and palliating his want of success by the issue of a pompous proclamation of victory in which the exploit of harrying the defenceless traders of Daulatabad was represented as the conquest of the city. The emperor's retreat was the signal for a general outbreak in the Deccan. The aged and unenterprising Ismail Fath had been found wanting, and at the instance of the rebel *amirs* he gracefully resigned his new-born dignity into the hands of Zafar Khan, better known as Hasan Gangu, the most able, active, and resourceful of those who had raised the standard of rebellion. Zafar Khan, the founder of the Bahmani dynasty which bore sway in the Deccan for about 150 years and lingered on afterwards for thirty years, was proclaimed king in 1347 under the title of Ala-ud-din Hasan Kangu (or Gangu) Bahmani, according to most historians. Only one well known historian gives him his correct title,

Bahman Shah, but the question is settled by the evidence of a temporary inscription and of legends on coins. It is more important than it might seem at first sight to be, for on the title of the first king depends the correct interpretation of the epithet Bahmani, applied to the dynasty which he founded. This is commonly connected with the caste name Brahman, and various stories are told of assistance received by Zafar Khan in early life from a Brahman, but the epithet was in fact derived from Zafar Khan's own name or title of Bahman which was borne as the assertion of a claim to ancient Persian descent.

Muhammad bin Tughlaq, on hearing of the serious turn which the rebellion in the Deccan had taken, would have returned, but affairs in Gujarat would not permit him to do so. He died in the course of his efforts to stifle the revolt in that province, and the affairs of the empire were in such confusion that Bahman Shah had ample leisure to establish his sovereignty in the south, and the Deccan was not wholly reunited to the empire of Dehli for more than three hundred years. Bahman Shah ignored the historic city of Deogir or Daulatabad, which had, not long before, been the official capital of India, and turning southwards selected Gulbarga as his capital. It is not easy to discover why he should have selected so unattractive a spot unless we suppose that it was because it had been his *jagir*. Daulatabad was associated with the brief and inglorious reign of Ismail Fath, and was probably considered to be too near the northern frontier of the Deccan to be a suitable capital for the newly-separated kingdom. Gulbarga had the advantage, in the eyes of a faithful Muslim, of being in convenient but not dangerous proximity to the great Hindu kingdom of the Peninsula. One historian tells us that Bahman Shah regarded Gulbarga as a fortunate spot, and his choice was probably regulated by superstition, for he was a firm believer in astrology. The next step, after the selection of a capital, was to make it a worthy residence for a king, and the great mosque was now built. The greater part of the fort, too, was probably built in this reign.

Gulbarga was the city whence, during the next eight reigns, large armies of the faithful marched, with varying success, against the Hindu Rayas of Vijayanagar, and the city held its place during the reigns of at least six of Bahman Shah's successors. The first to evince a dislike to the hot and dusty town was the eighth Sultan, Firuz Shah, known as

Ruz Afzun, who founded a town, which he named Firuzabad after himself, on the banks of the river Bhima, about twelve miles to the south of Gulbarga. In the reign of this Sultan a famous saint, popularly known from his long side-locks as Gisu Daraz, and from his practical charity as Banda Nawaz, came from Dehli to Gulbarga, and was adopted by Firuz Shah as his patron saint. But the zeal of the monarch for the saint cooled by degrees, and Banda Nawaz transferred his religous patronage to the Sultan's brother, Ahmad Khan, the Khan-i-Khanan. Ahmad Khan, a devout and scrupulous Musalman, with some knowledge of theology and casuistry, was a far more promising disciple than the cultured and pleasure-loving Firuz, who, though thoroughly orthodox, was apt to be impatient of saintly control. Ahmad Khan after a struggle overcame his brother, and, in spite of the incredulity of some historians, who will believe nothing wrong of so saintly a king as Ahmad, the sudden death of Firuz Shah within a very short time of his abdication must be pronounced too opportune to have been fortuitous.

Events on the northern frontier of the kingdom took Ahmad Shah away from Gulbarga for three years, and on his return he was attracted by the superior advantages of Bidar, which, in 1429, he made his capital. Gulbarga thenceforward necessarily declined much in importance as a city, but it gained great reputation as a place of pilgrimage, for Gisu Daraz, who did not accompany the court to Bidar, died and was buried here in the reign of Ahmad Shah, and his tomb is to this day the most famous shrine in the Deccan. But Gulbarga had so far lost favour as a seat of royalty that when Nizam Shah, the twelfth king, was forced in 1463 by the invasion of Mahmud Shah Khalji of Malwa to leave Bidar, he retired, not to the old capital, but to Firuzabad.

At the dismemberment of the Bahmani kingdom in 1490, when the provincial governors proclaimed their independence, each *jagirdar* continued to hold the lands which he had held under the Bahmanis, and those who were strong enough refused at first to submit to the new kings. Gulbarga was then in the possession of Dastur Dinar, an Abyssinian, who seems to have imagined that he could, with a little assistance, set at naught the authority of Yusuf Adil Shah of Bijapur, the founder of the Adil Shahi dynasty. In 1500 he formed an alliance with Khaja Jahan of Sholapur, a *jagirdar*, occupying a position similar to his own, and bade defiance to Yusuf. Yusuf Adil Shah marched against the presumptuous African and defeated and slew him, thereafter capturing the forts of Gulbarga and Sagar, which, together with all the territory which had been in the hands of Dastur Dinar, he annexed to his dominions.

In 1511, in the beginning of the reign of Ismail Adil Shah, Yusuf's son and successor, Kamal Khan, one of the principal nobles of Bijapur, entered into a conspiracy with Amir Barid of Bidar, the *maire du palais* of Mahmud Shah Bahmani, to take possession of and divide the Bijapur kingdom, and in pursuance of this design Amir Barid, taking with him Mahmud Shah Bahmani, invaded Ismail's territories, captured some of the forts in the vicinity of Gulbarga, and laid siege to Gulbarga itself. The rebellion in Bijapur was crushed and the principal rebels were slain. Ismail Adil Shah was now in a position to deal with the invaders. He defeated an army of 20,000 horse led against him by Mahmud Shah Bahmani and Amir Barid, while Jahangir Mirza, one of his nobles who had been forced to take refuge in Ahmadnagar during Kamal Khan's rebellion, relieved Gulbarga. The assumption of the royal title by the provincial governors of the Bahmani kingdom had been due not to disloyalty, but to the fixed determination of the governors not to serve the Barids, who were the *de facto* rulers of the Bahmani dominions. Accordingly we find Ismail Adil Shah, who was not inclined to abate a jot of his actual independence, paying homage to Mahmud Shah Bahmani immediately after he had defeated his troops, and making an effort to release him from the influence of Amir Barid. But the *roi fainéant*, who cared nothing for the business of the state or for actual power, so long as he had the means of gratifying his passions, hugged his chains and refused to be separated from the minister who was in fact his master. Ismail's intention to induce Mahmud Shah to visit him in Bijapur was thus frustrated, for Amir Barid was too wise to place himself in the power of the man whom he had wronged. The two kings repaired, therefore, to Gulbarga, where Ismail Adil Shah married his sister, Bibi Sati, with great pomp, to the young Prince Ahmad, son of Mahmud Shah. Soon after the ceremony Amir Barid gained possession of the persons of Mahmud Shah, his son, and the bride, and carried them off to Bidar.

In 1540 one of the numerous internecine wars which weakened the Muhammadan kingdoms of the Deccan broke out, and Burhan Nizam Shah of Ahmadnagar and Amir Barid of Bidar marched on Bijapur. Ibrahim Adil Shah I, the fourth of his dynasty, being unable to meet his enemies in the field, retired on Gulbarga, and the invaders, leaving a force to besiege Bijapur, followed him. Asad Khan Lari, one of Ibrahim's principal nobles, who had been compelled by force of circumstances to join the invaders, but who still remained at heart faithful to his old master, contrived to send a message to Ala-ud-din Imad Shah of Berar asking for assistance, and on his arrival joined him with his troops. The invaders were now compelled to retire from Gulbarga and retreated as far as Bir, followed by Ibrahim and Ala-ud-din, who encamped at Daulatabad. Near this place Amir Barid died, and Ibrahim Adil Shah thereupon made peace with Burhan Nizam Shah.

In 1554 Ibrahim Adil Shah I was involved in hostilities with Husain Nizam Shah of Ahmadnagar and was defeated in the battle of Sholapur owing to his failure to support Saif Ain-ul-Mulk, whom he distrusted. Saif Ain-ul-Mulk, who had formerly been commander-in-chief in Ahmadnagar, was himself compelled to seek safety in flight, and was refused admittance to Bijapur by Ibrahim who, to conceal his own deficiencies in the day of battle, affected to regard him as a traitor. Disgusted with this treatment Saif Ain-ul-Mulk, who no longer dared to show his face in Ahmadnagar, set up as a guerilla leader in the Bijapur dominions. He thrice defeated armies sent against him by the Sultan, the second battle taking place at Gulbarga. On the third occasion Ibrahim marched against him in person, and was defeated and hemmed in at Bijapur. He was compelled to seek assistance of Sadashivaraya of Vijayanagar, who sent an army which defeated and dispersed the rebels.

In 1581, Ibrahim Adil Shah II being still a boy, the affairs of Bijapur were thrown into confusion by quarrels between the two parties which were ever antagonists in the Deccan, the "foreigners" and the Deccanis, the Africans siding with the latter. Murtaza Nizam Shah of Ahmadnagar and Muhammad Quli Qutb Shah of Golconda took advantage of the disorganization of the state to enter into an offensive alliance against Bijapur. The plan of campaign was that the former should attack Naldrug and the latter Gulbarga, joining forces after these forts had fallen. For some reason this plan was not followed, and Muhammad Quli joined Murtaza at Naldrug without attacking Gulbarga. The allies were, however, unable to reduce this fortress and left it, proceeding at once to the siege of Bijapur. As they advanced the Bijapur *amirs* who had remained loyal to the young king, but who had withdrawn to their *jagirs* disgusted with the dissensions in the capital, collected their forces, and in conjunction with the Bargis of the Carnatic attacked the invaders, who now relinquished the task which they had deemed so easy and retired in the direction of their own dominions. Muhammad Quli returned to Golconda, but left his army in the field at Gulbarga where it was attacked by an army from Bijapur under the command of Dilawar Khan the African. A fiercely contested battle resulted in the defeat of the Golconda army, which fled, leaving in the hands of the victors much spoil, including 150 elephants.

Henceforward Gulbarga remained undisturbed by war's alarms until the tide of Mughal conquest advanced into the southern Deccan. In 1631, in the reign of Shah Jahan, Yamin-ud-Daulah invaded the Adil Shahi dominions. After capturing Bhalgi he continued his advance southwards to Sultanpur, near Gulbarga. Most of the inhabitants fled for refuge to Gulbarga, which was well stored with arms and provisions. A force was sent to attack the place and entered the city, which was plundered, but Yamin-ud-Daulah did not care to attempt a siege of the fort and pressed on with his army towards Bijapur. His attempts to capture the city were fruitless, and, after ravaging the surrounding country, he retired to Sholapur. In 1636 the imperial troops again invaded the territory of Bijapur and ravaged the country about Gulbarga, but could not obtain a foothold in the country sufficiently firm to enable them to lay siege to the fortress.

In 1686 Aurangzib carried into execution his long-cherished design of adding Bijapur to his empire and laid siege to the place. In October of that year Sikandar Adil Shah, the last of his line, surrendered and was sent into captivity at Daulatabad. In December Aurangzib marched to Gulbarga, where he halted for some time, engaged in devotions at the shrine of Gisu Daraz, and in attempting to induce Abul Hasan to surrender Golconda without a siege. His diplomacy was unsuccessful and he was compelled to attack the place, which fell after a siege of eight months. Since this period the history of Gulbarga has been uneventful.

The most striking of all the buildings of Gulbarga is the great mosque, built, as an inscription tells us, in A. H. 769 (A.D. 1367) in the reign of Muhammad Shah, the second king of the Bahmani dynasty, by Rafi bin Shams bin Mansur, Qazvini. This building is unique among Indian mosques, which usually consist of a large courtyard and a relatively small building, towards which the worshipper prays. What should be the courtyard of the Gulbarga mosque is all covered in. The building has a large dome in the centre of the western end and four others, slightly smaller, at the corners. The spacious roof consists of seventy-five small domes and twenty-seven gabled roofs. The front of the mosque consists of a range of eleven arches, and on each side is a range of fourteen arches, the last three towards the western end being closed. In the interior the effect of the long colonnades with their arches and vaulted ceilings is very striking. Meadows Taylor says that this building is a replica of the great mosque at Cordova, but this is not the case. Apart from radical differences of style the relative dimensions of the two buildings do not correspond, and the Gulbarga mosque could not compare with that of Cordova in point either of size or of richness of materials or wealth of decoration. The bazar consists of an arcade of sixty arches on either side with elaborately ornamented buildings at either end. The tombs of seven of the Bahmani kings who are buried here are unpretentious square buildings surmounted by domes. The tomb of Shaikh Gisu Daraz is more imposing. This is a large domed building with two ranges of arches, one above the other, running round it. But the doorway is small and mean, and the tomb has no pretensions to architectural beauty. To the west of the town is a large domed building standing on high ground and said to have been built by a money-lender and offered by him to Shaikh Gisu Daraz, who, however, refused to accept a building which had been erected with money gained by usury. It subsequently became the headquarters of a gang of robbers, from whom it received the name of *Chor Gumbaz*, which it retains to this day. The fort is interesting and picturesque in its decay. The citadel built by Bahman Shah is a square building of brick, eighty-five feet in height. It covers but a very small area and has the appearance more of a gigantic traverse than of a citadel. The fort received many additions from the Adil Shahi kings, particularly Ali I and Ibrahim II. In the reign of the latter, in 1624, a bastion was built to accommodate the great twelve yard gun, which now lies dismounted in the decaying fort.

II.—Bidar.

Legend, as well as etymology, identifies the town of Bidar with the old city of Vidarbha, the capital of a Hindu kingdom of the same name in the Deccan, whose Raja, Rukmin, rejected the demi-god Krishna as a brother-in-law and was at last forced to witness the abduction of his sister by the slighted hero and then to retire into seclusion at Bhatkuli, after the scornful refusal of the Pandavas, the heroes of the *Mahabharata*, to recognise his arrogant claims. Vidarbha is more pleasingly associated with the romance of Nala, Raja of Nishadha (Malwa), who loved Damayanti, the beautiful daughter of Bhima, Raja of Vidarbha. The story of their love, marriage, and subsequent misfortunes, is told at length in the great Hindu epic, and also by Faizi, Akbar's poet laureate, in his long and somewhat wearisome poem *Nal u Daman*. So far the legendary history of Vidarbha. Raja Vijaya Sena, one of the Valabhis of the solar line, who succeeded the Guptas in A. D. 319, is said to have founded Vidarbha, by which expression we may understand that he restored the ancient city. But Vidarbha never regained, during the Hindu period of history, its pristine importance, and remained a mere provincial town, unheard of for centuries after its restorer's reign.

In the course of the third expedition of the Musalmans to Warangal in 1322, the town was captured by Muhammad bin Tughlaq, then heir-apparent to the empire of Delhi, and it was an important centre of the revolt which took place in the Deccan after the accession of this prince to the throne and towards the end of his reign. It was seized in 1346 by the rebel Amir Ali, recaptured by Qutlugh Khan for the emperor, and again, in 1347, captured by Zafar Khan (Ala-ud-din Hasan), who was proclaimed king of the Deccan under the title of Bahman Shah.

The new king divided his kingdom into four *tarafs* or provinces, of one of which Bidar was the head-quarters, its governor receiving the *ex officio* title of *Azam-i-Humayun*.

In 1429, when Ahmad Shah Wali, the ninth king of the Bahmani dynasty, was returning from Berar, he halted at Bidar and was so charmed by the situation of the place that he resolved to make it his capital. The usual legend of the hunted fox or hare turning on the dog which was pursuing it is told to account for Ahmad Shah's choice, which is also said to have been influenced by the legendary and historical associations of the town; but its superiority over Gulbarga, in point of situation and climate was alone sufficient to account for the preference. Its central position and its situation on a rolling plateau gave it many advantages over the hot and low-lying town of Gulbarga, where Ahmad Shah's health had suffered, and it remained the capital of the Bahmanis as long as the dynasty lasted, and of the Barid Shahi kings who followed them.

Ala-ud-din II, the son and successor of Ahmad Shah, founded a large hospital at Bidar, and endowed it with *jagir* lands for the support of the Hindu and Muhammadan physicians attached to it and for the supply of medicine and food to the sick.

On October 4, 1461, Nizam Shah, the twelfth king of the Bahmani line, ascended the throne in Bidar, in the eighth year of his age. His mother, Makhduma-i-Jahan, governed the kingdom in his name, aided by the advice of Mahmud Gawan Khaja-i-Jahan. Early in this reign Sultan Mahmud Khalji of Malwa, having allied himself with the Rajas of Urisa and Telingana, invaded the Bahmani dominions, was defeated in his first engagement, but retrieved his defeat, fell upon the Deccanis as they were plundering, and utterly routed them. Nizam Shah was carried off by his mother to Firuzabad, near Gulbarga; while the invaders sacked and burnt the town of Bidar and laid siege to the citadel which was gallantly held by the Bahmani *qalahdar*, Mallu Khan. The besiegers daily attempted to fill the ditch with earth and rubbish, but their efforts were frustrated by the energy of the defenders, who cleared the ditch by night. In the meantime Nizam Shah's advisers had written for help to Sultan Mahmud of Gujarat, who now arrived at the northern frontier of the Bahmani kingdom with 80,000 horse. Mahmud Gawan, with five or six thousand Deccani horse, joined him by way of Bir, and occupied himself in raising more troops until he was able to take the field with an army of 40,000 Deccani and Gujarati horse. He sent

10,000 Deccani horse into Berar to harass the army of Malwa during its retreat, and marched on Bidar with the remainder of his force. Mahmud Gawan encamped between Bir and Kandhar and cut off Mahmud Khalji's supplies and raided his camp, but would not risk a battle, though the enemy could bring no more than 30,000 horse into the field. At length the army of Malwa was starved out, and Mahmud Khalji, after blinding his elephants and burning his heavy baggage, retreated through Gondwana, being afraid to venture into Berar. His trust in the Gonds whose raja was nominally his vassal, was misplaced. He was pursued and harassed by Mahmud Gawan, and, to avoid being cut off by him, attempted to reach his own dominions by way of the Satpuras. But he escaped the Deccanis only to encounter worse foes. His army died by the thousand from heat and thirst, and the Korkus of the hills, instigated by their raja, fell upon the exhausted force, slaughtering and capturing many and robbing the troops of all that they possessed. When the army at length emerged from the wild hill country Mahmud Khalji had the Korku Raja put to death.

After the retreat of the invaders Nizam Shah returned to his capital and the city was restored to its former grandeur. In the following year Mahmud Khalji again invaded the Bahmani dominions and marched towards Daulatabad, but the Deccanis prepared to meet him, and Mahmud Shah of Gujarat again marched to their aid whereupon Mahmud Khalji repented of the enterprise and retired. In 1471 Mahmud Gawan, the great minister of the later Bahmani kings, built a splendid college at Bidar and furnished it with a library of three thousand volumes. The ruins of this college are still standing, and though much dilapidated, still convey some idea of the former magnificence of the building. Nearly the whole of one side has disappeared and but one of the two stately minarets remains. The principal architectural ornament of the college was the exterior decoration in enamel and encaustic tiles and enough of this beautiful work remains, sadly mutilated though it is, to convey an impression of the whole design. The encaustic tiles of various colours are arranged in zigzag lines, and along the top of the building runs a frieze ornamented with texts from the *Quran* in coloured letters nearly three feet high on a ground of gold and green. On April 5, 1481, the great Mahmud Gawan was unjustly executed by order of Muhammad Shah Lashkari, and from this time the power of the Bahmani Sultans declined rapidly.

In October, 1487, Bidar was the scene of a serious revolt. The Deccani and African *amirs* rose suddenly in the night against the Sultan Mahmud Shah, of whose partiality towards the "foreign," or Turki, Persian, and Mughal *amirs*, they had long been jealous. They attacked the royal palace, but were repulsed by the desperate valour of a few foreigners in immediate attendance on the Sultan. In the morning Mahmud Shah ordered the foreigners to retaliate on the Deccanis and Africans. The slaughter lasted for three days, and the foreigners inflicted a terrible retribution for wrongs which they had suffered years before. The tombs of the unfortunate Africans, who fell on this occasion, are still pointed out. After these events Mahmud Shah took no further interest in business of state. He built a new palace and laid out a garden, and spared neither pains nor expense for the adornment of both. These being completed, he gave himself up entirely to luxury and pleasure, and Bidar became the resort of poets, singers, dancers, wantons, story-tellers, and wine-bibbers from all parts of India and Persia, so that "the city was the envy of Iran and Turan." All those who had any care for public business turned to the provincial governors, who were now practically independent. Qasim Barid, the minister, managed the affairs of the capital as he chose, and when he found that the *qalahdars* in his *jagir* declined to surrender to him the forts which they held immediately from the king he rose in revolt. Meanwhile, in 1490, Malik Ahmad Bahri Nizam-ul-Mulk, Fathullah Imad-ul-Mulk, and Yusuf Adil Khan proclaimed their independence in Ahmadnagar, Berar, and Bijapur, founding the Nizam Shahi, the Imad Shahi, and the Adil Shahi dynasties. Qasim Barid at the same time proclaimed his independence in Ausa and Kandhar, leaving little more than the capital to the voluptuary who sat on the throne of the Bahmanis, who, finding that he could not overpower the rebel, made terms with him, and in 1492 confirmed him as *Amir-i-Jumla* or prime minister. Henceforward the Bahmanis ceased in fact to be a ruling dynasty though Mahmud Shah had four nominal successors in Bidar, Ahmad, Ala-ud-din III, Wali-ullah, and Kalim-ullah, the last of whom died, a fugitive, in Ahmadnagar in 1527. Qasim Barid died in 1504, in the lifetime of Mahmud Shah, but he was succeeded by his son Amir Ali Barid who, on his father's death, obtained complete control of the persons of the remaining members of the royal family. His policy was to ally himself with the kings of Ahmadnagar, Berar, and Golconda against the Adil Shahi kings of Bijapur. This dynasty, however, established its pre-eminence and Ismail Adil Shah, the second of the line, with the assent of Burhān Nizam Shah, who dared not withhold it, resolved to punish Amir Ali Barid. In 1529 he set out for Bidar, and as he approached the place Amir Ali withdrew towards Udgir, leaving his sons, the eldest of whom was Ali Barid, to defend the city. Ismail Adil Shah laid siege to the fortress and defeated in the field both the defenders, who made a sortie, and an army sent from Golconda by Sultan Quli Qutb Shah. He also distinguished himself by slaying in single combat two noted warriors, the maternal uncles of Ali Barid. While the siege was still in progress Ala-ud-din Imad Shah came from Berar to intercede with Ismail Adil Shah for Amir Ali Barid, but was informed that the injuries which the intriguer had inflicted on Bijapur could not be pardoned. Ala-ud-din then advised Amir Ali to make the best terms he could with the invader, but Amir Ali returned to his camp and attempted to drown his sorrows. Asad Khan, who had been sent by Ismail Adil Shah to make a night attack on Amir Ali Barid, found his camp unguarded and the whole army drunk. He made his way carefully to Amir Ali's private tent and found him lying on a bed dead drunk, surrounded by dancing girls in the same condition. Asad Khan had the bed lifted up, and Amir Ali was carried swiftly away, still in a drunken sleep, towards Ismail Adil Shah's camp at Bidar. On the way he awoke, and cried out that he was being carried off by *jins*, but Asad Khan re-assured him and then read him a lecture on his debauchery which overwhelmed him with shame. In the morning he was brought before Ismail Adil Shah, who, after recounting his intrigues, ordered him to be put to death. Amir Ali Barid begged for mercy and promised to have Bidar surrendered if his life were spared. The execution was postponed, and Amir Ali was allowed to communicate with his sons in Bidar, who openly replied that their father was an old man, whose life was worth very little to them or to him, and that they would not surrender the fort. Privately, however, they informed their father that they would surrender the fort, but not until the last extremity. Accordingly, when Ismail Adil Shah ordered that Amir Ali Barid should be thrown to an elephant, the old man prayed that the sentence might be carried out before the bastion on which his sons usually sat. His request was granted, and when his sons saw the preparations for his execution they agreed to surrender the fort on the condition that their women were allowed to proceed unmolested to a place of safety. Ismail Adil Shah agreed to the condition, and the ladies withdrew from Bidar with the best part of the Bahmani jewels under their clothes. Ismail now entered the fort and seated himself on the throne of the Bahmanis. The treasures were brought forth, and the conqueror distributed them to his nobles and troops, to Ala-ud-din Imad Shah and others, reserving none for himself. He then restored to Amir Ali Barid all his former *jagirs* except Bidar, which he kept for himself, and required him to reduce the fortress of Mahur, the governor of which had declared himself independent, and to cede it to Ala-ud-din Imad Shah. Ismail then retired, leaving a garrison in Bidar.

Amir Ali Barid was in attendance on Ismail Adil Shah at the sieges of Raichur and Mudgal in 1530, and was deeply offended by being made, at a drinking party the subject of an Arabic jest which caused much amusement to the others present, but which he was not scholar enough to understand. Ismail Adil Shah, to heal his wounded vanity, promised to restore Bidar to him on his return to Bijapur, on condition that Kaliani and Kandhar were ceded to Bijapur. The promise was faithfully kept by Ismail, but Amir Ali never fulfilled the condition.

In 1540 Amir Ali Barid joined Burhan Nizam Shah in attacking Ibrahim Adil Shah I. They advanced to Bijapur and did much damage, while Ibrahim retired to Gulbarga; but, on being joined by his old servant Asad Khan Lari and by Ala-ud-din Imad Shah of Berar, he took the offensive and drove the invaders northwards as far as Daulatabad, where Amir Ali Barid died in 1542 His brother, the Khan-i-Khanan, took the corpse back to Bidar and buried it in the garden of Qasim Barid; and he was succeeded by his son Ali Barid, who was the first of his house who ventured, the last scion of the Bahmanis being now dead, to assume the title of Shah. In 1579 Sahib Khan, an unworthy favourite of Murtaza Nizam Shah, fell into disgrace and fled from Ahmadnagar to

Bidar, pursued by his master. On his arrival at Bidar the garrison, fearing lest his request for protection should be only a ruse to gain admission to the fort on behalf of his master, shut the gates in his face and fired on his troops, killing several. Meanwhile Murtaza arrived, and Sahib Khan found himself between two fires. He hastily tendered his submission to his master on condition that Salabat Khan, his principal opponent, should be dismissed, and that Bidar should be captured and given to him in *jagir*. The infatuated Sultan agreed to these terms, dismissed Salabat Khan to Bir, and, with the help of troops sent by Ibrahim Qutb Shah from Golconda, laid siege to Bidar. Ali Barid Shah applied for help to Ali Adil Shah of Bijapur, who sent a thousand horse and promised to send more on certain conditions. At this time Murtaza heard of the rebellion of his son in Ahmadnagar, and hastily returned to his capital, leaving Ibrahim Qutb Shah's troops with some of his own to continue the siege. The Golconda troops, however, very soon retired to their own country, and the Ahmadnagar troops under Mirza Yadgar were forced to abandon the siege.

Ali Barid Shah died in 1579, as appears from a chronogram in his beautiful tomb at Bidar. He was succeeded by his son Ibrahim Barid Shah, who reigned for seven years and was succeeded in 1586 by Qasim Barid II. In 1589 Qasim was nominally succeeded by his infant son, but a relative, Amir Barid, usurped the throne. He was expelled in 1601 by Mirza Ali Barid, another member of the family, and compelled to fly to Bhagnagar or Haidarabad. Mirza Ali Barid Shah reigned till 1609, and was succeeded by Ali Barid. In 1619, Ibrahim Adil Shah II marched to Bidar to punish Ali Barid, who had maintained the family tradition of hostility to Bijapur. Bidar fell, and Ali Barid and his sons were made captive by Ibrahim, who carried them to Bijapur, where they ended their days in captivity, Bidar being annexed to Bijapur. Bidar remained a part of the Bijapur kingdom until Aurangzib began to lay his plans for the entire subjugation of the kingdoms of the Deccan. Early in 1656 this prince, then viceroy of the Deccan for his father, the emperor Shahjahan, taking with him his son, Muhammad Muazzam, Mir Jumla, and Iftikhar Khan, marched from Aurangabad to Bidar, which was held by Malik Marjan, who had been *qalahdar* of the place under the Adil Shahi kings for 30 years. Aurangzib besieged the fortress, and in ten days succeeded in bringing his artillery to the edge of the ditch, and breached the bastion now known as the *Fath Burj.* Muazzam Khan and Mir Jumla then led a storming party against the defenders of the breach. Sidi Ambar Khan, one of Malik Marjan's lieutenants, had constructed a magazine within the *enceinte* and filled it with powder, rockets, and grenades. One of Mir Jumla's rockets struck this magazine, which exploded, severely burning Malik Marjan and his two sons. They were carried into the citadel, while Aurangzib entered the *Darwaza-i-Nauras*, which he re-named the *Fath Darwaza*, or "gate of victory." The sons of Malik Marjan asked for two days' grace in order that they might secure their property. On the second or third day Malik Marjan died and was buried in the tomb of Makhdum-i-Qadiri. His sons then surrendered the citadel, and Aurangzib made his triumphal entry on the 18th April 1656, and Bidar was annexed to the Mughal empire. With the fort were captured twelve *lakhs* of rupees in cash, ammunition worth eight lakhs of rupees, and 230 guns. There is now in Bidar a curious collection of old arms, most of which date apparently from the time when the fort was captured by Aurangzib, or from an earlier period.

In 1677, after Aurangzib had come to the throne, Qalandar Khan built a mosque in Bidar, the date of the completion of which was given in a neat chronogram. This mosque has apparently disappeared, but unfortunately the inscription which recorded the date of its completion has been removed and set up in the great mosque of sixteen arches, which is sometimes attributed to Ahmad Shah Wali, but was built, according to Khafi Khan, by Mahmud Gawan. It is a simple, but massive and imposing building in the Pathan style of architecture, with one large dome. It is an excellent example of the style in which it is built, but will not bear comparison with the great mosque at Gulbarga, and, unlike that building, labours under the disadvantage of being hemmed in by buildings which dwarf it and prevent the spectator from obtaining a view sufficiently comprehensive to convey a just idea of its admirable proportions and simple grandeur.

The ruins of the *Takht Mahal* or royal palace of the Bahmanis are more remarkable for their mass than for architectural beauty, but this building has suffered so much from neglect and from deliberate destruciveness that the ruin conveys no idea of the appearance of the palace before the destruction of its roof, undoubtedly domed, arcades, and terraced approaches. The Barid Shahi kings are blamed, by local tradition, for the deliberate destruction of monuments of the magnficience of their greater predecessors, the Bahmanis, and the *Takht Mahal* is cited as an instance of their vandalism.

The *Tirkash Mahal*, which was the hall of audience of the Barid Shahi kings; the *Gajan Mahal*, and the *Rangin Mahal* are all interesting buildings, and the mother-of-pearl inlaid work of the last is very beautiful. This building has unfortunately been disfigured in recent years by the whitewashing of some old carved work in dark coloured wood.

The old guns in the fort are numerous, and some of them are very large. The finest is a gun, twenty-four feet in length, made in 1580, in the reign of Ali Barid Shah. It bears some engraved inscriptions, one of which gives the weight of the ball which it carried as six maunds and half a seer, and of its charge as one maund and ten seers, to which ten seers were to be added if it were desired to increase the range.

The most interesting of the numerous tombs in the neighbourhood of Bidar are those of the Bahmani kings. These are, for the most part, large rectangular masses of masonry surmounted by heavy domes and adorned with tiers of arches. Their doorways are low and insignificant. The tomb of Ahmad Shah Wali, however, is beautifully adorned with enamel, and is in a very fair state of preservation. A yearly gathering is held at the tomb to commemorate the saintly king. The third tomb, that of Humayun the Tyrant, the grandson of Ahmad Shah, is in ruins, half the dome having fallen away. There is an interesting legend to the effect that the dome split immediately after the Tyrant's body had been placed in the tomb, as though refusing to shelter it. Unfortunately there are many still living who remember the tomb in an undamaged condition, and it is probably not more than twenty years since the dome collapsed. Between the Bahmani tombs and the town is an octagonal building without a dome, the tomb of Khalil-ullah (*But Shikan*, or the Iconoclast). This saint was adopted by Ahmad Shah as his patron after the capital had been removed to Bidar.

The most beautiful of all the tombs in Bidar is that of Ali Barid Shah. The older Bahmani tombs excite what admiration they deserve by their massive bulk, but this tomb rather by its proportions, which are so perfect that the eye is deceived as to the size of the tomb, which is not insignificant. It is square in plan with an open arch on each side, and it is surmounted by a beautifully proportioned dome, which terminates in a spire, the total height of the building from the ground being 106 feet. The tomb is adorned with exquisite enamel work, and the inscriptions in the interior consist of Persian verses and texts from the *Quran* beautifully executed. The tomb of Qasim Barid Shah, which stands next to that of Ali Barid, was evidently intended to be a replica of it, but it was never finished, and entirely lacks ornament. There are many other interesting monuments, for Bidar is truly a city of tombs, but the exigencies of space prevent even a passing notice of them. All those who care for relics of the past must regret that this delightful old city, which has stood eight sieges, stands so far from the beaten track of the traveller that the pleasure of visiting it falls to the lot of comparatively few.

CHAPTER VI.

RAICHUR.

A Bone of Contention.

THE old fort and city of Raichur lie in the Duab or interfluvial area between the Krishna and its principal tributary, the Tungabhadra. The scenery of this tract, the hottest part of the Deccan, would be dull and monotonous in the extreme but for the rocky hills with which it is dotted. These break the monotony of the horizon, and the toilsome ascent of any one of them is rewarded by a view to which spaciousness lends grandeur. The vast plain lies spread out in all its fertility beneath the spectator's feet, and even in the aridity of summer the heat vibrations give an appearance of variety to the expanse.

The history of the Raichur Duab is the history of the struggle between the Muhammadan kingdom of the Deccan and the Hindu kingdom of the Peninsula for supremacy in Southern India.

The fortress of Raichur was built, as an old Telugu inscription informs us, in 1294, by Gore Gangayya Ruddivaru, a servant of the Kakatiya kings of Warangal, of whose kingdom Raichur was, so far as is known, the western outpost, for no Kakatiya remains have been found further westward. The date of the foundation of the fort is interesting for two reasons. In the first place it coincides with the date assigned to the accession of Prataparudradeva II, who ascended the throne in Warangal on the abdication of his grandmother, Rudrammadevi. In the second place it coincides with the date of the first appearance of the Musalmans in the Deccan, for in 1294 Ala-ud-din Khalji, who afterwards ascended the throne of Delhi, led his daring raid on Deogir, the northernmost kingdom of the Deccan.

No chronicles enlighten us as to the considerations which led to the founding of the fort. In the absence of specific information we may be permitted to imagine the aged queen Rudrammadevi, weary of her long and lonely tenure of the reins of government, anxiously awaiting the time when her grandson would be ready to receive them from her tired grasp, and perturbed by reports of the new terror from the north, in the face of which she could not relax her hold on her husband's kingdom until she had seen it armed at all points. It is not unreasonable to suppose, from the history of the period, that it was in these circumstances that Raichur was founded and that the widowed queen who, according to the traditions of her race, should have immolated herself on her husband's pyre but chose the better part of holding his kingdom as he would have had it held, when she saw the noble fortress nearing completion cheerfully resigned to her young grandson the kingdom which was to cost him dear and the fortress which was to aid him little.

Raichur was strategically useless to the young king of Warangal, for when the Muslims came they paid no heed to his far western frontier, but marched direct on his capital from the north-west, by way of Bidar and Indur. It was not, however, destined to be left high and dry by the tide of warfare, for by a strange irony of fate it remained for many years a standing menace to the mightier Hindu kingdom which rose on the ruins of Warangal.

It was not until 1310 that the Musalmans travelled so far south as Raichur, and they did not actually attack the fortress until 1312, in which year Prataparudradeva II sent messengers to Delhi to intimate to Ala-ud-din Shah that the tribute was collected and that his vassal only awaited the arrival of a trusty official to whose care it might be consigned. Kafur Hazardinari, entitled Malik Naib, was the officer who was, at his own request, selected for this duty and for that of reducing affairs in the Deccan to order. There was Shankar, the son of Ramchandra of Deogir, to be dealt with. He was put to death. After performing this service Malik Naib devastated most of Maharashtra, as far as Gulbarga, Mudgal, and Raichur, and settled affairs in the Konkun and Telingana, besides carrying the imperial banners as far south as the Karnatik and the eastern coast of the Peninsula.

In 1317-18, in the reign of Qutb-ud-din Mubarak Shah of Delhi, Harpala Deva, the son-in-law of Ramchandra of Deogir, rebelled and was defeated and put to death with great cruelty. His rebellion had unsettled the whole of southern India and Mubarak Shah remained at Deogir until he had re-established his authority in the south, and placed garrisons in Gulbarga, Sagar, Dwarasamudra, and other places. Raichur was probably one of these, for Sagar lies in the Duab, and it is not likely that the principal fortress in that tract was neglected. The Deccan was then handed over to Malik Yaklaki, who shortly afterwards rebelled, but was captured. Malik Ain-ul-Mulk Multani was next appointed to the command in southern India, but we hear no more of Raichur in this reign, though an expedition to the eastern coast was undertaken.

In the expeditions to the south in the reign of Ghiyas-ud-din Tughlaq Shah of Delhi no account seems to have been taken of Raichur, which lay out of the beaten track between Deogir and Warangal, but Tughlaq's son and successor, Muhammad, very early in his reign, tightened his grip upon the outlying provinces of his empire, among which Dwarasamudra, the eastern coast, Warangal, and the Karnatak are mentioned, and Raichur was at this time certainly included in the empire of Delhi. When Deogir, now renamed Daulatabad, became in 1327 the capital of the Indian empire, Raichur was already an important town. In the confusion caused by the wild schemes hatched by Muhammad bin Tughlaq Vijayanagar was founded, and the new Hindu kingdom, with its capital in the neighbourhood of Raichur, became a power to be reckoned with, though the Hindus did not at once attempt to wrest the Raichur Duab from the Musalmans. Later in Muhammad Shah's reign when the centurions of the Deccan, apprehensive of his intentions towards them, resolved on rebellion, the officers serving in Raichur and Mudgal joined them and assisted them in raising Ismail Fath, the Afghan, to the throne of the Deccan under the style of Nasir-ud-din Shah. The choice was unfortunate and, after being defeated by the emperor, Ismail abdicated and Zafar Khan of Gulbarga was elected in his stead and was in 1347 proclaimed king of the Deccan under the title of Ala-ud-din Bahman Shah. Gulbarga was selected as the capital of the new kingdom and the Raichur Duab was included in the same province as the capital.

In 1365, in the reign of Muhammad I, Bahman's eldest son and successor, the Duab first suffered from the incursions of the Hindus of Vijayanagar. Muhammad Shah, at the wedding feast of his son Mujahid, grew merry in his cups, and, being pleased by the singing of a band of three hundred singers from Delhi, ordered Malik Saif-ud-din Ghori to draw up for their payment a draft on the Vijayanagar treasury. Malik Saif-ud-din regarded the order as a drunken boast, but was asked by the king on the following day whether the draft had been made out, and was compelled to offer excuses for his negligence. Muhammad read what was passing in his mind and said, "God forbid that a king so great and powerful as I should utter vain words. My order was not due to drunkenness or levity but to set purpose. Write the draft at once, seal it, and despatch it to the Raya of Vijayanagar, that he may honour it." The order was obeyed and Bukka I of Vijayanagar very properly resented the insult. The bearer of the draft was ridden round the city on an ass and expelled, and the Raya then assembled his armies and encamped at Adoni with 30,000 horse, 900,000 foot, and 3,000 elephants, and proceeded to ravage the southern districts of the Bahmani dominions. Muhammad Shah issued orders for the assembly of his forces, but Bukka was beforehand with him, invaded the Duab, and besieged Mudgal, the sister fortress of Raichur, at his leisure; secure in the protection afforded by the Krishna river, which was now swollen by the rains. Mudgal was garrisoned by no more than 800 Musalmans, and when the place fell the defenders, with the women and children, were massacred by the victors. Only one man escaped and hastened to Gulbarga with the tidings. Muhammad Shah mourned for his fallen heroes and, with oriental justice, ordered the fugitive to be slain instantly, for, he said, he could not endure the sight of one who had witnessed the death of so many of his companions in arms. Muhammad then crossed the Krishna with an army of 9,000 horse and Bukka and his cavalry fled before him to Adoni, leaving his camp at the mercy of the Musalmans, who slew there no less than 70,000 men, women, and children. With the details of the campaign we have little more to do, for the theatre of war was removed from the Raichur Duab, but the Hindus were defeated with terrible slaughter and Bukka was forced to honour the draft. No less than 10,000 Brahmans were slain in the campaign, and at its close the Hindu ambassadors stipulated that in all future wars the persons of women and children should be respected. This condition was frequently broken by the Musalmans in later times, but it is only fair to note that it was the Hindus who set the example in this respect when they dishonoured and slaughtered the wives of the garrison of Mudgal. At the same time Muhammad Shah swore that he would never again cause prisoners of war to be murdered.

Mujahid succeeded his father on the throne of Gulbarga in 1375. At this time some of the forts in the Raichur Duab were held by Bukka Raya while others were in the hands of the Muhammadans. Mujahid Shah wrote to Bukka and complained of the encroachment of the Hindus on the Duab. The Tungabhadra was, he said, the northern boundary of the kingdom of Vijayanagar, and he agreed, if this boundary were accepted, to leave Bukka in unmolested possession of the country to the south of that river as far as the coasts of peninsular India. The acceptance of these proposals would have involved the cession of Bankapur and other forts to the Bahmani kingdom. Bukka Raya replied that Raichur and Mudgal and all the country as far north as the Krishna had formerly been part of the dominions of Vijayanagar and that the Krishna should be the boundary between the Deccan and the Peninsula. He then demanded the surrender of Raichur and Mudgal and the return of the elephants which had been captured by Mujahid's father. These conflicting claims to the extensive Duab and to the two important fortresses of Raichur and Mudgal could only be decided in the field. Mujahid Shah, who was in the flower of his youth, active, energetic, and athletic, lost no time in assembling his troops from Berar, Daulatabad, and Bidar, and advanced into the Vijayanagar territories as far as Adoni. This place had not yet fallen to the Musalmans, and although the young Mujahid was anxious to acquire the honour of capturing a maiden fortress he was too impetuous to brook the restraints imposed by necessity on besiegers. It thus happened that Saffdar Khan Sistani, with the army of Berar, was left before Adoni with instructions to reduce it, while Mujahid Shah followed Bukka Raya down the valley of the Tungabhadra. The only story of the campaign which has come down to us illustrates the extraordinary value attached to mere brute courage and manual dexterity in the commander of an oriental army. Mujahid, while following the enemy, beguiled the time with sport, and on one occasion attacked and slew, with one arrow, a fierce tiger. The fame of this exploit so unmanned the Hindus that they would not abide Mujahid's onset. Bukka Raya fled towards the forests to the south of

Vijayanagar, hoping to entrap the Musalmans in defiles and forest paths. Mujahid marched straight in Vijayanagar, but found that the reduction of the rambling city with its many defensible posts, the attacking of which resembled street fighting on a large scale, would occupy him for so long that the enemy would have time to recover heart of grace. He therefore pursued Bukka to his forest refuge. The result of the expedition is all that concerns the history of Raichur. The Hindus were completely defeated, more than 40,000 of them being slain in the campaign, which decided the fate of the Raichur Duab. Henceforth this tract of country belonged to the Muslims by right of conquest.

Mujahid Shah was assassinated almost immediately after the termination of hostilities, but his successors reaped the benefits of his conquest, and the Raja of Vijayanagar never thenceforward laid claim as of right to the Duab, which enjoyed a long period of peace.

In 1399, during the reign of Firuz Shah, the eighth king of the Bahmani dynasty, Harihara II made an attempt to conquer the Raichur Duab, which he invaded with an army of 30,000 horse and 900,000 foot. Firuz Shah, on learning of this invasion of his dominions by the Hindus, marched from Gulbarga and assembled his forces at Sagar, where they mustered 12,000 horse. With this force he proceeded against a disaffected Hindu *zamindar* of that district, who could place in the field a force of seven or eight thousand Hindu infantry, mostly Kolis. The *zamindar* was defeated and put to death and Firuz Shah then awaited the arrival of troops from Berar and Daulatabad. The conspiracy against the peace of the Bahmani kingdom was, however, more widespread than had been anticipated. Harihara had taken care, before he took the first step towards hostilities, to enter into an agreement with Narsingh Deo, the Gond ruler of Kherla, who invaded Berar and ravaged it as far south as Mahur, thus detaining the armies of Berar and Daulatabad in the northern part of the kingdom. Firuz Shah, nothing daunted, marched against the vast host of the Hindus with the 12,000 horsemen whom he had been able to muster in the province of Gulbarga. The rainy season was at its height and the Krishna river was in flood, while Harihara, occupying the Duab, encamped on its southern bank to oppose the passage of the apparently insignificant army arrayed against him. Firuz could neither devise nor receive any plan which would enable him to cross the river in the face of the enemy until one of his lesser nobles, Qazi Siraj, a commander of a hundred horse, unfolded a bold design which, with his master's sanction, he put into execution. He volunteered to cross the river with a few companions and to assassinate either Harihara or his son, who was present with the Hindu army, thus affording to Firuz Shah an opportunity of crossing the river while the Hindu host should be plunged into confusion owing to the death of its leaders. Qazi Siraj, with seven companions disguised as religious mendicants, crossed the river secretly. They hung round the wine shops and Qazi Siraj sedulously made love to a courtesan whom he found in those haunts. It so happened that the woman was engaged to sing that night at a feast given by Harihara's son, and when she had arrayed herself in her finery Qazi Siraj professed that he could not bear the idea of being separated from her and implored her to allow him to accompany her. She replied that none but minstrels and dancers would be admitted to the feast, whereupon Qazi Siraj avowed himself a noted minstrel. The damsel, to test him, gave him her rebeck, on which he acquitted himself so well that she gladly allowed him and his companions to accompany her, conceiving that she would gain honour by introducing the accomplished strangers to the prince's notice. Qazi Siraj and one of his companions, dressed as women, were introduced at the proper time as singers and jugglers and, after exhibiting the usual antics of such entertainers, proceeded to perform a dagger dance, in which each brandished a pair of naked daggers. They approached the prince as though to give him a better opportunity of appreciating their dexterity, and when they were within striking distance, drove all four daggers into him. The six Musalmans who had been left without the tent cut through the canvas with their daggers, rushed into the assembly and laid about them, doing much execution among the Hindus, most of whom were confused with wine. Before the Hindus could recover themselves the eight adventurers extinguished the lights and withdrew during the confusion to a landing place where they awaited the passage of Firuz Shah's army. The encampment of the Hindu army was much scattered, and extended in each direction to a distance of more than five leagues. This dispersion only increased the confusion, and the various rumours current could not be verified. Some said that the whole Muhammadan army had crossed and that Harihara and his son had been killed. Others said that the infantry only had crossed and had inflicted severe losses on the Hindus in a night attack. As may easily be conceived there was much talk and no action, and under cover of the confusion three or four thousand Muhammadan horse crossed the river in basket boats covered with hide, swimming their horses across. The Hindu sentries fled before them, and with the dawn of day Firuz Shah with the rest of his army effected the passage in good order, their passage being covered by the troops which had crossed during the night. The Hindus were too scattered to be able to offer effective resistance at any one point to the compact army of Firuz Shah; and Harihara, having succeeded in gaining possession of the bier on which lay the body of his son, fled, followed at more leisure by the whole of his army. The pursuit was maintained through the Raichur Duab and even to the gates of Vijayanagar, the fugitives only adding to the slaughter by turning at times in a futile attempt to arrest the advance of the Muslims. Vast quantities of spoil fell into the hands of the victors, and Firuz Shah laid siege to Vijayanagar, at the same time despatching his brother Ahmad Khan, the Khan-i-Khanan, and Mir Fazlullah Anju with a force to lay waste the districts to the south of Vijayanagar. Qazi Siraj was made an *amir* and was attached to the Khan-i-Khanan. This expeditionary force captured about 10,000 children, male and female, of the Brahman caste, and retained them with the object of bringing them up as Musalmans. The Brahmans of Vijayanagar were now seriously alarmed and approached Harihara with the demand that all the treasure that could be collected should be offered to the invaders as a ransom for the captives. Mir Fazlullah was appointed to treat with the Hindus, who offered him ten lakhs of *huns* to be paid into Firuz Shah's treasury and one lakh for himself in consideration of his accepting these terms on behalf of the Sultan. The faithful servant concluded the negotiation and laid before his master the whole sum of eleven lakhs of *huns*. By the treaty now entered into the terms of former treaties prohibiting interference with women and children and the slaughter of prisoners of war were confirmed, and Firuz Shah's tenure of the Raichur Duab was formally recognized. Firuz Shah then hastened back to Gulbarga in order to march against Narsingh

Deo of Kherla, who had invaded Berar, and left Fulad Khan as governor of the Duab.

The peace of the Duab was next disturbed by reason of a lady. A poor goldsmith of Mudgal had a beautiful daughter of whom it is said that when her parents wished to marry her in her childhood to a youth of their own caste, the girl, conscious of her great beauty, persuaded them not to press her to marry, adding that she was convinced that her comeliness would bring her a higher prize than an obscure goldsmiths. At this time an old Brahman, who was returning to Vijayanagar from a pilgrimage to Benares, lodged at the goldsmith's house. The parents asked him to bestow a blessing on their daughter and he required the girl to be brought into his presence. When he was told that she was behind the *parda* he expressed surprise that a Hindu girl should deem it necessary to hide her face from any, most of all from a Brahman, and called her. After much hesitation the girl Partahal came forth and stood before him. The old Brahman was struck with her beauty and realized that her vague hopes were not unlikely to be fulfilled, could she only be introduced at court. He remained in the goldsmith's house for a year and instructed Partahal in Hindu music, in which he was well skilled. When he had perfected her in the art he left the goldsmith's house and returned to Vijayanagar, where he sedulously spread abroad the news of his late pupil's beauty and accomplishments. The report at length reached the ears of Harihara Raya, who sent for the Brahman, questioned him, and persuaded him to make an attempt to procure the girl for the royal seraglio, promising to make her his principal wife. The Brahman had no difficulty in persuading Partahal's parents to accept the offer, but when he attempted to place round her neck a necklace which the Raja had sent for her acceptance she declined the proffered honour. Her parents were much surprised and urged her to explain her conduct. After much hesitation she said that she had been assured in visions that she was to become a follower of Islam, and the honour destined for her would come to her as a Musalmani, and she finally rejected the offers of the Raya of Vijayanagar. Harihara Raja was much incensed by the news of Partahal's obduracy and resolved to obtain by force the beauty whom his blandishments had failed to entice. He hesitated openly to break the treaty by which Firuz Shah was recognized as the lawful sovereign of the Duab, and hovered on the south bank of the Tungabhadra on the pretext of enjoying the chase. Something more than the love of an unseen girl is needed to explain his subsequent boldness and we must turn aside for a moment to the domain of authentic history in order to discover its cause.

In 1398-99 Timur had invaded India and captured Delhi. Firuz Shah Bahmani, who was an acute and far-seeing ruler, presumed, with good reason, that the marauder would never reach the Deccan, and at the same time conceived that the recognition of his kingship by the *de facto* ruler of Delhi would enhance his prestige. He therefore hastened to make his submission to the invader and despatched to him an embassy which acknowledged him as overlord of all India, including the Deccan. In return for this compliment Timur, with the insolence of a conqueror, conferred on his vassal, by a stroke of his pen, the sovereignty of the Deccan, Gujarat, and Malwa. This empty grant was much resented by Dilawar Khan Ghori of Malwa, the governor who shortly afterwards assumed the royal title, and Muzaffar Shah I of Gujarat, and both rulers assured Harihara of Vijayanagar, who sent a secret mission to them, that their support would not be lacking when he chose to attack the Bahmani kingdom from the south. Even with these assurances Harihara still hesitated, and his wisest counsellors warned him of the danger of invading the territories of Firuz Shah. At length, however, impelled either by the hope of assistance from the north or by an unconquerable longing to possess the goldsmith's fair daughter, Harihara sent a force of 5,000 horse and a large body of foot across the river to raid Mudgal and capture the goldsmith and his family. The inhabitants, including the objects of Harihara's search, had in the mean-time, become apprehensive of the designs of the large Hindu army assembled in their neighbourhood, and had fled. Harihara was now in the awkward predicament of having provoked a powerful enemy without attaining his object. The matter had gone too far for an honourable compromise, for the force sent against Mudgal had plundered and ravaged many villages in the Duab. Fulad Khan, the governor of the district, pursued the raiders with such troops as he could collect and suffered an unimportant defeat on the bank of the Tungabhadra before he could assemble his full force. The indecisive victory gave the

Hindus confidence, and when Fulad Khan, having been joined by the rest of his troops, found that the enemy's army was unprepared for an attack, he fell on them and gained a signal victory which he duly reported to his master. He then pursued the Hindus to the gates of Vijayanagar, where he besieged them Firuz Shah resolved to press home the advantage gained by his lieutenant, marched with his army on Vijayanagar, and attempted to take the city by storm. The attempt failed, and the Musalmans were subsequently defeated, though not seriously, in an action fought under the walls of the city. After this check Firuz Shah was content to establish himself in an entrenched camp over against the city while he sent his brother, Ahmad Khan, with a force of 10,000 horse, to ravage the country to the south of Vijayanagar and his lieutenant Mir Fazlullah to besiege Bankapur, then held by the Hindus. Firuz Shah was hard pressed by the Hindus in his camp before Vijayanagar, but beat off their attacks. Bankapur was captured and Ahmad Khan plundered the principal cities lying to the south of Vijayanagar. In the meantime Harihara had vainly applied to the king of Gujarat for the assistance promised by him. Firuz Shah now altered the disposition of his troops. Leaving Ahmad Khan to watch Harihara in Vijayanagar, he marched in person against Adoni. This movement greatly disconcerted the Hindus and envoys were despatched to the camp of Firuz Shah, then seven leagues distant from the city. After some difficulty terms of peace were arranged. Harihara Raya was compelled to submit to the indignity of giving his daughter in marriage to the Muhammadan king, and to pay a large indemnity, and in order that there might be no future dispute regarding Bankapur it was included in the dowry of the Hindu princess. The wedding was celebrated with great magnificence, but the conclusion of the ceremonies renewed the enmity between the Raya and the Sultan. The former, when accompanying Firuz Shah on his way back from the city to his camp after the ceremony, turned back half way, instead of escorting his son-in-law to his tent, and Firuz Shah although unwilling to renew hostilities at such a time, swore to be revenged at some future time for the slight to which he had thus publicly been subjected. The beautiful Sonarin who had been the cause of the war, was given in marriage to Hasan Khan, the eldest son of Firuz, and the Muhammadan army returned to the Bahmani dominions.

In 1417 Firuz Shah attacked Pangul, then in the possession of Vira Vijaya Raya of Vijayanagar, grandson of Harihara II, who had died in 1406. Vira Vijaya at once declared war on Firuz Shah, attacked him with a large army, and utterly defeated him. The Musalmans fled and the whole of the southern and eastern districts of the Bahmani kingdom, including the Raichur Duab, fell into the hands of the Hindus. Firuz Shah sought help from Gujarat, but Ahmad Shah of that kingdom was not yet so firmly seated on his throne that he could venture on a campaign so far from his border, and no help came. Ahmad Khan recovered part of the lost territories, but the prestige of the Musalmans had received a severe blow from which it did not recover until after the accession of Ahmad Khan as Ahmad Shah in 1422.

Ahmad Shah, shortly after his accession, declared war against Vira Vijaya Raya, marched through the Raichur Duab with 40,000 horse, and encamped on the bank of the Tungabhadra. Vira Vijaya, who expected to overcome Ahmad as easily as he had overcome his brother, marched to meet him, and encamped on the south bank of the river with a million infantry. The armies lay watching one another for forty days without engaging in anything more serious than insignificant skirmishes, and at the end of that time Ahmad Shah called a council of war to consider whether he should cross the river and attack the enemy. It was unanimously resolved that the attempt should be made, and when the news of this resolve spread among the enemy the Raja of Warangal, who had come to the assistance of Vira Vijaya, at once withdrew, with his whole army. Vira Vijaya ordered his troops to prepare for battle, and meanwhile a force of ten thousand horse under Alam Khan and Lodi Khan, two officers of Afghan descent, forded the river some distance above the Hindu camp and, following a circuitous route, came round by the rear of the camp to a field of sugar-cane, where Vira Vijaya with a few attendants happened to be taking his ease. The attendants dispersed and Vira Vijaya, believing that the Musalmans had received information of his whereabouts and had come to the field for the express purpose of capturing him hid himself among the sugarcane. The Musalmans dismounted and began to cut the sugarcane in order to refresh themselves. They soon came upon Vira Vijaya, but failed to recognize him and took him for the owner of the field. They gave him a bundle of sugarcane to carry and drove him on before them. In the meantime the rest of Ahmad Shah's army had crossed the river, and the Hindus, after the fashion of oriental armies on the disappearance of their leader, fled in confusion. The division which had captured Vira Vijaya, having ascertained that the Hindus were in flight, pressed onwards in search of plunder more valuable than sugarcane and left the supposed husbandman behind. Vira Vijaya, finding himself free, hastened to join his army, and his officers, finding him once more in their midst, collected their scattered troops and were prepared to make a stand, but the narrow escape, and possibly the unwonted exertion of carrying a head-load, had unmanned the Raya and he refused to lead his troops against the enemy and ordered a retreat to Vijayanagar, where he shut himself up. Ahmad Shah would not waste his time in a siege but marched through the Vijayanagar kingdom laying waste the country, levelling temples, slaughtering kine, and putting Hindus to the sword without respect to age or sex, halting for three days for each 20,000 Hindus slain. On one occasion the Sultan had a very narrow escape when attacked by a body of Hindu horse while out hunting. He was saved by the valour of his immediate atttendants, and at once made preparations for laying siege to Vijayanagar. Vira Vijaya, on learning of these preparations, sued for peace, which was granted on payment of arrears of tribute. This campaign secured the possession of the Raichur Duab to the Bahmanids for many years, and Vijayanagar lay crushed until Ahmad Shah's death in 1435.

Very early in the reign of Ala-ud-din Ahmad Shah II, Ahmad Shah's son and successor, a rebellion broke out in the Raichur Duab. Vijayanagar had paid no tribute for five years and Prince Muhammad, the new king's younger brother, was sent with some of the principal nobles of the kingdom to collect the arrears. His army invaded the Vijayanagar dominions from the Raichur Duab and began the usual work of indiscriminate slaughter. Deva Raya II, the son and successor of Vira Vijaya, at once paid the arrears and the invaders withdrew to Mudgal. While the army halted here some restless spirits persuaded Muhammad that it had been his father's intention to divide the kingdom equally between his two eldest sons, and instigated him to send a message to his brother demanding either that he should be allowed to sit on the throne with him and should be associated equally with him in the government of the kingdom, or that the kingdom should be divided into two parts by metes and bounds, and that one should be given to him. The young man listened to this evil counsel and tried to persuade the two principal nobles with him to be the bearers of his message to his brother, and, on their refusing, put them to death. He then, by means of the large sum which had been collected from the Vijayanagar treasury, increased his army until he was strong enough to capture from his brother's officers Mudgal, Raichur, Sholapur, and Naldrug. The king marched southwards against his brother and defeated him in a closely contested battle. Prince Muhammad fled from the field with a few followers and took refuge in the forests, where he lurked until the king contrived to convey to him a message of forgiveness. The rebel returned to court and was shortly afterwards made governor of Raichur, where he lived a life of luxurious idleness for many years and troubled the peace of the kingdom no more.

Later in his reign Ala-ud-din Ahmad Shah was engaged in warfare with his father-in-law, Nasir Khan, Sultan of Khandesh, who had fomented a rebellion in Berar and invaded that province. Deva Raya II was not slow to recognize his opportunity. He first consulted his advisers as to the cause of the superiority in warfare of the Musalmans, whose armies were very much less numerous than the hosts of Vijayanagar. The Brahmans, after the manner of their kind, replied that the superiority of the Musalmans had been decreed by Heaven, and that the Almighty had granted them dominion over the Hindus for 30,000 years or more. The soldiers would have none of this blind submission to fate and attributed the frequent victories of the enemy to their better horsemanship and archery. Deva Raya accepted this sound and practical view and ordered that Musalmans should be freely enlisted in his army. He built a mosque for them in Vijayanagar and decreed that they should be free to practise the rites of their faith without molestation. To conquer their prejudice against making obeisance to an idolatrous master he had a copy of the Quran placed in a reading stand before his throne in order that they might salve their consciences by the excuse that when they bowed before him they were in fact bowing before the sacred book. The Hindu army was sedulously reorganized and improved on Muhammadan lines, the Musalmans enlisted were employed as instructors, and the pay of the Hindu *silahdar sawars* was raised in order that they might provide themselves with steeds better than the sorry nags on which they had hitherto been mounted.

Having thus reformed his army Deva Raya in 1443-44 imagined himself strong enough to bid defiance to the Bahmani king. He invaded the Raichur Duab and captured the fortress of Mudgal without difficulty. Having by this feat established his prestige, he left two of his sons to besiege Raichur and Bankapur while he in person, with the main body of his army, advanced to the southern bank of the Krishna. Ala-ud-din Ahmad Shah, on receiving information of the invasion of his territories by the Hindus, assembled his troops from the four provinces of his kingdom, and Deva Raya, who had been under the impression that the campaign in the northern Deccan had left the Muhammadan army too exhausted to take the field, was undeceived. He retired to Mudgal, where he prepared to stand a siege, and left an army to oppose the entry of the Musalmans into the Duab. Ala-ud-din Ahmad brushed this force aside, entered the Duab, and advanced to within twelve miles of Mudgal, where he halted and disposed his forces. To the Daulatabad army corps, commanded by Khalaf Hasan Basri, was entrusted the duty of dealing with the besiegers of Raichur and Bankapur, while the army corps of Bidar and Berar and the Bijapur division of the army corps of Gulbarga were despatched against Deva Raya in Mudgal. Khalaf Hasan marched first on Raichur and raised the siege of the fortress, compelling the besiegers to concentrate on Mudgal. He then turned his attention to Bankapur, but before he could reach this post the other son of Deva Raya, having heard of the march of events, had abandoned the siege and joined his father at Mudgal. The war was thus focussed in the neighbourhood of Mudgal, where three battles were fought. In the first the Hindus and in the second the Muhammadans gained indecisive victories, but in the third the Hindus suffered a crushing defeat. The Hindu prince who had been driven from Raichur by Khalaf Hasan was slain, and his death was the signal for flight. His corpse was taken to his father in Mudgal, whither the Hindu army, closely pursued by the Musalmans, fled for refuge. So hot was the pursuit that Fakhr-ul-Mulk Dihlavi and his brother, two of Ala-ud-din Ahmad Shah's principal nobles, with a few of their troops, followed the fugitives into Mudgal and found the gates shut upon them before they could escape. They were taken before Deva Raya, who ordered them to be kept in chains. As soon as Ala-ud-din missed the two *amirs* he sent a message to Deva Raya to the effect that he valued each of the two at a thousand horsemen, and that ten thousand Hindus would be slain for every Musalman put to death. Deva Raya, on receiving this message, proposed terms of peace. All that he required was that Ala-ud-din Ahmad should refrain from invading his dominions, and in return for the fulfilment of this condition he agreed to return his prisoners, to vacate the Duab, and to pay a yearly tribute. These terms were accepted. Deva Raya returned to his own dominions and regularly remitted the stipulated tribute, and peace reigned in the Raichur Duab until the Bahmani dynasty had ceased to be a force to be reckoned with.

In the reign of Muhammad Shah III, the thirteenth king of the Bahmani dynasty the four great provinces of the kingdom were divided into eight, and under this arrangement the old province of Gulbarga was subdivided into the provinces of Gulbarga and Bijapur, the Raichur Duab forming part of the latter. This fact is important, for it determined the destiny of the Duab on the dissolution of the Bahmani kingdom. The province of Bijapur was first given to the great minister Khaja Mahmud Gawan, the author of the partition, who was murdered in 1482 in consequence of the machinations of those who were opposed to his reforms. Muhammad Shah died shortly afterwards, stricken with remorse for his share in the death of his faithful servant, and was succeeded by his young son Mahmud, a weakling who was king only in name. The government of the province of Bijapur was given to Yusuf Adil Khan, the Turk, after the death of Mahmud Gawan.

During the reign of Mahmud Shah Bahmani all real power in the kingdom passed into the hands of the great nobles, and in 1490 three provincial governors, Yusuf Adil Khan of Bijapur, Ahmad Nizam-ul-Mulk of Ahmadnagar, and Fathullah Imad-ul-Mulk of Berar, disgusted with the arrogance of Amir Barid, who as minister at the capital kept his king in confinement and governed in his name, proclaimed themselves independent and assumed the insignia of royalty. In Golconda Sultan Quli Qutb-ul-Mulk remained nominally faithful to the *roi faineànt* until 1512, when he too declared himself independent. Amir Barid, the actual ruler of Bidar, did not assume the royal title until 1526, when the Bahmani dynasty ceased to exist.

Yusuf Adil Shah's assumption of independence was a severe blow to Amir Barid, who had expected to govern the whole of the Bahmani kingdom in his master's name and hankered especially after the province of Bijapur. He went so far as to write in Mahmud Shah's name to Timma, the virtual ruler of Vijayanagar, and to cede to him the Raichur Duab on condition that he punished Yusuf Adil Shah for his assumption of the royal title. At the same time Bahadur Gilani, the governor of the Konkan, was instigated to attack Yusuf from the west and captured the fortress of Jamkhandi, about thirty-six miles south-west of Bijapur, while a large Hindu host invaded and overran the Duab, capturing both Raichur and Mudgal. Yusuf, who was by religion a *Shiah*, was in sore straits and registered a vow that if he came safely through his troubles he would do what no Muhammadan ruler in India had hitherto ventured to do and would establish the *Shiah* religion in his kingdom. The situation was one which called for diplomacy and timely concession. Affecting to recognize the title of Vijayanagar to the Duab, Yusuf made peace with Timma, who had been recalled to his capital by affairs of state, and directed his efforts against the root of the evil, Amir Barid. Historians differ as to the course of the campaign against Bidar, but there is no doubt as to its result. Yusuf Adil Shah was left free to deal with Vijayanagar and marched on Raichur. When he reached the Krishna river the effects of a prolonged course of debauchery confined him to his bed for two months, during which period Timma, taking with him the son of Virupaksha I, the last king of the first dynasty of Vijayanagar, hastened to the relief of Raichur. Yusuf Adil Shah, having recovered from his sickness, marched against the Hindus without observing the most ordinary military precautions, and one day, when he was taking his ease with a few attendants, Timma fell upon his army and put it to flight. The Hindus failed to follow up their advantage and dispersed throughout the camp of the Musalmans, intent only on plunder. A fugitive brought news to Yusuf that Timma was near at hand with a few attendants whom he had been able to restrain from the general rush for the spoil and Yusuf collected his own attendants and such stragglers and fugitives as passed by the way and made for the Hindu prince. The movement rallied the Musalmans, who gained strength each moment, while the Hindus could not be recalled from the scene of plunder. Victory finally declared for the Musalmans, and Timma and the heir to the glories of Vijayanagar made the best of their way towards their capital, but the young prince, who had been wounded by an arrow, died by the way, and Timma, or "Timraj" as Firishta calls him, was able, on his return, to assume the style as well as the power of royalty.*

This campaign secured the possession of the Duab to the Adil Shahi dynasty. The fugitive who had led Yusuf into the path of victory was made an *amir*, with the title of Bahadur Khan, and received fifty elephants and a large sum of money. He was then deputed to recapture Raichur and Mudgal while Yusuf Adil Shah returned to Bijapur. The Hindu defenders of these fortresses were in no condition, after the defeat of their master, to sustain a protracted siege, and Bahadur Khan captured the two forts within six weeks and returned to Bijapur. Yusuf Adil Shah died in 1510, and after his death affairs in the kingdom of Bijapur fell into great confusion. Kamal Khan, one of the most powerful nobles of the state, made a determined and all but successful attempt to usurp the throne, and Krishnaraya, the grandson of Timma, taking advantage of this state of affairs, invaded and annexed the Raichur Duab. Kamal Khan was overcome, but Ismail Adil Shah, who succeeded his father Yusuf in Bijapur, was not strong enough to attempt to recover the Duab until 1521. In the rainy season of that year he marched against the Hindu army then occupying the Duab and halted on the bank of the Krishna with a small force. Krishnaraya, after calling up his vassals, was able to put into the field an army of 50,000 cavalry and 600,000 infantry, and Ismail was inclined to retreat and to postpone the attempt to recover the Duab to a more favourable time,

* There seems to be some confusion of names, or of dates, here. Timma actually acquired the supreme power in Vijayanagar about 1455 and Virupaksha, the last king of the first dynasty succeeded, nominally, in 1483. Timma, however, had died long before 1492, the date of this campaign, his successors being (1) Ishwara, (2) Nrisimha in 1473, and (3 Vira-Nrisimha between 1473 and 1508. Firishta perhaps uses Timraj as a generic term for the rulers of the usurping dynasty.

but some of the more adventurous spirits among his advisers succeeded in persuading him that this prudent course would ill consort with the prestige and dignity of a Muhammadan king who had marched a long distance in order to meet an infidel foe. Nevertheless Ismail was unwilling to attempt to force the passage of the river in the face of the Hindu host until one evening, when drunkenness had conquered prudence, he mounted his war elephant, and, without acquainting his companions with his intention, had the animal driven across the river, in order, he said, that he might enjoy both air and water. His troops, seeing the king cross the river, armed themselves with haste and some two thousand of them contrived, with great difficulty, to follow him across the river. The Hindus were able to meet this small force with 30,000 horse and 200,000 infantry. Of the result of the conflict there could be no doubt. The Musalmans were out-numbered and were overpowered almost at once. Those who escaped from the field were drowned in attempting to swim their horses back across the swollen river. Ismail himself was turned back against his will, and his elephant succeeded in reaching the opposite bank in safety, but of all who attempted to accompany him only seven horsemen were saved. This drunken freak entirely destroyed the spirit of the Muhammadan army and Ismail sought counsel of his trusty adviser Asad Khan Lari. Asad Khan advised him to retire at once to Bijapur, cement an alliance with Burhan Nizam Shah of Ahmadnagar, and then, before thinking of recovering the Duab, crush Amir Barid, who had originally instigated the Hindus to cross the Tungabhadra. Ismail, after taking a solemn oath to abstain from wine until Raichur and Mudgal should once more form part of his kingdom, returned to Bijapur and sent an embassy to Ahmadnagar.

In 1524 Ismail Adil Shah and Burhan Nizam Shah met at Sholapur, and Mariyam Sultan, Ismail's sister, was married to Burhan, her brother agreeing to surrender Sholapur to Ahmadnagar as her dowry. After the marriage he declined to fulfil his part of the contract, and the alliance between the two houses was thus rendered nugatory, much to the advantage of Vijayanagar. Burhan Nizam Shah entered into an alliance with the kings of Berar and Bidar and the allies attacked Ismail Adil Shah at Sholapur, but were defeated.

In 1529 Ismail Adil Shah, Burhan Nizam Shah, and Amir Barid were engaged in an attempt to expel Bahadur Shah of Gujarat, who had invaded the Deccan, and Ismail, on his return to his dominions after the retreat of Bahadur Shah, discovered that Amir Barid had been attempting, during the campaign, to detach the nobles of Bijapur from their allegiance and had suggested to them that they should overthrow the Adil Shahi dynasty. It was now quite clear to Ismail that he could enjoy neither peace nor security until this inveterate intriguer should be made powerless for evil, and he approached Burhan Nizam Shah with a proposal that Amir Barid, who was constantly intriguing with Golconda and Vijayanagar, should be crushed. The proposal was agreed to, and the allies marched on Bidar and captured it, in spite of assistance rendered to Amir Barid by Sultan Quli Qutb Shah of Golconda. Ismail pardoned Amir Barid, created him an *amir* of Bijapur, and restored to him his former territory, except Bidar itself. He was compelled, however, to renounce his pretensions to independence, to profess himself the vassal of Bijapur, and to promise to provide a contingent of 3,000 horse whenever his liege lord should require it. He was also obliged to undertake to capture the fortress of Mahur, after Ismail's business with the infidels of Vijayanagar should be completed, and to hand it over to Ismail's ally and brother-in-law, Ala-ud-din Imad Shah of Berar.

Ismail Adil Shah was now at length in a position to make another attempt to wrest the Raichur Duab from the Hindus. He was once more on good terms with Ahmadnagar, he had formed an alliance with Berar, he had recently defeated the troops of Golconda, and he had reduced Amir Barid to the position of a vassal. The time was, in other respects, favourable for his enterprise. Krishnaraya of Vijayanagar had just died and had been succeeded by his son Achyutaraya, and the internal affairs of the Hindu state were in considerable confusion. In 1530, therefore, Ismail Adil Shah, Ala-ud-din Imad Shah, and Amir Barid invaded the Raichur Duab, which had been in the hands of the Hindus for seventeen years, and recovered it without much difficulty, both Raichur and Mudgal being captured within three months. Ismail was now freed from his vow of abstinence and enjoyed a drinking bout in Raichur in company with his commander-in-chief, Asad Khan Lari, and Ala-ud-din Imad Shah. The two latter joined their entreaties that

Amir Barid should, in recognition of his services, be admitted to the symposium, and Ismail agreed. As Amir Barid entered and took his seat, thus making the number of the party up to four, Ismail handed him a cup of wine, with the words, "Here we have an example of the Arabic saying, 'the fourth of them was their dog.'" Ala-ud-din burst out laughing and Amir Barid, though he did not understand Arabic, perceived that he was the butt of the company and began to weep. Ismail was touched by his humiliation and promised to restore Bidar to him when they reached Bijapur. The promise was fulfilled, but Amir Barid failed to cede to Bijapur, as he had promised to do, Kaliani and Kandhar.

Ismail Adil Shah died on August 28, 1534, and was succeeded by his eldest son Mallu, who was deposed after a reign of a few months and was succeeded by his younger brother Ibrahim Adil Shah I.

In 1536 Ibrahim took advantage of the disturbed condition of Vijayanagar to send an army under Asad Khan Lari to invade that kingdom. Asad Khan was, however, defeated and compelled to return to Bijapur. It is not necessary to follow the tortuous course of politics and warfare in the Deccan during the next few years, in the course of which Ibrahim Adil Shah was attacked by Burhan Nizam Shah, Amir Barid, and Jamshid Qutb Shah. In 1543 Sadashivaraya, who had succeeded to the throne of Vijayanagar in the previous year, took advantage of Ibrahim's difficulties and sent his brother Venkatadri to besiege Raichur. Ibrahim, assailed on all sides, was doubtful where to strike, but recognized that Burhan Nizam Shah was his most bitter and Sadashivaraya his most dangerous enemy. He therefore set himself to conciliate these two while Asad Khan Lari marched against Jamshid Qutb Shah. Of the details of this campaign we have conflicting accounts, but Jamshid was driven back to Golconda and Bijapur was freed from the apprehension of immediate attack. The danger was not, however, past and Ibrahim's diplomacy seems to have succeeded but indifferently, for in 1544 Burhan Nizam Shah, at the instigation of Sadashivaraya marched on Gulbarga. Ibrahim at once marched to meet him and inflicted a crushing defeat on him on the banks of the Banathora, and Burhan was forced to flee to Ahmadnagar. In the following year Ibrahim assisted Ali Barid Shah of Bidar against Burhan and sustained two severe defeats, which he attributed to the treachery of his officers. This suspicion, probably unjust, was the parent of cruel and indiscriminate punishment, which bred disaffection in the state. Abdullah, the king's younger brother, was put forward as a candidate for the throne, and when his partisans lost heart, fled to Goa, where he was received with royal honours by the Portuguese, while Burhan Nizam Shah and Jamshid Qutb Shah marched on Bijapur. The invasion was a fiasco and the two Sultans returned to their own dominions, but the bitter hostility of Burhan Nizam Shah towards his wife's nephew underwent no change, and when Ibrahim strengthened his position by giving his daughter, Bani Bibi, in marriage to Ali Barid Shah and entering into a close alliance with Bidar, Burhan Nizam Shah replied by concluding a treaty with Sadashivaraya of Vijayanagar. Ibrahim at once complained to Burhan's envoys at his court of their master's conduct in entering into an alliance with an infidel against a Muslim, whereupon the envoys fled to Vijayanagar. War once more broke out between Ahmadnagar and Bijapur, and in 1552 Sadashivaraya, in fulfilment of his treaty with Burhan Nizam Shah, invaded the Duab and besieged Raichur. Burhan at once marched southwards through Ibrahim's territory and effected a junction with the Hindu army. He entered into an agreement with Sadashivaraya, in accordance with the terms of which the latter was to be allowed to annex the Duab while Sholapur was to be annexed to Ahmadnagar. Raichur and Mudgal now fell, and Sadashivaraya sent a large army under his younger brother to assist Burhan Nizam Shah in taking Sholapur. Burhan, after taking this fortress, rebuilt it and, leaving a strong garrison there, returned to Ahmadnagar, where he presently died. The advisers of his son and successor Husain Nizam Shah negotiated a treaty of peace with Bijapur, but quarrels soon broke out afresh and Ibrahim lost no time in following the example of Husain's father and entered into an alliance with Vijayanagar. He then proclaimed Ali, Husain's younger brother, who had fled to Bijapur for refuge, king of Ahmadnagar and despatched him towards Ahmadnagar with two thousand horse and a letter inciting the nobles of that kingdom to rise against Husain. Husain Nizam Shah collected his forces and marched on Sholapur, where he met and defeated Ibrahim. Ibrahim's failure to recover Sholapur concluded this campaign and in 1557 Ibrahim died and was succeeded by his son Ali Adil Shah I.

Ali Adil Shah in 1564 despatched to Husain Nizam Shah a demand for the rendition of Sholapur and Kaliani, with which Husain refused to comply. The quarrel ended in war and Ali Adil Shah and Sadashivaraya of Vijayanagar invaded the Ahmadnagar kingdom The Hindus during this campaign outraged the feelings of both their allies and their enemies by destroying copies of the *Quran*, burning mosques, and slaughtering Musalmans, and Husain Nizam Shah, no longer able to endure this desecration of his kingdom by the unbelievers, surrendered Kaliani to Ali Adil Shah, and thus ended the war. He foresaw, however, that peace would not endure, and entered into an alliance with Ibrahim Qutb Shah of Golconda, to whom he gave his daughter, Bibi Jamal, in marriage. Ali Adil Shah chose to regard this alliance as a menace, and again sent to Vijayanagar for assistance. Sadashivaraya welcomed another opportunity of weakening the power of the Muhammadan kingdoms of the Deccan and speedily joined Ali Adil Shah in Bijapur with 50,000 horse and 200,000 foot. The allies then marched on Kaliani, in the neighbourhood of which fortress Ibrahim Qutb Shah, who had just received his bride, was then encamped with Husain. Ibrahim, whether alarmed by the superior force of the allies or disappointed in his bride, at once forsook his alliance with Ahmadnagar and openly joined Ali Adil Shah and the Hindus. Husain Nizam Shah, finding himself thus basely deserted by his son-in-law, fled to Ahmadnagar, towards which place the allied armies pursued him. On their approach Husain fled to Junnar and the allies laid siege to Ahmadnagar and despatched foraging parties into the surrounding country to collect supplies and waste the land. The Hindus again took advantage of the opportunity of insulting the Musalmans and desecrated mosques by stabling their horses in them and using their woodwork as fuel. Meanwhile circumstances combined to render the position of the allies difficult. The rains broke with great violence and not only put the besiegers to the greatest discomfort in their camp but, by rendering the country impassable, prevented the arrival of supplies. Moreover Ibrahim Qutb Shah had veered round again and showed his sympathy with Husain-Nizam Shah by secretly conveying supplies of grain to the beleaguered force, and the excesses of the Hindus had deeply disgusted the Muhammadan armies. Ali Adil Shah perceived that the siege of Ahmadnagar could not be sustained under these conditions and retired to Sholapur, for the possession of which he had entered upon the war. On his way thither his chief noble, Kishwar Khan, represented to him that his Hindu allies had deeply wounded the feelings of all true Musalmans in his army and deprecated the alliance with the unbelievers. Sholapur could not, however, be besieged without their help and it was therefore decided to abandon, for the present, the idea of recovering that fortress and, as an alternative, to construct a strong fortress at Naldrug. At Naldrug, therefore, the allies separated and Sadashivaraya departed, deeply chagrined, to his capital. He had hoped to hold the balance between the Muhammadan kingdoms and to profit by their internecine strife until each dropped like a ripe pear into his hands, but the excesses of his troops had inflamed the religious zeal of the Musalmans to such an extent as to make it impossible for any Muhammadan sovereign again to seek his alliance. He therefore assumed the *rôle* of arbiter. He had, he conceived, been indispensable to Ali Adil Shah and he now affected to regard the two Muhammadan kings as his vassals, and treated them as subordinates when taking his departure to his capital. On his arrival there he demanded important cessions of territory as the price of the aid which he had given against Ahmadnagar. The Raichur Duab had already been ceded; probably when Ali Adil Shah first called in Sadashivaraya as an ally, and Ali was now compelled to cede the Hippargi district while Ibrahim Qutb Shah ceded the fortress of Pangul and the country surrounding it, thus destroying his scientific frontier, which lay along the Krishna. Sadashivaraya, not content with these concessions, provoked the Muhammadan kings still further by issuing an ordinance to the effect that when they appeared before him in future they would not be allowed to sit in his presence. This arrogance could not be borne, and Ali Adil Shah, who was responsible for the insults which the faith had suffered at the hands of his allies, at once remodelled his foreign policy. In the first place he approached Ibrahim Qutb Shah of Golconda, who had suffered much from the insolence of Sadashivaraya and besought him to use his good offices as an intermediary between Bijapur and Ahmadnagar. Ibrahim readily undertook this office and also agreed to see that Sholapur was restored to Bijapur. Mustafa Khan Ardastani, who was sent as an ambassador from Golconda to Ahmadnagar, impressed upon Husain Nizam Shah the folly of continuing his quarrel with Bijapur, and supported the case for an alliance by arguments drawn from history. When the Bahmani dynasty was at the height of its power and the whole of the Deccan was united under one Muhammadan king the Musalmans had never, he said, been able to crush the power of Vijayanagar. All that they had been able to do was to hold it in check by occasionall ydefeating the Hindus in the field. Now that the Deccan was divided into five independent kingdoms it was necessary for their existence that they should show a united front to Vijayanagar.

Husain was already tired of the strife with Bijapur and it scarcely needed these arguments to induce him to enter into a treaty of peace. His daughter Chand Bibi, "the noble queen," was to be given in marriage to Ali Adil Shah and was to receive as dowry the fortress of Sholapur, while Ali's sister, Hidiyah Sultan, was to be married to Murtaza, the eldest son of Husain. The two marriages were celebrated amid great rejoicings and at the same time Ali Barid Shah of Bidar declared his adhesion to the Muhammadan confederacy.

Ali Adil Shah now felt himself strong enough to open negotiations with Vijayanagar and sent an ambassador to Sadashivaraya to demand the retrocession of the Duab and the Hippargi district. The ambassador was received contemptuously and was turned out of the city. This was regarded as a *casus belli* and Husain Nizam Shah, Ibrahim Qutb Shah, and Ali Barid Shah joined Ali Adil Shah at Bijapur with their forces. On Christmas day, 1564, the confederates marched from Bijapur.

According to one account Sadashivaraya, now eighty years of age, made overtures of peace, but the truth seems to be that he was neither disconcerted nor alarmed by the news of the advance of the four kings. He sent his youngest brother, Timma, with 20,000 horse, 500 elephants, and 100,000 foot to hold the line of the Krishna and prevent the passage of the Musalmans into the Duab. Timma was followed by his next brother, Venkatadri, with another large army, and Sadashivaraya, after allowing time for his vassals to assemble, followed Venkatadri with the main body of his army. His numbers are said to have amounted in all to 100,000 horse and 3,000,000 foot, with 2,000 elephants and 1,000 guns. The two armies now lay facing one another on the Krishna, all the fords of which were strongly held by the Hindus. The Musalmans sent out a reconnoitring party to a distance of eighty miles to seek for a ford, but the party returned and reported that the only ford fit for the passage of troops with their artillery and transport was the principal ford between the two armies. The confederates therefore had recourse to a stratagem. They spread the rumour that another ford had been discovered and then marched up the river for three days. The Hindus, in order to oppose the passage, followed and marched abreast of the Musalmans, without even taking the precaution of leaving a force to guard the ford opposite to which they had originally encamped. Having thus misled the Hindus the allies left 20,000 horse opposite to them and marched back rapidly and secretly to the unguarded ford, covering the distance of their three days' journey in one day, and reached their destination in the evening. Their advanced guard crossed the river before sunset and covered the passage of the remainder of the army on the morning of the following day, January 24, 1565. The Hindus had now turned back towards the ford and the two armies formed for battle. The Muhammadan right was commanded by Ali Adil Shah, the centre by Husain Nizam Shah, and the left by Ibrahim Qutb Shah and Ali Barid Shah ; and in the Hindu army Sadashivaraya commanded the centre, Timma the right, and Venkatadri the left. Sadashivaraya refused to leave his litter and when urged by his attendants to mount his horse replied that there was no need for him to mount a horse in order to play with children, and that the Musalmans would flee at the first onset. The confederates then advanced to the attack ; their archers, spearmen, and swordsmen being ordered to devote their attention chiefly to the enemy's elephants. Many of these were wounded and threw the ranks of the Hindus into some confusion, and when Sadashivaraya perceived that the Musalmans were not overawed by his superior numbers he left his litter and took his seat on a jewelled throne under a splendid canopy. He then had gold, silver, and jewels heaped up on either side of him and promised rich rewards to all who should render themselves conspicuous by their valour. The Hindus, animated by the hope of gain, pressed forward with great determination and the confederates were beaten back and their wings were separated from their centre. Authorities differ as to the circumstances in which the tide of battle was turned. One account says that Ali Adil Shah, finding himself separated from Husain Nizam Shah, turned the mishap to advantage by working round the left flank of the Hindus until he reached the rear of their centre, and thus threw them into confusion, but according to the generally accepted account it was Husain Nizam Shah alone who saved the fortunes of the day. He made a determined stand and stayed the advance of the Hindus, while Kishwar Khan, who had been separated from his master, Ali Adil Shah, joined him Husain then caused an enormous howitzer, which had been cast in Ahmadnagar by Rumi Khan in 1548 and was known as *malik-i-maidan*, or " the king of the plain, " to be loaded to the muzzle with copper coin and fired into the midst of the Hindu masses. This terrible discharge was followed by a determined charge of the Muslims which threw the. Hindus back in great confusion. Sadashivaraya made all haste to quit his throne and regain his litter. Meanwhile the Muhammadans pressed on: one of their elephants overturned the litter, and the bearers were put to flight. The driver of the elephant resolved to take the jewelled and gilded litter as a prize, but as he bore down on it a faithful Brahman, who was in attendance on his master, cried out that Sadashivaraya was in the litter, and that if the *mahaut* would save him he should be made one of the chief nobles of the kingdom of Vijayanagar. The *mahaut*, on learning who was in his power, made his elephant pick up Sadashivaraya in his trunk and carried him off to Rumi Khan, the commander of the artillery of Ahmadnagar. Rumi Khan carried the captive to Husain Nizam Shah, who caused him to be beheaded on the spot and paraded his head on a pike before the troops. The Hindus broke and fled, and were pursued with great slaughter, the tale of the slain reaching the enormous number of 100,000.

Thus ended one of the most decisive battles ever fought in India, and the power of the Hindus in the south was for ever broken.

The allies halted for ten days after the battle, collected their plunder, and refreshed their troops with rest. They then advanced through the Duab to Anagondi, in the neighbourhood of Vijayanagar.

The maiden city of the Hindus was ravaged and destroyed, and the empire of the Carnatic was broken up.

Raichur and Mudgal still held out under Hindu commanders, and three generals, Mustafa Khan of Golconda, Inayatullah of Ahmadnagar, and Kishwar Khan of Bijapur were sent to reduce them. The fortresses surrendered at once and Mustafa Khan, as a matter of course, made over the keys to Kishwar Khan, regarding the Duab as part of the Adil Shahi dominions. Husain Nizam Shah, however, considered that he as the leader of the confederacy should first have been consulted, and he called Ibrahim Qutb Shah to account for his general's action. Ibrahim did not agree with Husain but feared to withstand him, and imprisoned Mustafa Khan for a time and afterwards allowed him to depart on a pilgrimage to Mecca. This incident rekindled the embers of strife between Bijapur and Ahmadnagar, and though Husain Nizam Shah died at this time, Ali Adil Shah continued the quarrel with his son and successor, Murtaza Nizam Shah I., and hostilities ensued. With these we are not concerned, for they did not affect Raichur.

The Sultans of Bijapur were now at length confirmed in the possession of the Raichur Duab, and the only power which had gone near to depriving them of it permanently was annihilated.

The Duab now enjoyed a long period of peace and was undisturbed until 1662, when an African *amir* named Sidi Jauhar and entitled Salabat Khan rebelled in Karnul, and Ali Adil Shah II, the seventh king of the Adil Shahi dynasty, marched through the Duab to quell the rebellion. Sidi Jauhar sent a message to the commander of Mudgal urging him to oppose the advance of the royal forces and promising him assistance, but the commandant could not be seduced from his allegiance and received Ali Adil Shah with all honour. The royal forces encountered Sidi Jauhar in the neighbourhood of Mudgal, and the rebel was defeated and fled to Raichur, the commandant of which fortress was related to him. Here he was well received, and his relative resolved to close the gates of Raichur against Ali Adil Shah, but the loyal officers in the garrison rose against him, imprisoned him, and carried the keys of the fortress to Ali Adil Shah while Sidi Jauhar fled beyond the Tungabhadra. Here his troops were defeated and he died.

After this rebellion the Duab enjoyed another period of tranquillity. On September 23, 1686, Aurangzib captured Bijapur and sent Sikandar Adil Shah, the last of his dynasty, into captivity at Daulatabad. Ruhullah Khan was appointed *subahdar* of the new imperial province of Bijapur, and, shortly after his appointment, took the field against those who still held out, for the fort of Raichur was still held by one of Sikandar's officers but was captured without much trouble by Ruhullah Khan in 1688, or, according to another account, on November 20, 1689.

The Duab was never seriously disturbed after this time. Under the treaty of 1853 between the East India Company and the Nizam it was assigned, together with Berar and other districts, to the Company, in payment of debts due chiefly on account of the maintenance of the Hyderabad Contingent, but in 1861 all the districts so assigned, except Berar, were restored to the Nizam.

Raichur contains no fine buildings, except the fort and its gates, and its numerous inscriptions are somewhat disappointing, for little is to be gathered from them, as a rule, save the names of local governors and deputy governors, most of whom signalized themselves by the erection of mean buildings bearing grandiloquent inscriptions. The Telugu inscription already mentioned stands apart from the others as a document of exceptional interest, but of the Arabic and Persian inscriptions, very few bear dates earlier than that of the establishment of the kingdom of Bijapur. The Hindus have marked their occupation of the place at various times by the erection of a stone elephant in one of the streets of the town, and by some carvings which display more indelicacy than art.

CHAPTER VII.

AN OLD DECCAN FORTRESS.

AT one point in its course the Penganga, the southern boundary of the modern province of Berar, turns suddenly northwards, and, after flowing in a northerly direction for upwards of thirty miles, resumes its course eastwards. In the curve thus formed, and to the south of the river at a distance of rather more than two miles, are situated the old town and fort of Mahur. About a mile from the river the ground rises abruptly and a rocky road leads up to a plateau. Scattered over this plateau is a medley of tanks, shrines, and mosques, most of them ruinous but some still in good repair. The extent of the ruins enables us to judge of the size of the ancient town, now a dreary and sleepy village, but at one time the capital of a province of the Muhammadan empire of the Deccan. Narrow roads, ankle deep in dust, lead us now between mean houses, and anon between the ruins of more pretentious buildings, taking us at length out to what were formerly the suburbs of a large town. Here in days of old we might have found stately pavilions and luxurious summer-houses, half hidden in cool gardens, kept green by pleasant tanks. Of all this the tanks alone remain, and even they are for the most part dry. The rest is dust and decay. To the south-west and north the Penganga may be seen winding through its fertile valley. Beyond this valley the low hills which lie between it and the Berar valley on the north, and form the Balaghat of Berar, stretch away to the horizon. Immediately behind the town rises a steep and, in most parts, inaccessible hill. Half way up its side rises the glistening white dome of a Mahanubhava temple; its crest is fringed with battlements, the battlements of the old fort of Mahur, which has played its part in the history of Berar and the Deccan. It is an imposing structure, but has long since lost its strategical importance. Its walls, still in good order, are built of blocks of dressed stone, some of which are as much as six feet in length, and encircle the hill crest. The fort is entered on the north by a gate well provided with flank defences and approached by a road which must surely resemble the roads of the Highlands of Scotland before the advent of General Wade. Other entrance there is none, save a postern near the southern bastion, which is approached by a path which branches off from a road crossing a *col* or neck between that bastion and a knoll on which stands a Hindu temple.

The fort is disappointing to the antiquary who is not intimately acquainted with local history, for it contains not a single inscription. The half of an old cast piece of ordnance which lies on the ground, and is the only relic of the former armament of the fort, raises delusive hopes in the breast of the inscription-hunter. It is difficult to understand how such a tempting piece of metal can have escaped the graving-tool, but it has. Of the buildings in the fort the guard-house in the gate, the elephant stables, and a mosque are the only ones that call for any notice. All are in a fair state of preservation. The mosque is a building of no architectural beauty, and lacks even the grandeur which mere vastness can give. It has three domes in the Pathan style, and its pillars betray traces of Hindu influence if, indeed, they were not filched from a Hindu temple. The gate and guard-house are excellent examples of the more severe style of Pathan architecture, and the same may be said of the fort generally. The workmanship is excellent, the carefully dressed and fitted stones recalling the characteristics of Roman handiwork. Where the hill-side below the rampart is less steep the fort is strengthened by what may best be described as ancient equivalents of the modern horn-work. There is but one tank, certainly insufficient for the needs of a garrison sufficiently strong to defend the fort, to say nothing of elephants, horses, and cattle. A hypercritical soldier would at once remark that the interior of the fort is commanded by adjacent hills. A civilian critic has remarked that the knoll to the south commands the southern bastion. The former observation is just, and is sufficient to condemn the fort as indefensible against modern artillery. But it has no applicability whatever to former conditions. The latter remark is one to which the saw *ne supra crepidam sutor judicaret* applies. The knoll is so close to the bastion that a lodgement could not possibly be effected thereon whether the fort were equipped with ancient or modern artillery. It might be of service to the defenders either as a suitable situation for an outwork, affording flank defence to the two long faces of the fort, or as a trap for impetuous and unwary assailants.

Of the date of the foundation of the fort nothing can be said with certainty. There is a tradition to the effect that it was founded by one Anand Deo, a Kshatriya Raja of Malwa who, migrating to the Deccan after the death of Raja Partab Chand of Malwa, extended his sway throughout Berar, Malwa, Gujarat, Kanara, and the Deccan generally, and founded, besides Mahur, the fortress of "Deogarh or Deogir." This myth does not call for serious investigation, and wiser men than retailers of mediæval legends have confused Deogarh with Deogir. A Rajput may have built a fort on the Mahur hill. No Rajput built the fort that now stands there. Nevertheless the Hindu pillars of the mosque may betoken more than mere imitation. They may be the remains of a temple which previously existed on the site of the mosque; for the temptation to convert an idol temple into a mosque where *Allah* would be worshipped was ever too strong for the predominant Muslim. The fort itself is certainly the work of a Musalman architect. Who he was and when he lived is not known. It might be expected that some mention of the building of the fort would be found in the annals of the Bahmani kings of the Deccan, but the earliest mention of Mahur in the authentic history of this dynasty implies that there was already a strong fort on the site. It may have been built by one of the governors of the Deccan under Sultan Ala-ud-din Khalji of Delhi, the pioneer of Muhammadan conquest in the Deccan, or in the time of one of his more immediate successors. Perhaps it was built in the earlier days of the Bahmani kingdom as a menace to the Gond rulers of Chanda. But Barani and Firishta, our principal authorities for the early history of Muhammadan rule in the Deccan, are silent on the point, and all that can be said with certainty is that the fort of Mahur existed in the early days of the Bahmani dynasty, which was founded by Ala-ud-din Bahman Shah in 1347.

In the reign of this Sultan the Bahmani kingdom was divided into four *tarafs* or provinces: Gulbarga, Daulatabad, Berar "including Mahur" and Bidar. The importance of Mahur, shown by its being specially mentioned as being included in Berar will be emphasised later, when, on the sub-division of the four original *tarafs* into eight, it became the capital of a *taraf* to which it gave its name.

In 1362 the Telinga Raja of Warangal, after being severely defeated by Muhammad Shah Bahmani, sent messengers to Firuz Shah Tughlaq, emperor of Delhi, beseeching him to order the rulers of Malwa and Gujarat to march against Muhammad Shah, and promising to support them and to enlist also the active sympathy of the Hindu Raja of Vijayanagar in the south. Firuz Shah, as might have been expected, paid no heed to this absurd request, but the Bahmani Sultan, who had his spies in Delhi and was informed of all that passed, was furiously angry at the idea that a Hindu Raja should have presumed to request the emperor of Delhi to aid in restoring Hindu supremacy in the Deccan and in ousting him, the independent sovereign of the south. He collected troops from all parts of his dominions, those from Mahur being specially mentioned, and despatched them against the Raja of Warangal, who, disappointed of the assistance which he had hoped to receive from Delhi, fled to the jungles, and obtained peace only on payment of a tribute of three hundred elephants, thirteen lakhs of golden *huns*, and two hundred horses; and the cession of the town and district of Golconda.

Three years later, in 1365, Muhammad Shah was engaged in a bloody *jihad* against the idolatrous Raya of Vijayanagar, and, having slaughtered in one battle no fewer than 70,000 Hindus, men, women, and children, resolved to subdue utterly the Hindu kingdom. With this object in view he formed a siege train for the reduction of the fortresses in the Vijayanagar country. Mahur was called upon to furnish its share of the artillery required. The account of this campaign is singularly interesting for two reasons. It was, we are told, the first campaign in which cannon were used by the Musalmans of the Deccan. We are also told that the park and arsenal were placed under the charge of a nobleman bearing the title of Muqarrab Khan who had under him some *Farangis*, or Europeans. Who these can have been is not clear. No Portuguese ship reached Indian shores till nearly a century and a half after this time. Possibly they were wandering soldiers of fortune who had travelled to India by way of the Eastern Empire, or slaves who had been captured and dispatched by Arab vessels to India. The authority for these facts is Firishta.

Later in Muhammad Shah's reign we find the Daulatabad nobles and some of those of Berar in revolt. Mahur did not fall into the hands of the rebels. The movement had its centre in Daulatabad, and there the disaffected gathered. It was suppressed without much difficulty, but shortly afterwards the disbandment of the numerous troops, which had been employed by Muhammad Shah in his foreign and intestinal wars, and the absence of any supervision of the civil administration led to a wholesale and alarming outbreak of highway robbery throughout the empire. The king issued orders to the *tarafdars*, the provincial governors, to the effect that robbers were to be hunted down like wild beasts and their heads sent to the capital, Hasanabad Gulbarga, "as a warning". About 20,000 heads were received and were piled in heaps on all sides of the city. The *taraf* of Berar probably sent its share. In 1398 the Bahmanid was hard pressed. Firuz Shah Bahmani "Ruz Afzun" was then on the throne. Harihara II, the Hindu ruler of Vijayanagar, anxious to regain his lost terrritory in the Raichur Duab, assembled an army of 30,000 horse and 900,000 foot and invaded the Bahmani dominions from the south. Then a rebellion broke out among the Kolis of Sagar. This was speedily suppressed; but no sooner had Firuz Shah assembled his army, which included the troops of the two provinces of Daulatabad and Berar, at the capital, than Nar Singh, the Gond raja of Kherla, whose territory marched with the northern frontier of Berar, invaded that province and, advancing southwards, ravaged the country as far as the environs of Mahur. This movement was prompted and aided by the Muhammadan Sultans of Malwa and Khandesh, who held the forts of Mando and Asirgarh, as well as by Harihara II of Vijayanagar. Mahur seems not to have been left defenceless, for the fort was not taken, or even attacked. Firuz Shah at once despatched the troops of Daulatabad and Berar northwards to expel the invader, while he, with the remainder of his army, marched southwards to encounter Harihara, who was encamped on the banks of the Krishna. One Qazi Siraj, with seven companions, managed to gain admission in the guise of minstrels to a *nach* in the camp of the Raja's son and heir-apparent, whom they stabbed to the heart. In the meantime the Muhammadan army had been crossing the river, and they fell upon the Hindus during the confusion caused by the assassination of the prince and defeated them with great slaughter. Harihara took refuge in his capital, and his country was ravaged till he was glad to make peace on any terms. Firuz Shah then returned to his capital, Gulbarga, and after a rest of two or three months marched to Mahur. Things had gone ill in Berar. The Muhammadan troops had been unable to expel the Gonds, and, what was worse, the governor of Mahur had turned traitor and declared for Raja Nar Singh. He repented on the king's approach, and was pardoned. Firuz Shah stayed more than a month in Mahur to settle the affairs of the surrounding country and then continued his march northwards to chastise Nar Singh. When the imperial army neared Kherla, Nar Singh in his terror appealed to the Sultans of Malwa and Khandesh for help. They declined to assist their former tool in any way, and put him off with ambiguous answers. Firuz Shah himself encamped at Ellichpur in Berar, while the Khan-i-Khanan and Mir Fazlullah Anju attacked the Gonds outside the fort at Kherla. The Muslims were at first repulsed with great slaughter and were in full retreat, when Mir Fazlullah caused the great kettle-drums to be sounded, as though the king himself had appeared on the scene. The Muslims rallied. The son of Nar Singh was captured and Nar Singh himself, with the remnant of his army, was pursued into Kherla. Nar Singh after standing a two months' siege submitted, and, being conducted to Ellichpur, swore allegiance to Firuz Shah. He promised to pay regularly a yearly tribute, and paid on the spot a tribute of fifty elephants, five maunds of gold and fifty maunds of silver. He was not only pardoned but was honourably treated as a feudatory prince of the kingdom. The siege of Kherla was abandoned, and the king returned to his capital, leaving Mir Fazlullah as governor of Berar.

Nine years later, in 1407, we find Firuz Shah overrunning Gondwana. Mahur must have been his base of operations, and his principal objective was probably Chanda. The fort is not mentioned again for eighteen years, but Firuz Shah's invasion of Gondwana evidently bore bitter fruit, for in the reign of Ahmad Shah Wali, or "the saint," his brother and successor, we find that the fort had by 1425 "somehow or other" passed out of the hands of the Bahmani Sultans, and was held by a local chieftain, an "infidel." This local chieftain was doubtless a Gond, perhaps the ruler of Chanda himself. Ahmad Shah marched against Mahur and induced the defenders to capitulate by offering them their lives. They surrendered, and the royal saint had them at once, to the number of five or six thousand, put to the sword. Ahmad Shah then busied himself with settling affairs in Berar, building and repairing forts on his northern frontier, to which he paid special attention. On his return to his capital, after a sojourn of more than two years in Berar, Nar Singh, his vassal, accompanied him as far as Mahur. We find Ahmad Shah, later in his reign, giving Mahur, Kalam, and Ramgarh in *jagir* to his son Shahzada Ala-ud-din Ahmad on the occasion of his marriage with the daughter of Nasir Khan Faruqi, Sultan of Khandesh. Ala-ud-din succeeded his father Ahmad Shah, and in 1452, towards the end of his reign, when he was in feeble health, his brother-in-law, Jalal Khan, who held the fief of Nalgunda in Telingana, rebelled, and despatched his son, Sikandar Khan, whom he wished to place on the throne as a descendant of Ahmad Shah in the female line, to Mahur, in order that he might hold it against the Bahmani king and so, by creating a diversion, give his father an opportunity of consolidating his power in Telingana. In pursuance of these designs Mahmud Shah Khalji of Malwa was invited to invade the kingdom. He marched southwards and encamped in the plains about Mahur, perhaps on the Mahur plateau itself. It had been falsely represented to him that Ala-ud-din Ahmad II was dead; and he was disagreeably undeceived by the news that the Bahmani king was marching on Mahur at the head of his army, and decamped by night. In the meantime the rebellion was crushed through the zeal and activity of the minister, Mahmud Gawan. Jalal Khan submitted and was allowed to retain his former fief, while Mahur was taken from Sikandar Khan and given to its former governor, Fakhr-ul-Mulk, who, we may surmise, had not willingly surrendered it to the pretender.

In the reign of Muhammad Shah III the Bahmani kingdom, which had originally been divided into four great *tarafs*, or provinces, was subdivided into eight. The province of Berar, of which the two chief fortresses were Gawilgarh and Mahur, was divided into the two provinces of Gawil and Mahur. Fathullah Imad-ul-Mulk, the viceroy of Berar who afterwards declared his independence, retained the province of Gawil only, and Mahur was bestowed on Khudawand Khan the African. When this subdivision was made the powers of the *tarafdars*, who had hitherto been practically supreme in their provinces, were considerably curtailed. They were allowed to retain possession of their fortified capitals, but all other forts in their provinces were to be commanded by officers appointed directly by the king. Mahmud Gawan's wise reforms came, however, too late to save the Bahmani kingdom from dismemberment, and excited discontent among some of the older *tarafdars*. A plot was hatched against Mahmud Gawan and Muhammad III, while under the influence of wine, ordered him to be executed without hearing him in his defence. The sentence was immediately carried out and Imad-ul-Mulk and Khudawand Khan, who were with the armies of Gawil and Mahur in the royal camp, withdrew from its neighbourhood. The King sent a message asking them for their reason for this step and they replied, in effect, that they preferred to keep their distance from a master who could treat his faithful servants as Mahmud Gawan had been treated. Muhammad III died in 1482, leaving his kingdom, now in the greatest confusion, to his twelve-year-old son Mahmud Shah.

In 1490 Fathullah Imad-ul-Mulk and the *tarafdars* of Ahmadnagar and Bijapur declared themselves independent sovereigns and Fathullah was so proclaimed in the mosques of Berar. His power over the southern portion of his kingdom was dependent principally on the good will of Khudawand Khan, who held the districts of Mahur, Paunar, Kalam, and Mehkar. The African, who was not strong enough to stand alone, had to choose between the *fainéant* Bahmanid and the new Sultan of Berar. He became the vassal of the latter, for whom he seems to have had a real regard. Thirteen years later, when Mahmud Shah Bahmani, who had been too weak to assert his authority over his rebellious vassals, by the advice of his minister, Amir Barid, invited Sultan Quli Qutb-ul-Mulk of Golconda, Fathullah Imad Shah, and Khudawand Khan to aid him against Yusuf Adil Shah of Bijapur; the two latter disregarded the summons, apparently on account of the friendship which had always existed between Fathullah and Yusuf, but also, perhaps, owing to mutual distrust. In 1517 we find Khudawand Khan still in possession of Mahur. He had been raiding some forts on the northern frontier of the Bahmani dominions, and Mahmud Shah Bahmani, led to battle by Amir Barid, captured Mahur and killed Khudawand Khan and one of his sons. As soon as Ala-ud-din Imad Shah of Berar, the son and successor of

Fathullah, heard of the fall of Mahur he hastened southwards with an army, to prevent the permanent occupation of so important a fort by the Bahmani troops. Mahmud Shah and Amir Barid were in no condition to oppose the Sultan of Berar. They therefore made the fort over to Ghalib Khan, another son of Khudawand Khan, and acknowledged that Mahur, as well as the forts which had been raided by Khudawand Khan, belonged to the kingdom of Berar.

Nine years later, in 1526, when Ghalib Khan was still holding Mahur for Ala-ud-din Imad Shah, Burhan Nizam Shah of Ahmadnagar, who had had a quarrel with Ala-ud-din Imad Shah concerning the *pargana* of Pathri, the home of Burhan's ancestors, marched with Amir Barid on Mahur, and captured it. He then prepared to march on Ellichpur, the capital of the Berar kingdom. Ala-ud-din Imad Shah was greatly alarmed and sought help from Miran Muhammad Shah Faruqi of Burhanpur, who readily came to his assistance. A fiercely contested battle was fought and ended in the total defeat of the Sultans of Berar and Khandesh, who fled leaving their stores, equipment, and artillery in the hands of the enemy, who was now master of Berar. The fugitive kings sought help from Bahadur Shah of Gujarat, who, glad of an excuse for interference in the affairs of the Deccan, came to their assistance with an army both numerous and well found. It was now Burhan's turn to be alarmed. He sent a letter to Babar at Delhi, imploring his aid, or at least an authoritative assertion of suzerainty, such as might deter the confederate Sultans from attacking him. Had Burhan Nizam but known it Babar had more than sufficient occupation in settling those parts of his newly-acquired empire which lay nearer to his capital, and the time for Mughal intervention in the Deccan was not yet. So great was the dread of Bahadur Shah's interference in the affairs of the Deccan that Ismail Adil Shah of Bijapur, at whose instance the Sultan of Berar had originally attacked Burhan Nizam Shah, endeavoured to persuade Sultan Quli Qutb Shah of Golconda to join him in assisting Burhan Nizam Shah, and, failing in that endeavour, despatched 6,000 picked horsemen with Amir Barid to the help of the Sultan of Ahmadnagar. He would doubtless have done more, but that he feared that Krishnaraya, the Hindu ruler of Vijayanagar, would invade his dominions at the first favourable opportunity. The details of the campaign which followed need not be gone into. Ahmadnagar was occupied by the confederate Sultans and the fort of Daulatabad was invested. Burhan Nizam Shah and Amir Barid attacked the invaders but were defeated, and Burhan was compelled to resort to diplomacy. He sent envoys to Ala-ud-din Imad Shah and Miran Muhammad Shah pointing out to them that Bahadur Shah had evidently no intention of leaving the Deccan, and that it was no more to their interest than to his own that the invader should remain where he was. The two Sultans went in alarm to Bahadur Shah's minister and revealed their suspicions of his master's designs. He cynically told them that the Sultans of the Deccan would be more powerful than they were, were they less given to quarrelling among themselves, and added that they should have considered what Bahadur Shah's designs were likely to be before asking for his help. Bahadur Shah, however, found it necessary to return to his own country. He could not count on supplies in the Ahmadnagar country and the rainy season was close at hand, when the Tapti and other rivers were likely to be so swollen that communication with Khandesh and Gujarat would be difficult. There was, too, the possibility that Ala-ud-din Imad Shah and Miran Muhammad Shah would turn against him, in which case his position would be far from enviable. Ala-ud-din Imad Shah had already retreated to Ellichpur. It was now agreed that Burhan Nizam Shah should cede Mahur and Pathri to Berar and should return to Miran Muhammad all the elephants, horses, and stores which had been captured by the Ahmadnagar troops, and Bahadur Shah returned to Gujarat. Miran Muhammad, before leaving, demanded the fulfilment of the treaty, and Burhan Nizam Shah, knowing that he was eager to return to Khandesh before the rains broke, restored to him the elephants, horses, and equipment, as had been agreed, but took no notice whatever of the demand for the retrocession of Mahur and Pathri to Berar. The wily Burhan had rightly estimated his man. Miran Muhammad, as soon as his own demands were satisfied, returned to Khandesh, leaving the unfortunate Ala-ud-din Imad Shah stripped a large slice of territory. Thus the only result of the war was to leave Ahmadnagar more powerful than before.

A few years later we find Ala-ud-din Imad Shah accepting the office of mediator with Ismail Adil Shah on behalf of Amir Barid, who had been plotting with Sultan Quli Qutb Shah of Golconda and the Hindu nobles of Vijayanagar against Ismail. He accepted this office the more readily for that it would give him an opportunity of enlisting Ismail Adil Shah's assistance in recovering his lost territory, the districts of Mahur and Pathri. He succeeded in his advocacy of Amir Barid's cause, and also accompanied Ismail in a successful campaign against the "infidels" of Vijayanagar. It was agreed that Amir Barid should assist Ala-ud-din in recovering Mahur, but just as they were about to march northwards to besiege the fort news arrived that Bahadur Shah was preparing for another descent on the Deccan. The design had to be abandoned. Ala-ud-din Imad Shah hurried back to Berar and Amir Barid was sent to Bidar, which had been generously restored to him by Ismail. The danger passed, and shortly afterwards Amir Barid again began to show signs of contumacy. Ismail Adil Shah was about to set out to punish him when Burhan Nizam Shah interfered. Ismail Adil Shah refrained from attacking Amir Barid, but hinted to Burhan that he would do well to mind his own business, adding to the message a scantly veiled threat. War ensued, and the king of Ahmadnagar was worsted. Ala-ud-din Imad Shah probably hoped that one of the conditions of peace would be the retroccession of Mahur to Berar, but this question was not brought forward and the fortress remained in the possession of the Nizam Shahi Kings until 1572, when they annexed the whole of Berar.

On the cession of Berar by Chand Bibi to Akbar's army under Sultan Murad and the Khan-i-Khanan, Mahur was expressly excluded from the territory to be ceded, but was subsequently annexed to the Mughal empire, for we find the *Sarkar* of Mahur returned in the *Ain-i-Akbari*, with eighteen parganas, a revenue of Rs. 10,72,172 and Rs. 2,448 *suyurghal*, as an integral part of the imperial province of Berar. The fort is briefly described as "a fort of considerable strength, situated on a hill." We are told that the *zamindar* was a Rajput named Indrajeo, and was entitled *Rana*. He commanded 100 horse and 1,000 foot. This short notice is not without its significance. The word *zamindar* in Muhammadan histories frequently means an independent chieftain. It is very probable that Indrajeo was a commandant of the fort of Mahur who was not strong enough to establish his independence, but whose tractability varied with the proximity and activity of the imperial troops. It is not likely that the full amount of revenue shown in the *Ain* was paid annually with any degree of regularity.

We now come to the reign of Akbar's successor Jahangir. The year 1623 found his son, Sultan Khurram, who had already received the title of Shahjahan, under which he subsequently ascended the throne, in rebellion against his father. He had been, in the previous year, in command of the army destined for the complete subjugation of the Deccan, but had marched from Mando in Malwa with the design of seizing the throne. He had first failed in his attempt and subsequently suffered a series of reverses from an army commanded by his brother, Sultan Parviz, and Mahabat Khan. Shahjahan was pursued across the Narbada and fled to Asirgarh, and thence to Burhanpur, deserted daily by one band of followers after another. They had indeed, every inducement to leave him. Those who gave themselves up of their own free will and made their submission were liberally treated, while those who were taken in arms were, by Jahangir's orders, trampled to death by elephants. Shahjahan, with the miserable remnant of an army which had consisted of 27,000 horse, fled to Mahur, perhaps with the idea of holding it against Parviz. He found, however, that most of the few followers left to him were on the point of deserting, and resolved to forestall them. Leaving his elephants and baggage in Mahur he fled secretly to the court of Muhammad Qutb Shah of Golconda. His subsequent adventures, though full of interest, form no part of the history of Mahur, which has not figured prominently in history since the old fort afforded a temporary refuge to the princely fugitive.

CHAPTER VIII.

TWO HILL FORTS.

(1)—Gawilgarh.

"THE fort of Gawilgarh is situated on a range of mountains between the sources of the rivers Purna and Tapti. It stands on a lofty mountain in this range, and consists of one complete inner fort, which fronts to the south, where the rock is most steep, and an outer fort, which covers the inner to the north and north-west. This outer fort has a third wall which covers the approach to it from the north by the village of Labada, all these walls are strongly built and fortified by ramparts and towers. The communications with the fort are through three gates, one to the south with the inner fort, one to the north-west with the outer fort, and one to the north with the third wall." Thus wrote the Duke of Wellington, then the Honourable Arthur Wellesley, in his despatch written after the storming of this fort by the troops under his command on December 15th, 1803.

Gawilgarh, somewhat more dilapidated than when it was captured by the great soldier, still overlooks the fertile Berar valley, and is a prominent object from the plains. From the fort itself, which stands at an elevation of 3,595 feet, a magnificent view of that valley is obtained on a clear day. The plains do not melt away into the dim distance, for the southern plateau of Berar rises on the horizon to the south-east, and the Yeotmal hills, about eighty-four miles distant as the crow flies, can be plainly distinguished.

The rocky hill on which the fort stands is actually steepest on the northern side of the inner fort where the natural escarpment of sheer rock overlooks the Kichak Dara. So steep is the face of the hill in this direction that the only defence is a parapet of stone, barely breast high, and probably designed rather for the purpose of preventing the defenders from falling over the precipice than for that of checking the ingress of assailants. The gates are not fully enumerated in the despatch. The outer fort is entered by two gates, while the inner fort has three large gates and a postern. One of these is the gate "to the south" known as the *Fath Darwaza ;* another is the *Kichak Dara Darwaza*, leading down into the Kichak Dara valley on the north, and now nearly blocked up with rubbish; and the third is the *Delhi Darwaza*, which forms the communication between the inner and the outer forts. The postern gate opens to the south-east. The Delhi gate consists of no fewer than three gateways, all, but especially the innermost, adequately provided with flanking defences. The outermost of these three gateways is adorned with curious reliefs. On either side is a tiger, holding in its claws and mouth five elephants, above each tiger is a tolerably well executed double-headed eagle, not "a half human figure," as the *Berar Gazetteer* has it. These birds are strangely similar to the heraldic "eagle displayed double-headed," familiar to all as the arms of Austria and Russia. Each eagle holds, in each of its beaks, a small animal. The mistake in the *Gazetteer* seems to be due to the faulty execution of the legs of the eagles, which are unduly thickened so that they somewhat resemble human legs. We are told in the *Gazetteer* that these reliefs are probably Gond emblems, but this is not so. The eagles are the *gandabherunda*, the fabulous two headed eagle of Vijayanagar, which preys upon elephants, and their presence on the gate is explained by the fact that Fathullah Imad-ud-mulk, the first independent king of Berar, was by birth a Brahman of Vijayanagar who was captured in early youth by one of the Bahmani kings of the Deccan and brought up as a Musalman. His use of the *gandabherunda* as an emblem is an indication that he was proud of his origin. In the centre of the gate, immediately above the point of the arch, is a palm tree.

The fort was built, according to Firishta and the author of the *Gulzar-i-Ibrahim*, by Ahmad Shah Wali, the ninth king of the Bahmani dynasty of the Deccan, in 1425-26, when he was encamped at Ellichpur. Tradition says that there was, even then, a fort on the site, built in the days of old by Gaoli or Ahir chieftains, and the legend, as in the case of Gaoligarh in Khandesh and the more famous Asirgarh, or Asa Ahirgarh, seems to be supported by etymology. A local historian, the late Sayyid Amjad Husain, tells us that this old fort was merely a building of mud, erected by the pastoral Gaolis as a protection against cattle-lifters, and the fort as it stands is certainly an example of Pathan architecture, which cannot well be assigned to an earlier date than that given to it by Firishta. Additions have been made at various times. The south gate mentioned by Wellesley and known as the *Fath Darwaza* bears an inscription partly defaced owing to the scaling of the stone by the action of the weather. So far as I know this inscription has not hitherto been deciphered : no reference is made to it either in the Berar Gazetteer or by the local historian mentioned above; yet enough of it remains to tell us that the gate itself was built by Fathullah Imad-ul-Mulk in the reign of Mahmud Shah, the fourteenth king of the Bahmani dynasty, in A. H. 893 (A. D. 1488) according to the following chronogram :—

بیا ببیت سرور

" Come to the house of joy."

It also records the fact that " Ulugh Imad-ul-Mulk, " as the inscription styles him, "rebuilt with the old stones the *jami masjid.*" This is the great mosque in the fort, which will be noticed hereafter. Fathullah Imad-ul-Mulk was governor of Berar in the reign of Mahmud Shah Bahmani. As has been said he was, by birth, a Brahman of Vijayanagar who was captured in his boyhood and brought up as a Musalman in the service of the Khan Jahan, then governor of Berar. When the province of Berar was divided, in the reign of Muhammad Shah, Mahmud's father, into the two provinces of Gawil and Mahur, he retained the northern province of Gawil. The Vijayanagar emblems on the Delhi gate of the fort indicate that Imad-ul-Mulk repaired or rebuilt this gate also when he built the *Fath Darwaza* and restored the great mosque. He had a motive for the rebuilding of Gawilgarh, for the position of the provincial governors in the reign of Mahmud Shah Bahmani was intolerable. Two years after the restoration of the fort, in 1490, Imad-ul-Mulk, together with Malik Ahmad Nizam-ul-Mulk of Ahmadnagar and Yusuf Adil Khan of Bijapur declared his independence, established a mint, and caused the *khutbah* to be read in his name in all the mosques in Berar. He made Gawilgarh his residential capital though Ellichpur was the most important town in his small kingdom. Imad-ul-Mulk's use of the Turki title *Ulugh*, or "great" is strange for the native Deccanis, of whom he was one of the chief, had long been at feud with the foreign officers, who were mostly Persians or Turks and Mughals from Central Asia, but Imad-ul-Mulk, though one of the principal Deccani nobles, was never a partisan, and his great influence was always exercised in the interest of peace.

The great mosque mentioned in the inscription over the *Fath Darwaza* was originally built by Ahmad Shah Wali on the highest point in the fort. It is a very fine building in the Pathan style of architecture and its situation enhances its imposing appearance, for the arches and colonnades of its approaches are placed on the hillside below it, and the mosque overtops them. In front of the entrance to the courtyard is the tomb of its restorer, Fathullah Imad-ul-Mulk. The *façade* of the mosque is formed of seven arches, the centre arch being slightly larger than the rest, and the building was formerly three ranges of arches deep and was covered in by a roof consisting of twenty-one domes. The western wall has, however, fallen away owing to the subsidence of the steep hillside, and has carried with it a complete row of domes, so that only fourteen now remain. This same catastrophe had apparently happened before Imad-ul-Mulk's time and had necessitated the rebuilding of the western portion of the mosque. There is no Imad-ul-Mulk now. Of the two minarets of the mosque only that at the north-eastern angle of the building remains. It rises very little above the domes of the mosque but has apertures filled in with very handsome stone lattice-work.

The Imad Shahi dynasty, founded by Fathullah, was short-lived. It expired with his great-grandson, and Berar, with its fortress capital, passed into the hands of the Nizam Shahi king of Ahmadnagar.

In the south-west face of the fort is a fine bastion bearing the following grandiloquent inscription in Persian :—

"In Gawil Bahram built a tower.

"The like of which the eye of time hath not seen.

"He raised it to such a height, that the planet Saturn takes refuge under its shelter.

"When I considered the date of it it was found (to be contained in the words).

That tower of Bahram is complete."

The chronogram gives us the date A.H. 985 (A.D. 1577). In the

Berar Gazetteer of 1870, the inscription is ludicrously mistranslated and misinterpreted. The translator, whoever he may have been, makes the date A.H. 453 (A.D. 1061 !). There was certainly no Bahram in Berar then, and it does not seem to have occurred either to the translator or to the editor that if the reading of the date was correct they had discovered something unique in the way of Persian inscriptions in the Deccan. The old *Berar Gazetteer* was not far behind other publications of its class in strange misreadings of history, and the strictures of that accurate oriental scholar, the late Major Raverty, on what he styles "Gazetteer history" are not without justification.

Bahram Khan was commandant of Gawilgarh under Sayyid Murtaza Sabzavari, who was governor and commander-in-chief of Berar under Murtaza Nizam Shah of Ahmadnagar. The fort was probably thoroughly repaired at this time in expectation of the invasion of the Deccan by the emperor Akbar. In the previous year Murtaza Nizam Shah had received news that the emperor had reached the borders of Malwa on his way to the Deccan, and marched to meet him. All was activity in Berar, and Murtaza Nizam Shah was firmly resolved to encounter the Mughals, though his nobles attempted to dissuade him from risking a battle. The news, however, was false. Akbar had but marched from Agra to Ajmer and was at the time too much engaged with affairs in Bengal and elsewhere to think of attacking the Ahmadnagar kingdom. Berar was ceded to Akbar in 1596, but the forts of Gawilgarh and Narnala remained in the hands of commandants appointed from Ahmadnagar, and were not surrendered. The heroic Chand Bibi of Ahmadnagar made an all but successful endeavour to regain the lost province, and the safety of the latest addition to the Mughal empire was jeopardized by the drunken sloth of Sultan Murad, Akbar's fourth son, which so disgusted the Khani-Khanan, the actual commander of the army of occupation, that he was recalled and was replaced by the learned freethinker, Shaikh Abul Fazl, who captured both Gawilgarh and Narnala from the troops of Ahmadnagar.

From the days of Akbar to the beginning of the nineteenth century no very noteworthy incident is connected with Gawilgarh. On the disruption of the Mughal empire Berar passed into the hands of Asaf Jah Nizam-ul-Mulk, the great viceroy of the Deccan, and thenceforward was the prey alternately of Mughal and Maratha. When Major-General Wellesley had on September 23rd, 1803,

"Against the myriads of Assaye clashed with his fiery few, and won,"

he moved eastwards through Berar, and, after being joined by Colonel Stevenson with his siege train, defeated the combined forces of Raghuji Bhonsla and Daulat Rao Sindhya at Argaon and marched on Gawilgarh, then held by the Rajput Beni Singh for Raghuji Bhonsla.

The best description of the capture of Gawilgarh is to be found, of course, in Wellington's despatches. Colonel Stevenson took his guns up by Dhamangaon and probably followed very closely the line of the road which now runs through the village of Mota to the little hill station of Chikalda. The fort was invested on December 5, 1803, the northern wall of the outer wall was breached by the 14th, and the place was carried by escalade and assault on the 15th. The garrison fled by way of the Kichak Dara ravine and on the 19th Raghuji Bhonsla who masquerades in some of the Anglo-Indian chronicles of the time as "the Bouncello", signed at the little hamlet of Deogaon, below Gawilgarh, the treaty which closed the war so far as he was concerned.

From 1803 to 1853 Berar was administered by the Nizam's Government and in the latter year it was assigned, with other districts, since restored, to the East India Company. Gawilgarh was dismantled in 1858 lest it should be seized by Tantya Topi, who in that year unsuccessfully attempted to break from the Satpura hills into the Deccan in order to stir up the country.

There still remain in the fort many old guns, all of which, with one exception, are manufactured of longitudinal strips of metal bound by transverse hoops. The exception is the half of a gun (muzzle portion) lying in front of the small mosque in the fort. This is a fair example of a light field gun on the European model of a century since. The old magazine still contains many round shot of stone of various sizes.

There are no less than eight tanks within the walls of the fort, but only four of them contain water during the hot season.

In what is now the Chikalda cemetery, near the site of the deserted village of Labada, is a tomb bearing the following epitaph:—

In memory of—
Lieutenant G. Young,
H. M. 7th Foot,
Who fell at the assault of Gawilgarh.
Sir Arthur Wellesly (*sic*)
On the 15th December 1803.

This inscription, on a slab of white marble, was placed on the tomb by the late Major (afterwards Colonel) Kenneth Mackenzie, Deputy Commissioner of the Ellichpur District, some twenty-five years ago. Lieutenant Young's contemporary epitaph, cut on a rough slab of trap, is now barely legible. All that can be deciphered is the following:—

G. YOUN...
7...
15th December 1803.

The slab bearing this inscription has been let into the head of the tomb. The inscription on the marble slab is erroneous in one particular, for the 7th Foot took no part in the storming of Gawilgarh and were not even in India in 1803. Lieutenant Young was an officer in the 2nd Battalion of the 7th Madras Native Infantry, now the 19th Carnatic Infantry, one of the regiments which took part in the storming of the fort. The mistake on the tombstone is probably due to the fact that officers of the native Infantry, being British, were included under the head of Europeans, *i.e.*, among the European regiments, as is explained in a note to Wellesley's despatch from Ellichpur, dated December 18, 1803. The General wrote on the 15th the day on which the fort fell, from Deogaon: "This service has been performed, I hope, with small loss on our side. No officer has been killed and but few wounded that I have heard of, excepting Lieutenant-Colonel Kenny, of the 11th Regiment (now the 81st Pioneers), and Lieutenant Young, of the 2nd of the 7th." He wrote three days later from Ellichpur to say that Lieutenant Young had since died. Lieutenant-Colonel Kenny also died of his wounds, and was buried in what is now the Ellichpur cemetery.

The glories of Gawilgarh have departed under the *Pax Britannica* but it remains an interesting monument of the brave days of old for those who care for such things.

(2)—NARNALA

Some ten miles to the north of the field of Argaon, where the combined armies of the Marathas in 1803, met with their second severe defeat in the open field at the hands of Arthur Wellesley, and on one of the southernmost of the detached hills of that offshoot of the Satpura range which overlooks the Berar valley, stands the old fort of Narnala. It would, perhaps, be more correct to speak of this fort in the plural, for the whole series of fortifications consists of three distinct forts stretching in a line from east to west; Jafarabad on the east, Narnala itself in the centre, and Teliyagarh on the west. These forts are enclosed, except in those places where the natural escarpment of roek renders artificial defences unnecessary, by stone walls well and strongly built and surmounted by battlements. The bastions are numerous. The fort commands fine views of the hill ranges to the north and of the plains to the south. The scenery is at its best during a break in the rains, or just after the rainy season, when the wooded slopes of the hills are green and the atmosphere is clear, and free from dust and haze, the plains spread out below like a map, dotted with villages with their fringes of dark green foliage, and intersected by streams running southward down from the hills to join the Purna, the river which, draining the valley of Berar, flows westward till it joins the Tapti.

The three forts have twenty-two gates in all, but this number includes wicket gates, and also those separate gateways situated on the same main entrances to the fort. The main entrances to the fort are but four in number, the *Delhi Darwaza*, the *Sirpur Darwaza*, the *Akot Darwaza*, and the *Shahnur Darwaza*. The last named gate is the most important approach from the south, and boasts of three separate gateways; the Shahnur gate proper, the *Mehndi Darwaza*, and a gate called by Hindus the *Mahakali*, and by Musalmans the *Muhammadi Darwaza*. This last is the most interesting and historically the most important monument in the fort, and will call for further notice. The other gates have no special features. They are fair specimens of the heavier style of Pathan architecture, with a certain grandeur in their massive simplicity.

Of the twenty-two tanks in the three forts most are contained in the central fort. The system of water supply here was admirable. Of the old waterworks there still remain a part of the aqueduct and some of the stone drains constructed for the purpose of conveying surface water into the tanks, and the overflow from one tank into another.

The *jami masjid*, or principal mosque in the Narnala fort, is in ruins. It occupies a commanding position and was, perhaps, an imposing structure, but what is left of it does not enable us to form an opinion on this point. A local historian tells us that it was built in A. H. 915 (A. D. 1509) by one Mahabat Khan, and that it bore an Arabic inscription to this effect, but the inscription has now disappeared. There is also in the fort a small mosque in good repair, with three arches and a high Pathan dome. Its foundation is uncommemorated by any inscription but a slab let into the wall of the building records the unimportant fact that a nobleman of Haidarabad visited the fort in 1873. This slab might well be removed, for the inscription is in bad taste, and a mosque is no place for it.

Another building is the *baradari*, used as a dak bungalow. The alterations were made with unnecessary vandalism, and the decoration of the fine old domed interior consisted at one time of a coat of bright blue set off by a stripe of whitewash. Other buildings are the mint, *sarrafkhana*, and elephant stables. There are also the ruins of a *mahal* erected for one of the Bhonsla rajas of Nagpur, and in Teliyagarh stands a small mosque.

The *Mahakali* gate is the most beautiful piece of Pathan architecture in Berar, in fact its fault is that it is not in harmony with its severely simple surroundings. The gateway itself, built of white sandstone, is highly ornate, being adorned with conventional lotus flowers, a rich cornice, ornamental crenellations, and those most effective of architectural ornaments, finely executed Arabic inscriptions. It is flanked by projecting balconies, the window openings of which are filled in with panels of lattice work displaying considerable variety of design. There is nothing effeminate in the general design and the artist has succeeded wonderfully in harmonising profusion of ornament with the stern outlines of the Pathan style, however much the gateway may differ from those in its neighbourhood. The inscriptions have failed to excite the curiosity of the editor of the *Berar Gazetteer*, though they are as clear as though they had only recently been cut. He refers to them as "extracts from the *Quran*."[1] That perhaps, is, for the gazetteer historian, a good enough definition of any Arabic inscription. Extracts from the *Quran*, however, form the smallest part of these inscriptions and one short text calls for more than passing notice, for it is very dexterously used as a chronogram which gives the date of the building of the gate as A. H. 892 (A. D. 1487) which is also expressed in words. The upper of the two inscriptions then goes on with the creed of Islam and blessings on the heads of prophets, angels, *khalifahs* generally, and the four successors of Muhammad in particular. By this we know that the builder of the gate, Fathullah Imad-ul-Mulk, was a *Sunni*. The lower inscription informs us that the gate was built in the reign of the great and exalted king, the *Ghazi*, Shahab-ud-dunya-wa'd-din, Mahmud Shah, the son of Muhammad Shah, the son of Humayun Shah, the son of Ahmad Shah, the son of Muhammad Shah Bahmani, and concludes with a prayer for the endurance of his rule. Both inscriptions have an important bearing on two or three questions which, though of little importance to the general reader, occupy the attention of students of Indian history. It might, at least, have been expected that they would have been examined when the *Berar Gazetteer* was being compiled.

One of the objects of interest is the fort in the *khuni burj*, or "bloody bastion." This was the place of execution. Criminals sentenced to death were bound hand and foot and pushed over the edge. Some idea of what used to happen may be obtained by rolling a large stone over the edge and watching its progress. An execution by this method must have been a sickening sight.

On a knoll in the fort is a gun known as the *nau-gazi top*, or "nine-yard gun". The name refers to the length, and not to the range of the gun. It is an iron gun of the old faggot pattern, and points southward over the plain. Engraved on it is a Persian inscription which runs as follows :—

"He (God) is the Everlasting One. The Emperor Aurangzib Alamgir. This is the nine-yard gun, which was made during the rule of the Deccanis. Now Atlu Beg, the slave of the imperial court, having come to the fort of Narnala in the month of Jamadi-ul-Awwal in the year 1091 of the Holy Hijra (A.D. 1679), has mounted the above mentioned gun by the grace of His Majesty, the lord of the earth and the age, ruler of the world and its inhabitants, the true spiritual guide. Written by Pahlad Das, the Kayath. It is 150 years since this gun was captured and nobody has mounted it till now."

There are also in the fort the remains of two gun foundries. This completes the list of antiquities and we come to the history of the fort. It is not known when it was first built. Firishta tells us that Ahmad Shah Wali, the ninth king of the Bahmani dynasty, when he was encamped in Ellichpur for two years, "founded" the fort of Gawil and "repaired" that of Narnala in 1425. The local historian already referred to, takes exception to this statement and asserts that Gawilgarh was built long before Narnala But he is at the trouble of informing us that his authority, for this statement is the inscription on the *Mahakali Darwaza*, and argues that the date of the building of that gateway is the date of the foundation of the fort. That this is not so is evident from the fact that Narnala was a fort capable of affording to the governor of the province, long before the *Mahakali Darwaza* was built, protection from his rebellious nobles and from a foreign invader. There is a gate at Gawilgarh which was erected at about the same time as this gate at Narnala, but it does not follow that Gawilgarh did not exist before that gate was built. There seems to be no reason to doubt the accuracy of Firishta's statement and we may assume that the fort was in existence for some time before 1425.

Ala-ud-din Ahmad Shah, the son and successor of Ahmad Shah Wali, had married a daughter of Nasír Khan, ruler of Khandesh. This lady, who bore the title of Malika-i-Jahan, wrote to her father and complained that her husband neglected and slighted her. Nasír Khan, having first satisfied himself that Ahmad Shah of Gujarat would not interfere with him, resolved, in 1475, to invade Berar. He assembled his own troops and received as well the assistance of 2,000 cavalry and a large force of infantry, placed at his disposal by the "Raja of Gondwana," probably the Raja of Kherla. His next step was to foment disaffection among the nobles of Berar. Nasír Khan claimed descent from the second *Khalifah*, Umar, surnamed *al Faruq*, and his family was distinguished by the epithet *Faruqi*. He succeeded in persuading some of the officers in Berar that by fighting for the direct descendant of Umar they would be engaging in a holy war, and that all who fell would be certain of paradise. The Berar nobles must have been easily duped if they could be persuaded that to fight side by side with infidel Gonds against a Muhammadan sovereign was meritorious, or even permissible, according to the precepts of Islam. Nevertheless Nasír Khan's arguments prevailed with many, and the traitors plotted to seize the person of the Khan-i-Jahan, governor and commander-in-chief of Berar, who remained faithful to his master. He, becoming aware of their designs, withdrew to Narnala, where he was besieged by the rebels. Thence he contrived to send a letter to Ala-ud-din Shah, acquainting him with the state of affairs in Berar. The Sultan sent orders to Khalaf Hasan Basri, Malik-ut-tujjar, governor of Daulatabad, to march on Berar with an army of "foreigners," *i.e.*, Persians, Arabs, and Turks and Mughals from Central Asia, the Abyssinian and native Deccani troops being employed only in guarding the frontiers. The Khan-i-Jahan, on Khalaf Hasan's advance from Daulatabad, was able to break out of Narnala, and marched southwards as far as Mehkar to meet him. Khalaf Hasan despatched him with some Deccani troops to Ellichpur, and ordered him to guard that place and Balapur against the inroads of the Korkus of the Melghat, whose aid had been enlisted by Nasír Khan. He himself marched northwards to Rohankhed, near Buldana, and in the hills above that village fought a desperate battle with the invaders, who were utterly defeated. Nasír Khan fled to his capital, Burhanpur, and on being pursued thither by Khalaf Hasan took refuge in the fort of Laling*, leaving Khandesh to be laid waste and the fine buildings of Burhanpur to be levelled to the ground by the invaders. As Khalaf Hasan was returning to the Deccan Nasír Khan sallied forth from Laling and attacked his advanced guard with a greatly superior force, but was again defeated, many of the deserters from Berar who had taken refuge with him being slain. According to the *Berar Gazetteer* the Bahmani Sultan was present in person with his army in Berar and Khandesh. This is an error.

In 1490 Fathullah Imad-ul-Mulk, the governor of Berar who built the *Mahakali* gateway, proclaimed himself independent and founded the Imad Shahi dynasty, which lasted for about seventy years. The last

* Or Asirgarh, according to another authority.

of the line, Burhan Imad Shah, succeeded to the throne as a boy and soon after his accession was seized and closely imprisoned in Narnala by his prime minister, Tufal Khan, who, with the assent of Ibrahim Qutb Shah of Golconda and the Sultan of Khandesh, assumed the royal authority. Two or three years later, in 1565, Murtaza Nizam Shah of Ahmadnagar and Ali Adil Shah of Bijapur invaded Berar, devastating it with fire and sword as far north as Ellichpur. Tufal Khan ingratiated himself with Ali Adil Shah by means of rich presents, so that Ali not only withdrew his own force from Berar but persuaded Murtaza to retire likewise. Seven years later, in 1572, the same two Sultans entered into a compact whereby Murtaza Nizam Shah was to be free to extend his dominions by conquering and annexing Berar and the little kingdom of Bidar, while Ali Adil Shah was to be allowed to annex the equivalent of these two provinces from the ownerless dominions of the late kings of Vijayanagar. No sooner was this amicable arrangement concluded than Murtaza Nizam Shah set out for Berar, impatient to possess his share of the spoil. He first sent a message to Tufal Khan, demanding that Burhan Imad Shah, who must, so the message ran, have come to years of discretion by this time, should be set at liberty and placed in undisputed possession of his kingdom. The letter concluded with threats of what Tufal Khan might expect in the event of his not complying with these demands. Tufal Khan sought the advice of his son, Shamshir-ul-Mulk, who laughed at Murtaza's threats and advised his father to prepare for war fearing nothing. Murtaza Nizam Shah marched northwards towards Ellichpur, near which place a battle was fought between the armies of Ahmadnagar and Berar, and the latter was completely defeated. Tufal Khan and his son fled and were pursued through the jungles for six months until at last they contrived to make their way to Khandesh, where they took refuge in Asirgarh. Murtaza Nizam Shah marched to the borders of Khandesh and thence despatched a letter to Miran Muhammad Shah of that country warning him of the consequences of harbouring Tufal Khan. Miran Muhammad sent the letter on to Tufal Khan as a hint that his presence was not desired, and Tufal Khan fled back to Berar, avoiding the army of Murtaza Nizam Shah. He then sent a letter to the emperor Akbar offering him the province of Berar and representing himself as a vassal of the

Mughal empire whom the Sultans of the Deccan wished to eject from his fief on account of his not being, like them, a *Shiah.* He then sent his son Shamshir-ul-Mulk to Gawilgarh and shut himself up in Narnala and prepared to stand a siege. Murtaza Nizam Shah brought a large force, well found in artillery, against Narnala, and commenced systematic siege operations.

In the meantime Tufal Khan's letter had reached Akbar, who promptly sent an envoy to Murtaza Nizam Shah, to apprize him that the emperor regarded Berar as a fief of the empire and Tufal Khan as one of his vassals, and to warn the Sultan to evacuate the province and to refrain from molesting Tufal Khan. The envoy was unfavourably received and was sent back to his master, who was then at Agra. He informed the emperor of the failure of his mission, but Akbar was then too much engaged with affairs in Bengal to be able to punish Murtaza Nizam Shah.

Meanwhile the siege of Narnala dragged on. The guns of the besiegers could not be brought sufficiently close to the place to breach the walls, and the Sultan, heartily sick of the apparently hopeless task, was on the point of returning to Ahmadnagar, when an Afghan trader appeared one day in the camp, said that he had brought some horses and merchandise from Lahore by order of Tufal Khan, and asked that he might be allowed to enter the fort and deliver them. Changiz Khan, Murtaza Nizam Shah's chief adviser, perceived at once that this merchant could be made use of, and permitted him to enter the fort on condition that he accepted an appointment in the Sultan's service. The merchant jumped at the bait and took his horses and merchandise into the fort, where, by bribing the defenders to desert their posts at nightfall he rendered his first service to his new master. The guns were dragged up as close as possible to the walls, now denuded of defenders, and a breach was speedily made. The besiegers poured into the fort on one side while Tufal Khan with a few followers fled on the other, only to be pursued and captured. The unfortunate young Burhan Imad Shah and some other members of the Imad Shahi family were found in the fort and were made prisoners, Murtaza Nizam Shah's zeal for the young prince's interests having cooled with wonderful rapidity. In the meantime Shamshir-ul-Mulk had surrendered Gawilgarh on receiving a promise of his life. He was sent with his father, the young Sultan, and the other members of the Imad Shahi family, to a fortress in the Ahmadnagar dominions, and "in a short time all had left this transitory world, either by natural death or by some other means," as the historian naïvely remarks. The same historian (Firishta) is more explicit elsewhere with regard to the end of these unfortunates. He says that they all died in one night and gives the various stories current as to the mode of their death. Some said that they were strangled one by one; others that all of them, in number about forty souls, were shut up in a small room without ventilation. Thus, in 1572, ended the existence of Berar as an independent state.

Narnala is not mentioned again until 1596, when the imperial troops under Sultan Murad, Akbar's fourth, but second surviving, son and the Khan-i-Khanan, having defeated the Deccanis in a pitched battle, had their headquarters at Jalna, whence detachments were despatched to besiege Narnala and Gawilgarh. Matters progressed but slowly, owing to the constant bickering between Murad and the Khan-i-Khanan, and in the following year the emperor, weary of their quarrels, recalled the Khan-i-Khanan and sent Shaikh Abul Fazl to the Deccan. He captured both Gawilgarh and Narnala, but was assassinated on his way back to Agra. Sultan Murad died of drink shortly afterwards.

The inhabitants of the country about Narnala, unwilling, perhaps, to concede to the rival fortress of Gawilgarh any title to consideration not possessed by the fort which they regard as theirs, maintain that Narnala was stormed by Wellesley's troops after Argaon, and even point out the Delhi gate as that by which the storming party effected an entrance. Nevertheless Narnala was not captured by "England's greatest son," and does not seem even to have been held by the enemy. It may have been held by a detachment, but we are not told that it received even so much attention. The battle of Argaon was fought on November 29. On the 30th Wellesley wrote his despatch, in which he said that his intention was to proceed at once to Gawilgarh; "which he would lose no time in attacking." He kept his word, as we have seen, and Gawilgarh fell on December 15. When it is remembered that the distance between Argaon and Gawilgarh is thirty miles as the crow flies and much more by the road which Wellesley was compelled to take, and that the siege train which, after being dragged over almost impassable country in the hills, was in position at Labada on December 5th, it will be obvious that Narnala could not have been stormed in the interval. Legends, however, even when of comparatively recent growth, die hard, and the tale of the fierce attack on the Delhi gate by Wellesley's redcoats will probably still be told over the evening fire. In the fort is a Christian grave marked by a cross, but bearing no inscription. Tradition assigns it to an officer left by Wellesley in the fort with a detachment, but the story is not corroborated.

A striking object outside the fort is the shrine of Sayyid Ali, a saint of some celebrity in Berar. The tomb is situated on the summit of a steep knoll. Inside the fort is a tomb known as that of the famous saint Burhan-ud-din Auliya, a visit to which is said to be a sovereign remedy for, or a safeguard against, hydrophobia. Statistics of the percentage of cures are not available, but the results of one case of which I have heard lead me to believe that the pilgrimage is never likely to become a serious rival of the Pasteur treatment. It is sad to have to expose another Narnala myth, but it is a fact, if history is to be believed, that Burhan-ud-din is buried at Rauza or Khuldabad, near Daulatabad.

CHAPTER IX.

SOME FORGOTTEN BATTLEFIELDS OF BERAR.

IN India, which has been at times a vast empire, and at times a congeries of petty states bound by no close bonds and without a *de facto* overlord, there is not a province in which it is not possible to point out the sites of numerous battles fought in the olden days. Northern India has its battlefields, whereon the fate of the whole empire has not seldom been decided. In southern India the traveller may visit the sites of countless battles fought between the Musalman invaders and the Hindu inhabitants, and later between the established Muhammadan kingdoms of the Deccan and the great Hindu empire of the South, or between the various Muhammadan sovereigns themselves.

An attempt to connect scenes naturally dreary or monotonous with valiant deeds of olden days can hardly fail to lend an additional interest to those localities in the eyes of those whose lot is cast among them and of those who are led by curiosity, or love of sport or travel, to visit them. This must be my apology for an attempt to excite a small amount of interest in places obscure and uninteresting enough in themselves, but not wholly devoid of the interest which attaches to historical associations—some forgotten battlefields of Berar—a province which was for long the debatable land between northern and southern India, afterwards the frequent scene of conflicts between the states of Gujarat, Khandesh, and Malwa on the north, and the Bahmani empire or its disintegrated fragments on the south, and again the borderland between the great Mughal empire on the north and the independent Muhammadan kingdoms of the Deccan.

Rohankhed, a village situated a few miles north of Buldana, seems to have held in Berar in former days relatively the position held by Panipat in northern India. It was a town situated on the high road from north to south, commanding the ascent to the Balaghat or the table land of southern Berar and was the site of two notable battles. Ala-ud-din Ahmad II, the son and successor of Ahmad Shah Wali, and tenth king of the Bahmani dynasty, had married Agha Zainab, entitled

Malika-i-Jahan, the daughter of Nasír Khan Faruqi, Sultan of Khandesh. He subsequently received into his harem the daughter of the Raya of Sangameshwar in the Konkan, and gave her the title of Ziba Chihra or "Beautiful Face." His attentions to this lady aroused the jealousy of the senior wife, who sent a message to her father complaining of her husband's conduct. Nasír Khan's wrath was aroused at the idea that his daughter, the descendant of Umar the *Khalifah*, was slighted for a Hindu girl, and he formed the design of punishing his amorous son-in-law by invading his dominions and annexing Berar, the northern province of his empire. He did not consider it safe to take any steps without first assuring himself of the good will and approval of his powerful neighbour, Ahmad Shah of Gujarat, but it was not difficult to obtain his consent to a campaign, the object of which was the humiliation of the powerful king of the Deccan. Accordingly in 1437 Nasír Khan set out, having previously won to his interest several disaffected nobles of Berar, whom he seduced from their allegiance by exciting their cupidity. The rebels endeavoured to excuse their treason by persuading themselves that those who fought in the cause of a lineal descendant of Umar-ul-Faruq would, if slain, have the privileges of martyrs for the faith of Islam. These were probably *Sunnis*, ready to proclaim their orthodoxy by revolt against their latitudinarian master. They must purposely have ignored the awkward fact that the invader's active ally was the "infidel" Raja of Gondwana, with whom they proposed to fight side by side against a sovereign who was at least a Musalman. They plotted to imprison their leader, the Khan-i-Jahan, who remained true to his master, and to send him bound before Nasír Khan; but he perceived their designs and withdrew to the fort of Narnala, where, with such troops as remained faithful, he prepared to stand a siege. Although he was closely besieged by the insurgent nobles, who had the *khutba* read in the name of Nasír Khan, he contrived to send a message to his master acquainting him with the state of affairs. Matters were in a very unsatisfactory state at the capital, where the feud between the native Deccani and the African *Amirs* on the one hand and the foreign *Amirs* on the other led to quarrels at the royal councils. At last it was arranged that the foreign *Amirs* with their troops should advance under Khalaf Hasan Basri, the governor of Daulatabad against the invaders, and that the king should follow with the main body of his army. The flower of the army, consisting of picked foreign troops, was sent under Khalaf Hasan to Daulatabad, the native Deccani and Abyssinian nobles being posted along the northern frontier of the empire where it marched with Gujarat and Malwa, to guard against any irruption from that direction. Khalaf Hasan then entered Berar with seven thousand picked Arab troops, creating a diversion which enabled the Khan-i-Jahan to escape from Narnala and join him at Mehkar in Berar. Thence Khalaf Hasan sent the Khan-i-Jahan and some other Deccani *Amirs* to Balapur and Ellichpur, to guard against an invasion from the Satpuras and Gondwana on the north-east and east. In the meantime the invaders under Nasír Khan had advanced as far south into Berar as Rohankhed, where they were encamped. Khalaf Hasan marched northwards from Mehkar to meet them and fell upon them at the *ghat* just above Rohankhed, routing them utterly. Nasír Khan fled back to his capital, Burhanpur, closely pursued by Khalaf Hasan, who forced him to evacuate the capital and seek refuge in the fort of Laling.* The city and the surrounding country were plundered, and as Khalaf Hasan was returning with his spoil he inflicted one more severe defeat on Nasír Khan, who attacked him on his homeward way. In this last battle many of the treacherous nobles of Berar, who had fled with Nasir Khan, were slain. Very shortly after Khalaf Hasan's return Nasír Khan died, his death being attributed to mortification at the failure of his enterprise.

Rohankhed was once again the scene of a great battle in the reign of the emperor Akbar. Berar was then subject to the Nizam Shahi Sultans of Ahmadnagar. Husain Nizam Shah, who died in 1559, had four sons and four daughters. His eldest son, Murtaza Nizam Shah, succeeded him. He was a madman. His next brother, Burhan, coveted the throne, and in 1584 fled from Ahmadnagar to the Konkan, but finding the climate unhealthy left that country for Gujarat, and threw himself on the protection of Akbar. At this time Akbar was maturing his plans for the conquest of the Deccan, and the accession to his cause of Burhan and the governor of Berar, Sayyid Murtaza Sabzavari, who had fled from the mad Sultan Murtaza and sought refuge with the emperor, coincided exactly with his designs. It is indeed not unlikely that these

* Or Asirgarh, according to another authority.

circumstances hastened the execution of those designs. Akbar made his foster-father, Aziz Kuka, then governor of Malwa, commander-in-chief of the army of the south, the objective of which was Ahmadnagar. The operations of Aziz Kuka were fruitless from a political point of view. He advanced far enough into the Nizam Shahi dominions to plunder Ellichpur and Balapur in Berar, but, finding that the Sultans of Khandesh, Ahmadnagar, and Bijapur were unanimous, and that no help could be expected from the emperor, whose time and resources were devoted to other matters, more important at the time, he judged retreat to be the more prudent course, and Burhan and Murtaza Sabzavari gained no immediate advantage from their treachery to their country. Aziz Kuka had to retire before the superior forces of Ahmadnagar and Khandesh.

Shortly after this affairs in Ahmadnagar favoured Akbar's designs. Murtaza Nizam Shah's insanity assumed a more virulent type, and interested persons managed to persuade him that his son, Miran Husain, was plotting to supplant him on the ground that he was insane. He consequently attempted to murder the young man, but the plan failed and he was himself, on June 14, 1588, suffocated or, it would seem, roasted to death in the hot room of what we call a Turkish bath by his son, who succeeded him. Firishta, who was a faithful servant of Murtaza, the madman, gives an interesting, if painful, account of his end. Husain succeeded his father, but was assassinated after a reign of about two months. Mirza Khan then placed Ismail, the younger son of the fugitive Burhan, on the throne and the youth was instructed in the Mahdavi doctrines by Jamal Khan, much to the disgust of the *Shiah* nobles of the kingdom. Akbar, hearing that Ismail had been placed on the throne, sent for Burhan, his father, who was holding an appointment in the *tuman* of Bangash, and, reminding him that he was by right Sultan of Ahmadnagar, bestowed the kingdom, as a fief of the empire, on him, and offered him what troops he might consider necessary for the conquest of his country. But Akbar's guile was met with equal guile. Burhan thanked the emperor, but excused himself from accepting the offer of troops on the plea that the Deccanis would unite to oppose him with all the strength at their command, should he appear at the head of a foreign army to enforce his rights. He preferred, he said, to go alone and see what effect an appeal to the loyalty of his subjects would have. The truth was that Burhan had no intention of reigning merely as the Mughal's vassal surrounded by Mughal advisers and Mughal troops. The emperor let him depart to try his fortune, bestowed on him the *pargana* of Handiya, immediately to the north of Berar, in *jagir*, and sent orders to Raja Ali Khan, the vassal ruler of Khandesh, to assist him to the best of his ability. Proclamations were issued by Burhan to the Nizam Shahi nobles, many of whom, including Jahangir Khan, the Abyssinian, one of the wardens of the marches, promised to submit to him as their king. He accordingly entered Berar with a small force, when Jahangir Khan, repenting of his disloyalty to the king *de facto*, fell upon the king *de jure*, defeated him, and put him to flight. Burhan returned disappointed to Handiya, and remained there for a while, busily hatching plans for obtaining his kingdom. He managed to obtain promises of help from the *Sunni* ruler of Khandesh and the *Shiah* Sultan of Bijapur, the former assisting in obedience to the emperor's commands and the latter because he was annoyed at the spread of the Mahdavi heresy in the neighbouring state. Jamal Khan, hearing of the preparations of Burhan, held a council of the Mahdavi leaders, at which it was decided that Sayyid Amjad-ul-Mulk, the Mahdavi governor of Berar, should be commissioned to withstand Raja Ali Khan and Burhan in Berar: while Jamal Khan, with the young Ismail Shah, undertook the task of repelling the invasion from Bijapur. But Jamal Khan, having marched to meet Ibrahim Adil Shah II of Bijapur, and having defeated him in one battle, received the news that the nobles of Berar had declared for Burhan and had gone to Burhanpur, the capital of Khandesh, to meet him. He accordingly retreated towards Berar, closely followed by Ibrahim Adil Shah, who used his best endeavours to cut off all supplies from the retreating army. In these circumstances so many of Jamal Khan's men deserted him and joined Burhan that he could rely on none but those who had formally accepted the Mahdavi doctrines. At length he reached the *ghat* or hill-road of Rohankhed. Burhan Nizam Shah's advanced posts held the road itself, and Jamal Khan found it necessary to advance against the main body of Burhan's army by another road, very difficult. The heat was intense, and water was not obtainable. At last, when Jamal Khan's army was thoroughly exhausted in its search for a camping ground with water, information was received that there was within six miles a halting place with a plentiful supply. Weary though they were, the troops rushed on through the burning heat, and on arriving, worn out with fatigue and thirst, at their destination, they found that the plentiful supply of water of which they had been told consisted of a few wells in a palm-grove. Jamal Khan and his advisers agreed that it would be best to attack the forces of Burhan Nizam Shah and Raja Ali Khan at once. They accordingly pressed on, though the distance between the armies was considerable, and reached the allies on May 18, 1591. Burhan Nizam Shah and Raja Ali Khan drew up their forces to receive them, and the Mahdavis, fired with religious zeal, attacked so fiercely that the battle was on the point of ending in the defeat of the invaders when a musket ball struck Jamal Khan in the forehead, killing him on the spot. In oriental warfare the death of the leader invariably involved the defeat of his army. The Mahdavis fled, taking with them the young Ismail Shah. They were closely pursued by the victors and were forced to leave the young king in a village in their flight. Ismail, now merely the crown prince, was discovered and brought to his father, who expressed to him his delight at the result of the battle. The new king presented to his ally, Raja Ali Khan, a gift of horses and elephants, and after formally bidding him farewell, pressed on to his capital, Ahmadnagar. Thus ended the second battle of Rohankhed. Jamal Khan did not "stumble against" the army of Burhan Nizam Shah, as stated in the *Berar Gazetteer*. He marched directly to meet it, and, having met it, attacked it with great determination. The tradition of a great battle still exists at Rohankhed, where the field is shown, but they only know that it was fought long "long ago." The only trace of its former importance which Rohankhed still retains is a handsome mosque in the Pathan style of architecture, the gate of which bears an inscription recording the fact that it was erected by Khudawand Khan in A. H. 990, nine years before the second battle of Rohankhed. This Khudawand Khan fought in the battle on the side of Jamal Khan, and was one of those who endeavoured to convey the young Ismail Shah to a place of safety. Khudawand Khan was overtaken and slain by the victorious troops of Burhan Shah.

The small town of Shakarkhelda in the Buldana district was the scene of one of the battles in the civil wars which were the immediate cause of the disintegration of the Mughal empire. Asaf Jah Nizam-ul-Mulk, the governor of Malwa, left the imperial court in the year 1723 with the design of establishing his all but nominal independence in the Deccan, with Haidarabad as his capital. This design was perceived by the nobles at court, who consequently wrote to Mubariz Khan, *subahdar* of Haidarabad, urging him to oppose Nizam-ul-Mulk by force of arms. Nizam-ul-Mulk collected his troops and marched southwards to Daulatabad, and when Mubariz Khan, in obedience to the instructions from Delhi, invaded Berar, the northernmost province of the satrapy of the Deccan, he marched to meet him, and the armies met at Shakarkhelda. The battle, from accounts which have come down to us, seems to have been a one-sided affair. The bravery of Mubariz Khan himself is beyond doubt. He was slain, fighting bravely, after his two sons, Mas'ud Khan and Asad Khan, had been killed; of his followers three thousand were killed, but the resistance offered cannot have been obstinate, for it is said that the loss in killed on Asaf Jah's side was one only, the casualty being Zahir-ud-Daulah. It may be inferred that more execution was done by Asaf Jah's troops in the pursuit than in the actual battle. Asaf Jah Nizam-ul-Mulk, to commemorate his victory, changed the name of the village from Shakarkhelda to Fathkhelda, "the village of victory." It is still known indifferently by either name in Berar. There is in the village a fine mosque built in A. H. 989 (A. D. 1572), a year before the mosque at Rohankhed was completed. From the inscription which it bears there is no doubt that it was built by the same Khudawand Khan who built the Rohankhed mosque. The two mosques are evidently the work of the same architect. The battle of Fathkhelda does not occupy a prominent place in our histories of India, but it was nevertheless important, for it established the practical independence of the Nizams of Haidarabad, who, while they continued to style themselves vassals of the house of Timur, were, in fact, for several generations independent sovereigns, though they never adopted the royal style. The battle was fought in October 1724.

The next battlefield which calls for notice is Siwni, a small village in the Kelapur Taluq of the Wun district. In February, 1818, Appa Sahib (Mudaji) Bhonsla was seated on the *gadi* at Nagpur, having recently been restored after complete and unqualified submission to the Resident, Mr. Jenkins. But Mudaji, as treacherous as he was cowardly, was, at the very moment when he was subscribing to the terms of the agreement in which he confessed that he had forfeited all claims to consideration, intriguing to embarrass and if possible to destroy the British. He was found to be in treasonable correspondence with the Peshwa, Baji Rao, to whom he now appealed for help. In the middle of March news arrived that Ganpat Rao, with the advance guard of the Peshwa's army was advancing on Nagpur, and that the Peshwa himself was following with the main body. It was apprehended that Appa Sahib Bhonsla would escape and endeavour to join the Peshwa at Chanda. In these circumstances Mr. Jenkins found it necessary to arrest the Bhonsla. Ganpat Rao with the van of the Peshwa's army advanced in a north-easterly direction and encamped, on April 1 or 2, on the banks of the Wardha river, near Wun, in Berar, at a point a little above the confluence of the Wardha and Penganga rivers. Thence he cautiously crossed the Wardha, but his troops were immediately driven back by Lieutenant-Colonel Adams, who had, on April 3, reached Warora with a brigade of infantry, the 5th Bengal Cavalry, and some Horse Artillery. Baji Rao had already reached the south-east corner of Berar and was marching aimlessly backwards and forwards between the Wardha and Penganga rivers without venturing to cross either. Adams was delayed for want of supplies, which had to be sent from Nagpur. The delay, however, was advantageous, as it allowed time for Brigadier-Generals Doveton and Smith, who were advancing to cut off the Peshwa's retreat to the north-west and south, to come up. On April 14, Baji Rao ventured just to cross the Wardha, but a movement by Adams drove him back again. On April 16, Adams received a letter from Doveton ordering him to advance on Pandharkawada, now the *tahsil* town of the Kelapur *taluq* in Berar, so as to reach it on the 17th. On the evening of the 16th Adams began his march, and on the morning of the following day reached Popalkhuta, which Baji Rao had quitted barely twenty-four hours before. Adams, hearing that Baji Rao had retreated as far as Siwni, some twelve or fourteen miles to the south-west, followed him at once, with his cavalry, horse artillery, and a light infantry battalion. Meanwhile Baji Rao had discovered that he was advancing directly on Doveton's line of march, and promptly turned northwards, a movement which brought about an encounter between Adams' advance guard and the Marathas about five miles from the village of Siwni. Adams guessed from the number of elephants and standards that Baji Rao was present in person, and at once attacked with the 5th Bengal Cavalry and the Horse Artillery, driving the enemy back in confusion. The Horse Artillery secured a position on the rising ground to the north of Siwni, whence they were able to direct an effective fire on the disorganized Maratha army. The cavalry, led by Adams himself, then charged, still further disorganizing the Marathas. This charge brought the cavalry to a second ridge, in the valley below which the Marathas were seen in great numbers. The horse artillery again came into action with excellent effect, and Adams again charged the enemy with no more than two squadrons. The main body of the Marathas was by this time in complete confusion, but two bodies of horse seemed to be inclined to make a stand. The first, however, on receiving the fire of the horse artillery and on being threatened in flank by the remaining squadron of the 5th Bengal Cavalry, broke and fled. The second was dispersed by a third charge led by the indefatigable Adams, and the rout of the Marathas was complete. Baji Rao himself escaped with difficulty, quitting his *palki*, which had been pierced by a round shot, and mounting a horse. The victors captured five guns, the only artillery which the Peshwa had with him, three elephants, and two hundred camels. Of the treasure only Rs. 1,100 were captured. The Peshwa's troops, true to their Maratha instincts, had looted all the rest in the confusion. The pursuit was continued by Brigadier-General Doveton, who was at Pandharkawada when the battle was fought: but the Peshwa was unfortunately not captured. The battle of Siwni was a masterly piece of work. The Marathas left a thousand dead on the field, while of the victors only two were wounded. No determined resistance was offered by the Marathas, but this circumstance ought not to be allowed to detract from the credit due to the troops. They made a forced march of thirty miles over a difficult road in the burning heat of April in Berar, and at the end of this march attacked the immensely superior numbers of the enemy with such vigour and impetuosity as to paralyse his power of resistance. The honours of the day fell to the 5th Bengal Cavalry, the Madras European Horse Artillery, and the Bengal Native Horse Artillery.

Berar has other battle-fields, both mythological and historical, but the historical fields are not forgotten and the mythological fields are not historical, so that both lie without the scope of this chapter.

CHAPTER X.

AN OLD BATTLEFIELD OF BERAR.

THE early history of Balapur, like that of most respectable Indian villages, is "lost in the mists of antiquity." Even tradition is silent as to the name of its founder and the period of its foundation, helping us no further than the conjecture that it was founded by one of the rajas of olden times. But the old town was, from the date of its first mention in authentic history down to the time when British rule was firmly established in India, a place of importance from a military point of view. We are first introduced to it by Firishta, who informs us that when Khalaf Hasan Basri, in 1437 in the reign of Ala-ud-din Bahmani II, marched northwards from Daulatabad to meet Nasír Khan Faruqi of Khandesh, who had invaded Berar by the invitation of the treacherous nobles of that province, he sent the Khan-i-Jahan, governor of Berar under the Bahmani Sultan, to garrison Ellichpur and Balapur with his Deccani troops, apparently with a view to checking the irruptions of the Korkus with whom Nasír Khan had allied himself. Whether Balapur was attacked or not we are not told, but it is pretty certain that it did not fall; for Nasír Khan was, within a very short time, driven out of Berar.

More than a century and a half passes before we hear anything more of Balapur. In 1595 Ahmadnagar, the capital of the Nizam Shahi Sultans, was the scene of fearful struggles between the different parties in the state. Their mutual animosity reached such a pitch that one party committed the fatal error of appealing for aid to Sultan Murad, the second surviving son of the emperor Akbar, who was then in Gujarat awaiting the opportunity of interfering in the affairs of the Deccan. The prince and his commander-in-chief, the Khan-i-Khanan, at once marched southwards through Berar as far as Ahmadnagar, to which capital they laid siege. Those who had invited the prince to interfere now bitterly repented of their rash action, and, for a time at least, all parties were united in their opposition to the invader. The siege dragged on and the heroic endeavours of the Sultana Chand Bibi had already disheartened the Mughal leaders when news arrived that the eunuch, Suhail Khan, the commander-in-chief of the Bijapur troops, with an army of 70,000 horse, including, as well as his master's forces, the troops of the Golconda kingdom and such of those of the Ahmadnagar kingdom as were not shut up in the capital, was marching to the relief of the beleaguered town. The Khan-i-Khanan, as cautious as Sultan Murad was rash, made overtures of peace and a treaty was concluded, by the terms of which Berar was ceded to the Mughal empire, on condition that the imperial troops withdrew from the hereditary dominions of the Nizam Shahi dynasty, and refrained from molesting the independent kingdoms of the Deccan. The Mughals accordingly retreated into Berar, and Sultan Murad settled at Balapur, which he made his military headquarters. About ten miles from the town he built himself a palace, and named the village which grew up around it Shahpur. Of the palace it may now be said *perierunt etiam ruinæ.* Balapur thus became, for a time, the capital of Berar. Here Sultan Murad held his court, here he gave a splendid feast on the occasion of his marriage to the daughter of Bahadur Khan Faruqi of Khandesh, and hence issued the orders appointing Mughal officers to the administration of the latest addition to the empire. The peaceful sojourn of the prince and the Khan-i-Khanan in their new province was soon to be disturbed. The Ahmadnagar nobles, feeling perhaps that the Mughals had gained Berar too easily, again sought help from Bijapur and Golconda. The allied armies marched northwards and the imperial forces moved southwards to meet them as far as Sonpet on the Godavari. There a battle, which may best be described as an oriental Sheriffmuir, took place. At length the Mughals, many of whom had fled precipitately to Shahpur and Balapur, gained the day, very much more by good luck than by good management. The Khan-i-Khanan received fresh honours and returned triumphant to Shahpur. A series of quarrels between him and Sultan Murad ensued, during the course of which the prince was engaged in the congenial occupation of drinking himself to death. He succeeded so well that he died shortly afterwards of *delirium tremens*, and was buried at Shahpur; his body being afterwards exhumed and taken to Delhi, where it was laid beside the remains of his grandfather, the emperor Humayun, whose splendid mausoleum is a better resting place than the dissolute young prince deserved.

In the meantime the Khan-i-Khanan had been recalled from the Deccan, Sayyid Yusuf Khan and Shaikh Abul Fazl being sent to set matters right. Their efforts were not conspicuously successful, and Abdurrahim, the Khan-i-Khanan, was consequently re-admitted to favour. His daughter, Janan Begam, was given in marriage to Sultan Daniyal, the emperor's youngest son, and father and son-in-law were despatched to the Deccan, where affairs had begun to assume a serious aspect. The Sultan of Khandesh who had submitted to Akbar was now dead and his son had broken out into rebellion and seized the fort of Asirgarh. Daniyal and his father-in-law were sent on to Berar, with orders to reduce Ahmadnagar, while Akbar himself followed with the head quarters of the imperial army and proceeded to the siege of Asirgarh, which fort fell in 1599. Ahmadnagar was reduced in the following year by Khaja Abul Hasan, Sultan Daniyal's *divan*. Balapur and Jalna had been the principal cantonments of Daniyal's army during these operations. On the successful conclusion of the campaign, Sultan Daniyal was appointed to the government of the Mughal province of the Deccan, which at this time included Berar, Khandesh, and parts of the Ahmadnagar kingdom. Akbar, ever fond of quaint conceits, had changed the name of Khandesh to Dandesh in honour of his youngest son. The Khan-i-Khanan remained in the Deccan with Daniyal, as his tutor and adviser. In the meantime the peace between the empire and the Muhammadan kingdoms of the Deccan had been cemented by a marriage between Daniyal and a daughter of Ibrahim Adil Shah II of Bijapur, but neither marriage nor business of state was able to keep the prince from the delights of the wine cup, and in 1604 he died of drink at Burhanpur. Akbar, who was overwhelmed with grief at the death of his youngest son, died in the following year, and was succeeded by his eldest surviving son, Salim, who ascended the throne under the title of Jahangir. During his reign Balapur maintained its position as an important cantonment. In 1616, Man Singh, the brother of one of Akbar's most famous generals, died in Balapur of drink; a fate which seems to have overtaken many of those whose duties compelled them to pass much time in Berar.

The rise of Malik Ambar, the Abyssinian, was soon to arouse the Mughal *amirs* in Berar to the necessity for doing something more than drinking. Jahangir had, in the fourth year of his reign, sent his son, Sultan Parviz, to push matters on in this corner of the empire, but the prestige of the Mughals waned continually. History repeated itself. Parviz and his companion in the Deccan, the Khan-i-Khanan, quarrelled, until the latter was recalled and replaced by the Khan-i-Jahan. Matters did not improve. The Mughals were compelled to abandon the cantonment of Balapur and retreat to Burhanpur, leaving Berar to be overrun by the Deccanis. Things went from bad to worse till Malik Ambar came into prominence. To such good purpose did he arouse in the breasts of the old subjects of the Ahmadnagar dynasty that sentiment which among them did duty for loyalty that he was able to establish his authority in Berar. History again repeated itself, and the Khan-i-Khanan was sent to the Deccan. His efforts availed but little, and the Mughal *amirs* were glad to accept the offices of Ibrahim Adil Shah II of Bijapur, who acted as the "honest broker" in the matter of patching up a peace.

Eight years later, in 1619, Malik Ambar again made war on the Mughals, who were at this time holding Balapur and all the northern portion of Berar, besides the fort of Ahmadnagar where Khanjar Khan, the Mughal general, was besieged. The imperial army in the field, under Darab Khan, was successful, but was forced owing to the difficulty of obtaining supplies, to retire northwards to Rohankhed, and thence to Balapur, where they went into cantonments. They were followed by the Deccanis and a combat took place in the vicinity of Balapur, in which the Mughals were successful. Later in the same year another battle took place near Balapur. Darab Khan was in command of the imperial troops and was victorious over the Deccanis. His younger brother, Rahman Dad, was stricken down with fever in Balapur, but would not be restrained from joining his brother, but the brave young man overtaxed his strength and died a few days after the battle. The Deccanis now seemed to recognize that it was hopeless to attempt to dislodge the Mughals from Balapur, and we hear of no more fighting in the vicinity for a time. But shortly after this Jahangir complains of the rulers of the Deccan having broken faith, and of having, in violation of treaties, captured portions of the former Ahmadnagar dominions and Berar. Sultan Khurram, afterwards Shahjahan, had been sent against the Deccanis, but they were able to induce him to persuade the emperor to grant them peace on favourable terms. At this time Khurram was again appointed to command of the army of the Deccan, but could not be despatched at once, as Jahangir had set his heart on the reduction of Kangra, and the troops engaged in the siege of that place could not be spared.

At last despatches arrived from the Deccan containing the intelligence that the enemy's forces now amounted to about 60,000 horse, that they had conquered a large part of the imperial dominions, reducing military posts wherever they found them, and that they had advanced as far north as the old town of Mehkar in Berar where for three months the imperial troops withstood them, defeating them in three pitched battles. But by degrees the Deccanis laid waste the whole country round Mehkar so that the Mughals could no longer obtain supplies, and were forced to retreat northwards to Balapur followed by the Deccanis. Here the Mughals sent out a force of picked cavalry, between six and seven thousand strong, against the Deccanis, and a battle ensued in which about a thousand men were slain on either side, and the Mughals returned to Balapur laden with much spoil. They claimed the victory, but as they were followed by the Deccanis to the town, the victory cannot be considered as decisive. The Mughals held Balapur for about four months, at the end of which time supplies again gave out owing to the ravages of the Deccanis in the surrounding country. Berar was then abandoned and the Mughal forces retreated to Burhanpur. It is acknowledged in the official history of Jahangir's reign that most of the *parganas* of Khandesh and Berar were in the hands of the Deccanis, who collected the revenue therefrom. The Deccanis now besieged Burhanpur in such force that the imperial troops, thoroughly disorganized, could not even make an effective sortie. Kangra had by this time fallen, and Sultan Khurram set out at the head of a large army to redeem the situation in the Deccan, and was followed by reinforcements under Lashkar Khan. In the meantime the Deccanis had raided Malwa as far as Mando, but they were driven back to Burhanpur and fled thence without a battle. Khurram chased them through Berar and Murtaza

Nizam Shah was obliged to take refuge in Daulatabad. The Mughal commandant in Ahmadnagar still held out, and the siege was raised by Khurram's troops. Malik Ambar, in order to obtain peace, was compelled to make great sacrifices. Berar was restored to the Mughals together with a large tract of country adjoining its southern frontier and the Deccanis paid an indemnity of fifty lakhs of rupees.

Balapur does not again come into prominence during Jahangir's reign, though affairs in the Deccan again fell into great disorder, and Burhanpur was again besieged, but in 1626 death removed the able and implacable enemy of the Mughals, Malik Ambar, to whose ability and energy a generous tribute is recorded in the memoirs of Jahangir. Nevertheless, owing to the treachery of Pira the Afghan, at one time entitled Khan-i-Jahan, confusion reigned in Berar until Jahangir's death.

On the extension of the frontiers of the Mughal empire southwards, Balapur of course lost its importance as a cantonment and defensive post. In 1629 it was held in *jagir* by Buhlul Miyana, a commander of 4,000 horse. He had evidently been engaged in treasonable correspondence with Murtaza Nizam Shah, for in this year he fled from his *jagir* to the Balaghat. Balapur is mentioned later in the same year in connection with the operations against Buhlul, Pira, and their fellow rebels, but was not the scene of any event of importance. It continued to be a military cantonment throughout the reign of Shahjahan.

Early in Aurangzib's reign Suhrab Khan was the *faujdar* or military governor of Balapur, and was in high favour at court. Later in the reign he was removed from Balapur on promotion, being appointed commander of 1,500 horse and commandant of the fortress of Udgir, now in the Nizam's dominions. The *Berar Gazetteer* tells us that Muhammad Azam Shah, Aurangzib's third son, resided at Balapur and built a mud fort there, but the fact is not recorded in the standard histories of Aurangzib's reign. An elaborate *chhatri* or pavilion, overlooking the river, is ascribed to Raja Jai Singh, who was a commander of 4,000 horse under Shahjahan and was afterwards one of Aurangzib's best generals.

Henceforward we do not find much mention of Balapur until the reign of Muhammad Shah of Delhi. At the beginning of his reign the leading *amirs* of the empire were leagued against the two Sayyid brothers, Husain Ali Khan and Abdullah Khan, whose absolute power had for some time constituted a grave danger to the state. In 1720 Chin Qilij Khan, Asaf Jah Nizam-ul-Mulk, the ancestor of the Nizams of Haidarabad, was governor of Malwa. The Sayyids stirred up their nephew, Alam Ali Khan, governor of Daulatabad, to attack Asaf Jah, and Asaf Jah at once marched into Berar to meet him. Asaf Jah with some difficulty crossed the Purna river and thus turned the flank of Alam Ali Khan. He then took up a position at Balapur, where he was attacked by Alam Ali Khan. The latter was defeated and slain and at the same time the Sayyids were overthrown at Delhi. Asaf Jah returned to Delhi when the emperor's power was established, but his position there was like that of Clarendon at the court of Charles II, and he was the butt of frivolous and effeminate courtiers. Dissatisfied with the state of affairs at Delhi, he returned to the Deccan, and the *amirs* at court secretly instigated Mubariz Khan, *subahdar* of Haidarabad, to attack him. The *amirs* met at Shakarkhelda in Berar in October 1724, and Asaf Jah was victorious, and renamed the site of the battle Fathkhelda to commemorate his victory.

The most conspicuous object in Balapur is the fort, which is singularly like old pictures of the Hatras fort, *si parva licet componere magnis.* The outer or lower fort is a decagon with a bastion at each angle. Above this rises the inner fort, which is a pentagon, each angle terminating in a bastion, as in the lower fort. The structure is situated between the two rivers on which Balapur stands. Both the outer and inner forts are entered by fine Mughal gateways, and above the gateway of the outer fort is an inscription, now illegible, which, history tells us, records the building of the fort in 1757 by Ismail Khan, Nawab of Ellichpur. The fact that Ismail Khan should have gone to the trouble and expense of building this fort proves that Balapur, though no longer a frontier town between an empire and an independent kingdom, was not devoid of importance. The fort was probably of great service against the inroads of Marathas. The *Berar Gazetteer* says that the inscription records the completion of the fort by Ismail Khan. Local history says that the Nawab did not live to complete it, though he set up the gates and put the work in train. The fort is rightly described in the

Gazetteer as "the largest, and probably the strongest in Berar, the hill forts of the Melghat excepted. The *chatri* of Raja Jai Singh has already been mentioned. It is a graceful building on a high plinth, resembling in plan what is called by heralds a "cross quadrate," *i.e.*, the four arms of a cross issuing from the four sides of a square. It is surmounted by five *Pathan* domes, one large one in the centre over the square surrounded by four small ones. The superstructure is supported by twenty pillars and lintels, not arches. The ornament is principally of the leaf and dart pattern, with conventional lotus flowers, and the interior of the domes is fine. There seems to have been originally a flight of steps leading down from the pavilion to the river, but these have disappeared.

A fine *haveli* in the town was built by a local saint, Sayyid Amjad. An inscription over the principal gateway, a good specimen of Mughal architecture, informs us that it was built in 1118 A.H. (1703 A.D.).

The mosque in Kasarpura is a very fair example of Mughal architecture, though the arches are too squat to be graceful. A long and somewhat bombastic inscription, exceedingly well executed and well preserved, informs us that the mosque was built in 1150 A.H. (1737 A.D.). The mosque is known as the *Rauzah Masjid,* for it contains the tomb of a celebrated local saint, Maulavi Ma'sum Shah, of whom many wonders are related.

Balapur is out of the beaten path of tourists, and its monuments of the past are, perhaps, hardly possessed of enough magnificence to attract the sight-seer, though interesting enough to those who are able to associate them with the events with which they are connected.

CHAPTER XI.

GOLCONDA.

THE STORY OF A SIEGE AND A GALLANT DEFENCE.

THE citadel of Golconda stands on a rocky hill rising abruptly from the plain, on the north bank of the river Musi, about seven miles from the city of Haidarabad, the capital of the Nizam's dominions. The citadel itself, strongly fortified, is surrounded by stone walls enclosing a large area, within which the city of Golconda, once the capital of the Qutb Shahi kings, formerly stood. The city has long since been deserted, and the interior of the fort is a now a cantonment where some of the Nizam's regular troops are quartered with their followers. It also contains the state treasury and some other buildings still in use, but the citadel is deserted.

When the hill on which the citadel now stands was first fortified we do not know, but we are told that it was formerly the site of a mud fort built by one of the earlier Rajas of Warangal, or of Vijayanagar, the great Hindu empire of the Peninsula. Of its early history practically nothing is known, and it was probably a place of very little importance until the Qutb Shahi kings made it their capital. In the reign of Muhammad Shah Lashkari, the thirteenth king of the great Bahmani dynasty, which reigned in the Deccan for nearly two hundred years, troubles arose in Telingana, and a Baharlu Turk of Hamadan, Sultan Quli by name, who had been a slave in the household, was, after some hesitation, appointed to pacify the country and to clear the land of the robbers who overran it. He had formerly been employed as accountant-general to the imperial harem, to the ladies of which lands had been assigned in Telingana, and his faithful discharge of his duties in this post stood him in good stead, for, when Telingana was overrun by robbers so that the rents were never regularly remitted, and for long periods together were never received at all, those who suffered most from the anarchy prevailing in that province used their powerful influence to obtain for their faithful servant the post of pacificator. The young Turk's performance of the task thus entrusted to him surpassed the expectations of all. The condition of the kingdom at this time was such that an appeal to arms would probably have hastened its downfall, and the young man was consequently compelled to rely on his diplomatic tact and personal charm of manner. Notwithstanding the disadvantages under which he laboured, he soon succeeded in restoring order, thus securing the confidence placed in him by the ladies of the harem and winning useful friends among those *amirs* of the empire who had lands in Telingana.

In the reign of Mahmud Shah, the son and successor of Muhammad Lashkari, Sultan Quli became an *amir* of the empire, with the title of Qutb-ul-Mulk, receiving as his *jagir* Golconda with the surrounding country. Shortly after receiving this grant he was appointed commander-in-chief in Telingana, a position which strengthened his hands considerably. In 1512 Qutb-ul-Mulk, who had for some time been practically independent, followed the example which had been set by Yusuf Adil Khan, Ahmad Nizam-ul-Mulk, and Fath-ullah Imad-ul-Mulk, the governors of Bijapur, Ahmadnagar, and Berar, and, throwing off his allegiance to the now feeble house of Bahman, had himself proclaimed independent sovereign of the territory which he had hitherto ruled in the king's name, under the style of Sultan Quli Qutb Shah, and made Golconda his capital. Sultan Quli had already replaced the old Hindu mud fort with a substantial fortress of stone which the surrounding country yielded in large quantities. His fort received many and substantial additions at the hands of his descendants and successors. The Qutb Shahi kings of Golconda did not, like their neighbours, the Adil Shahi kings of Bijapur, run mad on architecture, but they built, and built well, in spite of a depraved preference for stucco for buildings other than fortifications. Muhammad Quli Qutb Shah, the fourth king of the dynasty, made extensive additions to the fort built by his ancestor, and also founded, as his residential capital, the city of Haidarabad, which he at first named Bhagnagar, after his favourite mistress, a Hindu girl named Bhagmati. Abdullah Qutb Shah, the successor of Muhammad Quli Qutb Shah, also devoted much care to the improvement of the fortress and constructed a spacious *ambar-khana* or store-house within the citadel. An inscription on black basalt, recording the erection of this *ambar-khana*, is still in an excellent state of preservation. It relates that the *ambar-khana* was completed, by the efforts of Khairat Khan, the faithful servant of the glorious King Abdullah Qutb Shah, in the month of Rajab, A. H. 1252 (A. D. 1642). Just within the gate of the citadel is an extensive armoury of three stories. The summit of the steep rocky hill on which the inner citadel is situated is crowned by a large hall with a flat roof, whence a magnificent view of the surrounding country may be obtained. Here, we may imagine, the successors of the resourceful and accomplished Turk were wont to sit in the cool of the evening, enjoying the fresh breeze and surveying the fair landscape spread out around them, and from this point of vantage Abul Hasan, the last of that kingly line, doubtless watched, with mingled apprehension and amusement, the efforts of the great host of the emperor of Delhi to wrest from him his fortress capital, the last possession that remained to him of all his dominions.

We now come to the most stirring and interesting event in the history of Golconda—its siege and capture by the Emperor Aurangzib, and the extinction of the Qutb Shahi dynasty. Aurangzib had, in his younger days, been viceroy of the Deccan in the reign of his father, Shah Jahan, and had made Aurangabad his capital. He had even then formed the resolve of overthrowing the two remaining independent kingdoms of the Deccan, Bijapur and Golconda, and in the case of the latter very nearly carried his purpose into execution. In 1665-6 Mir Jumla, the most powerful subject of Abdullah Qutb Shah, had by his arrogance deeply offended his master, to whom his great power and wealth rendered him an object of fear and envy. Abdullah Qutb Shah, on being informed that an improper intimacy existed between Mir Jumla and the queen-mother, lost control of his passion and declared that he would revenge himself on his presumptuous subject. Mir Jumla who was absent from Court, hearing of his master's anger, at once wrote a letter to Aurangzib, claiming his protection and offering to assist him in capturing Golconda, an enterprise which, he declared, would present no difficulties. Abdullah Qutb Shah's next move was to throw Mir Jumla's son, Mir Muhammad Amin, into prison. Repeated letters from Aurangzib, directing the release of the young man, produced no result, and the prince accordingly, with the consent of his father the emperor, who ordered the governor of Malwa and the neighbouring feudatories to render all the assistance they could, prepared to march against Golconda. The prince sent his eldest son, Sultan Muhammad, with a large following, in the direction of Golconda, cloaking his design by the pretext that he was sending him to Bengal in order that he might there wed his cousin, the daughter of Sultan Shuja. He followed his son with a larger force. Abdullah Qutb Shah, alarmed at the approach of Sultan Muhammad, who had now advanced to within six miles of Haidarabad, and disturbed by the news that the imperial army was following in his wake, collected what valuables he could and fled from Haidarabad to Golconda. The young prince encamped by the Husain Sagar tank, and Haidarabad, deserted by the king, was plundered. An encounter took place between the Mughal troops and a detached body of the Golconda army, in which the latter was worsted. Abdullah Qutb Shah then endeavoured to temporise, and sent presents to Sultan Muhammad who, however, refused to make any terms until the whole of Mir Jumla's property was given up. In the meantime Aurangzib was approaching with the main body of the army, and on his arrival preparations were made for laying siege to Golconda in regular form. As the siege progressed Shayista Khan, the governor of Malwa, and other chiefs joined Aurangzib's army. Golconda was reduced to serious straits when a message suddenly arrived from the old emperor at Delhi commanding Aurangzib to desist, and conveying an assurance of forgiveness to Abdullah Qutb Shah. Shah Jahan was at this time under the influence of his eldest son, Dara Shikuh, who was jealous of Aurangzib's success, and probably had no difficulty in persuading his father that the conqueror of the wealthy city of Golconda would lose no time in becoming the emperor of Delhi. He could cite a precedent by retailing the story of Ala-ud-din Muhammad Khalji and his too trusting uncle Jalal-ud-din Firuz Khalji. Aurangzib obeyed the command without a murmur, though the terms which he was able to enforce are sufficient to prove that Golconda could not have held out much longer. An indemnity which covered the cost of the expedition was recovered from the king, who also gave his daughter in marriage to Aurangzib's son, Sultan Muhammad, and designated his newly-made son-in-law heir-apparent to the throne of Golconda. All Mir Jumla's property and family were surrendered, and Abdullah gave as dowry to his daughter the district of Ramgir, which adjoined the southern dominions of the emperor of Delhi, and by this surrender became incorporated in them. He also agreed to insert the emperor's name in the inscription on his silver coinage, thus proclaiming himself, according to oriental custom, a vassal of Delhi. Mir Jumla entered the service of Aurangzib, and the Mughal troops were withdrawn from Golconda. Meanwhile Aurangzib bided his time. He had, as he thought, secured the reversion of Golconda, but he meant to have Delhi and Bijapur to boot. He must have seen by this time that Delhi should be his first objective, and the prompt obedience which he rendered to his father's order was, in all likelihood, merely a blind. Two years later he ascended the throne, having incarcerated or exiled his brothers and imprisoned his father. Circumstances prevented him from attending to the affairs of Golconda for many years after his accession, but the great object of his reign was to stamp out the independence of the two kingdoms yet remaining in the south and to establish an empire from Kabul to Cape Comorin.

The turn of Bijapur came first, and in 1686 Sultan Sikandar Adil Shah was besieged in his capital by the emperor. In the meantime Abdullah Qutb Shah had died, and had been succeeded by his son-in-law Abul Hasan. This king, presaging what his fate would be if the independence of Bijapur were destroyed, gave his neighbour what help he could afford. But it was all to no purpose—Bijapur fell and Sikandar Adil Shah was taken captive.

The siege of Bijapur interfered very little with Aurangzib's plans for the conquest of Golconda, and he had already, in 1684, before marching against Bijapur, commenced operations in the eastern kingdom. Troops were sent, first under Khan-i-Jahan Kukaltash, and then under prince Muhammad Mu'azzam, the emperor's second son, to wrest from Abul Hasan, the king of Golconda, some tracts of Telingana which he claimed as part of his dominions. An envoy, Mirza Muhammad, was also sent by Aurangzib to Abul Hasan, ostensibly for the purpose of demanding from him two large diamonds, the price of which, the emperor promised, should be taken into account in calculating the tribute due from Golconda, but really for the purpose of reporting upon Abul Hasan's administration, and, according to private instructions received from the emperor himself, with the object of goading the unfortunate king, by insolence, into some overt act or declaration of hostility against the emperor, and thus furnishing an excuse for an attack on Haidarabad. His mission was not unsuccessful. Abul Hasan protested that he had no such diamonds as those described by the emperor, and Mirza Muhammad's behaviour goaded him one day into saying, "I, too, am called a king in my own country." The envoy insultingly replied that the title was a misnomer, whereupon the cautious monarch replied, "It is you who are mistaken, for if I be not called a king, how can Alamgir be called the king of kings?" The envoy afterwards confessed that on this one occasion Abul Hasan got the better of him in controversy.

Meanwhile Muhammad Mu'azzam and the Khan-i-Jahan had advanced into the Golconda territories, and the troops of Abul Hasan went out to meet them. Mu'azzam, who had little taste for his mission, was anxious, if possible, to avoid bloodshed, but the only terms which he could offer were so humiliating, being no less than the surrender of all for which he had come to fight, the payment of all arrears of tribute, and a humble apology from Abul Hasan, that the king could not accept them. In the hostilities which followed the failure of the negotiations, the imperial forces were everywhere triumphant, and the parganas which had formed the subject of the dispute remained in their possession. But Mu'azzam, who was far from being convinced of the justice of his father's cause, and was personally well disposed towards Abul Hasan, deliberately failed to follow up the successes of the troops under his command, and in consequence of their supineness both he and the Khan-i-Jahan were severely rebuked by the emperor. The Deccanis, though they no longer dared to face the Mughals in the open field, harassed them with continual night attacks, and during a period of four or five months, throughout which Mu'azzam and the Khan-i-Jahan, who were disgusted with the emperor's severity, neither ordered nor permitted any action that might have been decisive. The Mughal troops scarcely knew what it was to get a good night's rest. The news of their inactivity only served to inflame still further the wrath of Aurangzib, who now wrote with his own hand a letter in which he severely upbraided his son, adding to it a note for the benefit of the Khan-i-Jahan, the substance of which was that the emperor well knew that his son's misconduct was the effect of the Khan's evil counsels.

The prince, reduced to tears by his father's letter, was at length stung into action. He called a council, but the result of its deliberations only increased his perplexity. The Khan-i-Jahan and the more influential officers, prompted partly by sloth and partly by cowardice, but chiefly by gratifications received from Abul Hasan and his officers, advised a continuance of the policy of inaction. Sayyid Abdullah Khan of Barh, however, warned the prince that it would be dangerous to hesitate any longer in carrying out the emperor's wishes, and counselled immediate action. Mu'azzam, who will henceforth be designated by his title, Shah Alam, followed a middle course, and sent a most undignified message to Muhammad Ibrahim, the commander of the Golconda forces, to whom he condescended to explain the dilemma in which he found himself, representing that his unwillingness to pursue hostilities had drawn upon him the wrath of his father, and that the time had come when it was no longer possible for him to remain inactive. He then proceeded in a more dignified strain to explain that he personally had no wish to proceed to extremities, and advised Muhammad Ibrahim to evacuate the districts occupied by the imperial forces. If this were done, he said, he would have grounds on which he could address his father, with a view to dissuading him from the design of destroying such independence as the kingdom of Golconda still possessed. With this message Shah Alam sent a valuable emerald as a present for Muhammad Ibrahim, an action which cannot but have been interpreted as that of a suppliant for peace. Consequently, although Muhammad Ibrahim himself was disposed to accept the prince's terms, the opinion of his officers, and especially of the Hindus among them, who were aware that Aurangzib would never rest while a state in which idolators enjoyed the indulgences allowed to them in Golconda remained independent, was too strong for him. Moreover, the Deccanis were inspirited by the arrival of a reinforcement from Golconda. A reply, the terms of which resemble the famous piece of French bombast, "Not a stone of our fortresses, not a foot of our territory," was sent to Shah Alam's pacific message, and the guns of the Deccanis opened a vigorous fire on his camp. Some damage was done and Shah Alam's spirit was at length aroused. He drew up his forces and advanced to the attack. The Deccanis were prepared, resisted most stubbornly, but were at length beaten back. In the course of the pursuit Shaikh Minhaj, one of Abul Hasan's generals, sent a message to Mu'izz-ud-din, Shah Alam's eldest son, imploring him as a fellow-Muslim to stay his hand until the wives and families of the defeated army could be conveyed to a place of safety. The young prince, after consulting his father, consented to a brief truce. The Deccanis, of course, utilized the time thus gained in re-forming for a fresh stand, and a second battle, more determined than the first, followed. The Deccanis were at length again put to flight, but, even while fleeing, had the incredible impudence to send a message to Mu'izz-ud-din deprecating the wholesale slaughter of Muslims on both sides, and proposing that the dispute should be settled by a combat between a few chosen champions selected from each army, an old device in southern India. The proposal was submitted to Shah Alam, who in reply proposed that the Deccanis who, having been put to flight in the open field now sought an opportunity of displaying the admittedly superior dexterity of their champions in sword-play, should engage the champions of the imperial army on elephants. This did not suit the Southerners, and they declined the challenge. Shah Alam received news the next morning that the officers of the Golconda army were in full flight towards Haidarabad, and, having caused the great drums to be beaten to celebrate his victory, he started in pursuit.

Meanwhile the Brahman advisers of Abul Hasan contrived to poison his mind against Muhammad Ibrahim, whom they accused of temporising with Shah Alam, and the conspiracy was so successful that it was resolved to throw its victim into prison and presently to put him to death on his return to Haidarabad. But Muhammad Ibrahim, before reaching the city, received information of the designs of his enemies, and immediately made his submission to Shah Alam, by whom he was received with every mark of favour.

Shah Alam had by this time arrived within striking distance of Haidarabad, and the news of his approach and of the defection of Muhammad Ibrahim struck dismay into the hearts of Abul Hasan and his advisers. It was now that Abul Hasan committed the only unkingly act recorded of him in the dark days which were beginning to fall upon him, the last of a kingly race. Smitten with sudden panic, he fled suddenly by night, with such of his valuables as could be transported by the slaves of his harem, from Haidarabad to the old fortress capital, leaving the bulk of his treasure and most of his harem behind. His flight was a signal for a rising of the mob in Haidarabad, who plundered the wealthy and respectable inhabitants indiscriminately, and for some time Haidarabad suffered as a city taken by storm. The mercantile community was plundered, according to Khafi Khan, to the extent of four or five millions sterling, while respectable citizens thought themselves fortunate if they could escape on foot, leading their unveiled wives and daughters by the hand to the fortress. Before the mob had well finished their work, the army of Shah Alam arrived, and gutted even the palace of the king. The prince did all he could to restore quiet. The provost-marshal of his army and the minister of Abul Hasan co-operated, and endeavoured, by patrolling the town with a body of five hundred horse, to check the plunderers, but neither the foreign army nor the native mob was to be restrained. The unfortunate king sent a message from the fort imploring that the hand of the spoilers might be stayed, and at length they were to some extent brought under control.

Shah Alam had next to consider the terms of peace with Abul Hasan Shah. He stipulated for the payment of an indemnity of ten crores and twenty lakhs of rupees, over and above the fixed annual tribute, and the exclusion of the two Brahman advisers of the king, Madanna and Yenkanna, from the councils of the kingdom. The districts of which the conquest had been the ostensible object of the war were to be ceded to the emperor. On these terms, which were perforce agreed to, Shah Alam consented to intercede with the emperor and to endeavour to dissuade him from the further prosecution of hostilities. Madanna and Yenkanna were not only excluded from the councils of the kingdom; two of the widows of Abdullah Shah, Abul Hasan's uncle and predecessor, were so enraged with the two Hindus, whom they held accountable for all the troubles that had befallen the state, that without consulting the king they caused them to be assassinated and had their heads sent to Shah Alam.

The news of the treaty with Abul Hasan was conveyed to the emperor, who was at Sholapur exercising a general supervision over the operations against Bijapur and Golconda. Openly he expressed himself satisfied, but in private he made no secret of his displeasure with what he considered the lame conclusion of a successful expedition. He recalled the Khan-i-Jahan from the field, and appointed Sa'adat Khan special envoy to recover the tribute and indemnity which Abul Hasan had agreed to pay. The Khan-i-Jahan, when he appeared before the emperor, was so bitterly upbraided that in disgust at the treatment which he had received he entered into treasonable correspondence with the Maratha Sambhaji, son and successor of Shivaji, who was aiding the Sultans of Bijapur and Golconda, and instigated him to fall upon the troops of I'tiqad Khan, Khaja Abu-l-Makarim, and Tahavvur Khan, who were conveying grain to the imperial forces.

Meanwhile Shah Alam was still encamped at Haidarabad. Some of the *amirs* of Golconda had joined his army, the presence of which was a menace to the fortress. Accordingly the troops of Abul Hasan, under the command of Sharza Khan and Abdur Razzaq Khan Lari, attacked the prince's army, inflicting upon it considerable loss. Shah Alam, still unwilling to make the attempt to reduce Golconda, and, deeming the forces under his command insufficient for the purpose, as indeed they were, withdrew, on the pretext that he could not obtain supplies, to Khir, where he encamped. Here he received a reinforcement under the command of Qilij Khan, who was the bearer of a message recalling him to the imperial camp.

Things were not going well with the imperial troops in the Deccan. The siege of Bijapur under Muhammad A'zam, the third son of the emperor, made but little progress, and his troops suffered severely from the want of supplies, and from the vigorous attacks of the besieged, and of their allies the Marathas. Sa'adat Khan was sent, as we have seen, with an army to collect the tribute and indemnity due from Abul Hasan, but the emperor wisely determined not to divide his forces by besieging Bijapur and Golconda simultaneously. He therefore advanced in person against Bijapur, taking with him Shah Alam, and arrived before the place on Sha'ban 21, A.H. 1097. (A.D. 1685). Shah Alam was unable to restrain his friendly feelings for the Sultans of the Deccan, and lost very little time in entering into correspondence with the nobles of Bijapur. The emperor, hearing reports of Shah Alam's treachery had his attendants watched, and one of them was detected. He was put to the question and implicated others, including Shah Alam, who was sent for and interrogated in private. Although he was guilty of the almost incredible meanness of disowning his agent, his protestations were not believed, and he was treated virtually as a state prisoner.

The siege was vigorously pressed, and late in the year 1686 Bijapur fell. The king, Sikandar Adil Shah, the last of his race, was brought in silver chains before Aurangzib, and was then sent to Daulatabad, where he ended his days in honourable captivity.

Aurangzib was now in a position to give his undivided attention to Golconda, the last of the independent Muhammadan kingdoms of the Deccan. He did not march immediately against the fortress, for on his way thither lay a noted shrine, which his piety could not afford to neglect. This was the shrine of Gisu Daraz Banda Nawaz, the patron saint of Ahmad Shah Wali Bahmani, at Gulbarga, the ancient capital of the Bahmani empire. The emperor duly performed his pilgrimage, but he was by no means so engrossed in the state of his soul as to be unable to find time to attend to wordly matters. Sa'adat Khan has already been mentioned as the special envoy who was sent to Haidara bad with the object of recovering the tribute and indemnity due from Abul Hasan. The emperor sent letters from Gulbarga both to his accredited agent and to Abul Hasan Shah. The latter was dishonestly led to believe that prompt payment of the dues would not only ensure the safety of his dominions, but would secure for him the emperor's special favour. The former received full and concise instructions. He was informed that the emperor was marching on Golconda with the intention of reducing it, but was instructed at the same time to spare no pains in collecting the tribute. Sa'adat Khan faithfully obeyed his master's order and led Abul Hasan to believe that the settlement of his cash account with the emperor would relieve him from all apprehensions. The unfortunate king found it impossible to raise the money necessary for the satisfaction of the emperor's demand, but in order to show that he was doing all that he could, he asked Sa'adat Khan to send a eunuch who could inspect the royal seraglio and remove the jewels of the women in part payment of the demand. Sa'adat Khan replied that he could not comply with this request, and in the course of the next few days Abul Hasan received the disquieting news that the emperor intended to advance from Gulbarga. He was now thoroughly alarmed, and collected from his harem sufficient jewellery to fill nine trays. These he sent, with a list of their contents, but without any valuation, to Sa'adat Khan, stipulating that they were only to be retained as a guarantee of good faith. With the trays was sent a quantity of gold on the same terms, which were that the valuables were to be returned in case the emperor's determination to besiege Golconda was found to be unalterable. At this time Abul Hasan took the opportunity of the emperor's presence at Gulbarga to send him a complimentary present of fruit. Sa'adat Khan, hearing of the despatch of this present, sent for the bearers, and despatched together with Abul Hasan's present the jewellery and gold which had been delivered to him in trust, thus making it appear that these valuables, as well as the fruit, were a gratuitous present from Abul Hasan. Immediately after the despatch of the jewels Abul Hasan heard that Aurangzib was marching towards Golconda with the avowed intention of reducing it. On receipt of this news he demanded from Sa'adat Khan the return of the property which had been entrusted to him, plaintively explaining that he had, by pledging the jewels of the ladies of his harem, sacrificed his honour in the vain hope of saving his country. Sa'adat Khan was forced to admit that he had sent the jewels to the emperor, and endeavoured to excuse his action on the ground that he had no certain news that Aurangzib was marching on Golconda. The defence would have been weak, even had it been true, for by the terms of the pact the envoy was bound to satisfy himself that his master would not attack Golconda before he sent the jewels to him. But there can be no doubt that Sa'adat Khan acted throughout on detailed instructions received from Aurangzib, and it is not easy to understand how some latter-day historians, who represent Aurangzib, as a simple-minded bigot, in whom was no guile, can palliate the baseness of his conduct on this occasion towards a sovereign who was, at least, with all his faults, a brother Muslim. It is not surprising to learn that Sa'adat Khan's breach of faith excited the deepest indignation in Haidarabad and Golconda. His house was surrounded by the troops of Abúl Hasan, and he lived for two days in a state of siege. At the end of that time he contrived to send a message to the king, in which he admitted that he had misconstrued the terms of the agreement and repeated his false and frivolous excuse. He added that he knew that Aurangzib had long been desiring a pretext for attacking Golconda, that no better pretext than the murder of the imperial envoy could possibly be supplied, and that he was quite ready to die in order to provide that pretext. At the same time he hinted that if his life was spared Abul Hasan need never despair of obtaining all that his good offices could procure from Aurangzib. This message had the desired effect, and the wily envoy was henceforth not only immune from personal danger, but was treated by the deluded king as an honoured guest.

Aurangzib, having finished his devotions at Gulbarga, and having made a short halt at Ahmadabad Bidar, which he had re-named Zafarabad, or the city of victory, marched towards Golconda. Abul Hasan now became seriously alarmed, but still hoped, by timely submission, to secure some measure of independence, and in this hope sent a message to the emperor, humbly asking pardon for past faults and promising amendment for the future. With the message were sent valuable presents. All the satisfaction that he obtained was an imperial *farman*, setting forth his misconduct in severe terms. His base actions, he was informed, were too numerous to be recorded, but it was still possible to mention one in a hundred of them. The commission of all power in the state to infidels, to whom holy Shaikhs and learned men were made subject, the open encouragement of vice, the Sultan's own love for wine, his employment of the infidel Marathas in war, against the holy law of Islam, and the payment of subsidies to "the accursed Sambhaji" were enumerated as offences for which no forgiveness could be expected either in this world or the next.

Abul Hasan, seeing that his submission availed him nothing, now set himself in earnest to prepare to meet his powerful foe. He sent a force under the command of some of his principal nobles, Shaikh Minhaj, Sharza Khan, and Mustafa Khan Lari,* to oppose the advance of the Mughals, and in bidding them farewell ordered them in the event of victory to use every endeavour to capture the emperor alive, and having captured him to treat him with all honour. The *amirs* replied that they would endeavour to capture him, but could not promise that they would treat him with honour, as they could not trust their feelings. They then marched out to meet the invaders with an army of forty or fifty thousand horse. The

* Better known as Abdur Razzaq Khan Lari.

imperial army was within two marches of Golconda when the Deccanis appeared in the distance. The latter did not venture to attack, and scarcely offered any serious opposition to the advance of the emperor, but hung on the flanks of the Mughals and committed themselves to nothing more than petty skirmishes. The emperor pressed on, and on the 24th of Rabi-ul-Awwal, A.H. 1098 (A.D. 1687) arrived within gunshot of Golconda. Preparations for the siege were immediately pushed on. The necessary material was collected and work was commenced on the batteries and trenches. The Mughals had to deal not only with the besieged within the fortress, but also with the field army of Abul Hasan Shah, under the command of the nobles already mentioned, which took up a position in rear of the besieging force and co-operated with Sambhaji's Marathas in cutting off supplies. At this time a famine, due to the failure of the rains, prevailed in the Deccan, and it would have been difficult for the Mughals to obtain sufficient supplies even had their convoys been unmolested. As it was the imperial army endured terrible privations throughout the siege, while the besieged, who had ample stores of grain in Golconda, lived in the midst of plenty.

The siege now began in earnest. The Mughals were harassed in the rear by the field army of Abul Hasan. A heavy and incessant fire was kept up from the fort, and the besieged made almost daily sallies. Firuz Jang was appointed to the command of the besieging army, and to him were entrusted all the dispositions for the siege. In the early days of the investment both the emperor and Firuz Jang suffered a serious loss. Qilij Khan, the general's father, and one of the most faithful and able servants of the emperor, was slain by a shot from the fortress. Shah Alam, though still in disgrace on account of his treasonable correspondence with the enemy at Bijapur, was mindful of his former sympathy with Abul Hasan, and now most imprudently entered into correspondence with the defenders of the fortress. Informers discovered to the emperor his negotiations with Abul Hasan, and even accused him of having formed the design of joining the besieged king, alleging that Nur-un-nisa Begam, his chief wife, an accomplished and virtuous lady, had visited Golconda in disguise in pursuance of her husband's treasonable designs. Some of Shah Alam's officers, who were believed to be true to the emperor's interests, were questioned as to their master's conduct, but replied that they had no reason to suspect his loyalty. At the most he intended, they said, to request the emperor to pardon Abul Hasan and abandon the siege, and to represent himself to Abul Hasan as the most influential of the emperor's advisers. They were not believed, and Shah Alam and his son Muhammad Azim were summoned to the imperial presence and disarmed. Shah Alam was then deprived of his title, rank, *mansabs*, and *jagirs*. Nur-un-nisa was imprisoned and insulted, and measures were taken to induce both her and her husband to confess that they had been guilty of treason; but these failed of their object. Aurangzib even had Nur-un-nisa's uncle and some of her principal eunuchs put to the torture, with a view to extracting confessions from them, but nothing was elicited. The prince, however, remained in disgrace, and Abul Hasan lost his best friend in the imperial camp.

Meanwhile the siege progressed, and the trenches were pushed forward daily. One day, as Firuz Jang was supervising the working parties in person, the besieged, led by Shaikh Nizam and Abdur Razzaq Lari, made a determined sortie. The slaughter on both sides was great, the Rajputs being the principal sufferers among the besiegers. After a most determined struggle the sortie was repulsed, and shortly afterwards Shaikh Minhaj, Shaikh Nizam, Muhammad Ibrahim, and most of the principal *amirs* of Golconda, realizing that their master was doomed, deserted to the Mughals, and were rewarded by the emperor with honours, titles, and important commands. Abdur Razzaq Khan Lari, who bore the title of Mustafa Khan, was the only one of the principal *amrrs* who remained faithful to his master to the last, resisting all attempts to shake his loyalty.

These defections had no immediate effect on the duration of the siege, which continued to drag its slow length along, for the fortress was so well found both in guns and ammunition that the besieged were able to maintain an almost unceasing fire of artillery and rockets, so that, as the historian says, " so heavy was the smoke that it was impossible to distinguish day from night, and scarcely a day passed on which there were not numerous casualties in the trenches. Nevertheless the imperial troops, prominent among whom were the deserters from Abul Hasan's army, displayed the greatest valour and determination, and succeeded in pushing on the parallels to the edge of the ditch." As soon as they had obtained a foothold in this position batteries were thrown up close to the wall, and attempts were made to fill the ditch with large sandbags. A constant cannonade was kept up by the advanced batteries, and at length the wall was breached. But meanwhile the Marathas and the field army of Abul Hasan, some of whom still remained faithful, had done their work so well that there was a famine in the imperial camp. The satirist Ni'mat Khan-i-Ali gives an amusing description of the wretched plight of the besieging army. The rains again failed and the Deccan produced no crops. In addition to this calamity a pestilence, probably cholera, broke out in the imperial camp, and numbers died daily from famine and disease.

The tide of desertion now ebbed. Many deserted to Abul Hasan, and many more who had not the courage openly to desert, but who heartily wished for an end to the apparently interminable siege, rendered the besieged what assistance they could. We do not read that any of the deserters from the fortress returned to their former allegiance. It would rather seem that Abul Hasan was the loser in this exchange of deserters, for, whereas he was forsaken by his principal nobles, no leaders of the first rank, and probably no one of any importance, left the emperor. The truth probably was that the superior officers knew that whatever hardships they might be called upon to suffer, the result of the campaign was certain. Those inferior to them in rank and intelligence were not so assured of this, and were less patient of hardships which pressed more heavily upon them than upon their superiors.

As the termination of the siege seemed no nearer than when it had first commenced, the emperor recalled his third son, Muhammad A'zam, who had been sent to Ujjain and Agra to regulate Shah Alam's *jagirs* when that prince fell into disgrace, and had by this time reached Burhanpur. Ruhullah Khan, to whom had been entrusted the administration of Bijapur, was also summoned to the imperial presence. The difficulty of obtaining supplies had in the meantime increased to such an extent that Mirza Yar Ali, an experienced and faithful officer who was appointed chief of the commissariat, declined the appointment in despair of being able to carry out its duties to the emperor's satisfaction.

Muhammad A'zam, who was an old enemy of Mirza Yar Ali, on his arrival in the imperial camp, represented that Mirza Yar Ali's refusal of the appointment was in fact an act of disobedience to the emperor, and so worked on his father's feelings that the unfortunate officer was beheaded. In his place one Sharif Khan, who had earned an unenviable notoriety in the collection of the *jizya*, or poll-tax on Hindus, was appointed chief of the commissariat.

Heavy rain and the flooding of the river Musi now added a fresh obstacle to the prosecution of the siege and reduced the besiegers to a plight far worse than that of the besieged. In the month of Rajab, as the third month of the siege was drawing to a close, Firuz Jang made an attempt to carry the place by escalade at night. Ladders were prepared and were placed in position, and the escalading party began to ascend them. Before they had reached the parapet, a dog, which was wandering round the rampart in search of corpses on which to feed, began to bark. The besieged were instantly on the alert, and ran with torches to the spot whence the sound proceeded. The ropes which fastened the ladders to the wall were cut, and the ladders were overturned, the escalading party being hurled into the ditch and overwhelmed with a shower of hand-grenades. But so sure of success had the Mughals been that a messenger, one Haji Mihrab, had been posted in order that at the moment at which the escalading party was expected to reach the parapet he might ride off to the emperor's tent with the news that the fortress had fallen. He carried out his instructions to the letter, and, without waiting to see whether the escalade had been successful, galloped off to the emperor and offered him respectful congratulations on the fall of the place. The satirist Ni'mat Khan-i-Ali has a most amusing poem on the reception of the news by the army. He describes their extravagant delight at the tardy termination of the long and arduous campaign in the Deccan, and the prospect of a speedy return to Hindustan, and then revels in the details of their disappointment when, in the morning, the rejoicing was found to be premature. The dejection of the imperial army on hearing the news of the utter failure of the attempt from which so much had been hoped was, indeed, extreme, and a less determined general than Aurangzib would certainly have abandoned the siege and awaited a more convenient opportunity for its prosecution. But the determined bigot had set his hand to the plough and would not look back. He recked little that his troops were dying like flies from disease, famine and exposure. His resources were practically limitless, and he would not admit that he was defeated. The attempt to capture the fortress by escalade had failed, but the extravagant gratitude displayed by Abul Hasan towards the dog, the saviour of his capital, sufficed to show how narrow had been the line which divided failure from success. The dog received a collar of gold, a jewelled chain, and a coat of cloth-of-gold, and was kept always in the royal presence. But to the emperor the failure of the escalade merely suggested a fresh method of attack. Mining was now commenced, and in a short time three mines were carried as far as the wall, and nothing remained but to charge them.

At this period of the siege Abdullah, the chief *qazi* of the empire and the recognised authority on all questions of ecclesiastical law, ventured to represent to Aurangzib that it was unlawful to continue the siege. He might have known that the open expression of his scruples would have no other effect than to bring about his own disgrace. His predecessor had ventured to express a similar opinion with regard to the siege of Bijapur, and the treatment which he had received had compelled him to resign his post and retire to Mecca. But Abdullah did not allow this consideration to deter him from doing what he believed to be his duty. He fearlessly contended that as Abul Hasan was a Muslim who had agreed to submit to the emperor's authority and that as the continuance of hostilities involved the daily destruction of a large number of Muslims in either army, the siege was unlawful. He was unceremoniously dismissed from the imperial presence and was ordered to busy himself with the settlement of disputes, and to refrain from expressing opinions as to the lawfulness of that which the emperor chose to do.

In the middle of the month of Sha'ban, the siege having then lasted for about five months, a deluge of rain fell. The tents of the besieging army were beaten down, and the massive batteries, which had been constructed with infinite labour and at infinite risk in the fierce heat and under the guns of the fortress, were washed away. The troops had no other shelter than "that tent of cloud which is supported by ropes of rain." While they were in this plight the garrison made a most determined sortie. The spirit of the imperial army was now thoroughly broken, and many of its leaders displayed the most contemptible cowardice. Salim Khan, the African, after attempting for a short time to withstand the attack of the Deccanis, fled and hid himself in a cave. Saff Shikan Khan, whose reputation for valour was great, and who had hitherto displayed unflagging energy throughout the siege, was in command of that portion of the trenches on which the attack was led by the valiant Abdur Razzaq Khan Lari. He lay down in the mud and feigned to be wounded. Jamshid and Ghairat Khan, the commander of the imperial artillery, fled disgracefully, and though the latter attempted to hide himself he was recognized and captured. Sarbarah Khan and twelve other *mansabdars* were also captured. That portion of the besiegers' position which was attacked was cut off from the camp of the main body of the imperial army by a *nala*, swollen by the recent rain. Endeavours were made to convey reinforcements to the combatants by means of elephants, but the water was deep, and the supports were unable to reach their hard-pressed comrades.

Meanwhile the Deccanis returned to the fortress with their prisoners, who were led before Abul Hasan. Ghairat Khan was so overcome with terror that he appeared as one dead, and showed no signs of life until a match was applied to his breast, a somewhat rude method of diagnosing his complaint. Abul Hasan treated the captives not only courteously, but generously. The principal *mansabdars* received each a horse, as a present, and all received robes of honour and were permitted to return to the imperial camp. Sarbarah Khan, before he was dismissed, was taken round the store-houses and magazines, when he saw great store both of grain and powder piled up to the roof. It is impossible not to admire Abul Hasan's policy on this occasion. He must have known that the captives had endured and would endure in the famine-stricken camp of the besiegers hardships which would make the lot of a prisoner of war in Golconda appear enviable in their eyes. He must also have guessed that they would be severely called to account by their master for their gross misconduct in the field, and, in fact, his apparently gracious dismissal of them was as ingenious a punishment as could have been devised. His display of his resources in the eyes of Sarbarah Khan was a hint that the emperor need not hope to reduce the place by mere persistence.

With the returned prisoners Abul Hasan sent to Aurangzib two messages, one written and the other verbal. The terms which he offered were extravagantly liberal, and gave Aurangzib the best possible opportunity of making peace with honour. Abul Hasan began by acknowledging that he was the emperor's vassal, or, in oriental phraseology, his slave. He besought forgiveness for any fault that he might have committed, and pointed out that he had already been severely punished. He then agreed to surrender the fortress on condition that he was appointed viceroy for the territories over which he and his ancestors had ruled as independent kings. He sought this favour, he said, on the ground that his people had already suffered much misery on account of the war, and he feared that an unsympathetic stranger would grievously oppress them by demanding imposts which they could not possibly pay. He desired, in short, to satisfy the emperor's demands from his own treasury, and save his people from the exactions of an imperial officer who would undoubtedly regard the conquered province as his special spoil, and would, after satisfying his master's demands, bleed the people to the utmost in order to satisfy his own. He then agreed to pay to the emperor a crore of rupees for every assault that the imperial troops had made on Golconda, and a like sum for every halt that they made within the territory of Golconda, on their return to Hindustan. He also offered to relieve the immediate needs of the besieging army with an offering of five or six hundred maunds of corn. These were terms which the emperor might well have accepted without disgrace, but with a ruthless disregard of the misery of his troops and a persistent determination to conquer what he affected to consider the pride of Abul Hasan, and to reduce Golconda by force of arms, he declined to listen to any message that might be sent. "If," he said, "Abul Hasan is, as he pretends to be, my vassal, the only course open to him is to come before me bound. Only thus can I listen to him." Henceforth there could be no question of peace, and the imperial army renewed their preparations for continuing the siege. Fifty thousand sacks, which were to be filled with earth and thrown into the ditch, were ordered from Berar. The refusal of the generous terms offered by Abul Hasan and the orders for the continuance of the siege, caused the liveliest discontent among the imperial troops, who, longing for rest and retirement after their prolonged and arduous campaigning, gave vent to their disappointment in complaints both loud and bitter.

On the nineteenth of Sha'ban the miners reported that the mines were ready to be exploded. It was accordingly ordered that the besiegers should man the trenches, advancing as close as possible to the walls, and should then utter loud shouts, in order to attract the garrison to the walls. The shouts had the desired effect, but Abdur Razzaq Lari guessed their object. He accordingly ordered countermines to be sunk as rapidly as possible. His operations were successful, and his miners abstracted from one mine both match and powder, and damaged the charges of the other two mines with water. Ignorant of the damage that had been done the besiegers fired one of the mines in preparation for an attempt to take the place by storm. But the powder in the direction of the fort was wet, and the mine consequently exploded in the wrong direction, killing over a thousand of the imperial troops, among whom were many officers of high rank. A scene of indescribable consternation and confusion ensued, and the garrison, seizing their opportunity, sallied forth and attacked the besiegers, capturing the trenches. After an obstinate fight the trenches were recaptured with much loss, but they were barely re-occupied when a second mine was fired, the effects of which were even more disastrous than those of the first. By the explosion itself and the stones which it threw up about two thousand of the imperial army were killed and wounded, and the explosion was followed up by the besieged with a second sortie, even more determined than the first. They were met by the Mughal commander, Ghazi-ud-din Khan, Firuz Jang, who was driven back with a loss of nearly three hundred and fifty men. So critical was the position of the imperial troops at this juncture that the emperor himself found it necessary to come to their relief with the reserves. As he advanced to the attack a heavy storm came on, the *nalas* filled rapidly, and the rain fell with such violence that it was impossible for the troops to manœuvre, and Aurangzib himself was repulsed. The principal battery was completely washed away, and the Deccanis, seeing the demoralisation of their assailants, poured forth from the fortress in ever increasing numbers. They again entered the trenches and rushed upon the siege batteries, capturing and carrying off several of the guns, and spiking those which they could not carry away. Having effected so much, they turned their attention to their own defences, and utilised the huge sandbags with which the ditch had for the second time been filled in repairing the breaches in the wall, thus, as Khafi Khan says, using the equivalent Persian proverb, killing two birds with one stone.

In the meantime, the imperial army, floundering in the heavy mud and impeded by the swollen *nalas*, were endeavouring to attack the fortress. They knew that one of the bastions had been battered to pieces. They did not know that the besieged had taken advantage of their successful attack on the trenches to repair the ruined bastion. When the attacking column advanced in the morning under a heavy fire, which carried destruction among their ranks, and neared their objective, the morning light disclosed no breach in the fortifications. Both Ni'mat Khan-i-Ali and Khafi Khan give an amusing account of the argument which ensued as to which bastion was the object of the attack. The argument so facetiously described by both authors was doubtless an accusation of treachery brought by the men against their leaders, met by them and their henchmen with an indignant denial. Many of the storming party believed that they had been betrayed, and led against the wrong bastion, and accused their leaders and those who were in the confidence of their leaders of having led them into a trap. The argument ended in a free fight, which was encouraged by the plaudits and delighted shouts of the garrison, who lined the walls and enjoyed the spectacle. This ridiculous conflict continued till nightfall, when the officers with much difficulty brought it to an end.

There still remained one mine to be fired, and the emperor, having directed that it should be fired the next morning, rode out to witness the spectacle, which was a miserable fiasco. This was the mine from which the besieged had removed the powder. A match was ignited, but the mine would not explode, and the miners were afraid to inspect the mine so closely as to discover what was wrong, but at last a spy brought information of what the besieged had done. The match had been cut, but sufficient was left to lead the miners to believe that the mine had not been tampered with. The emperor, bitterly disappointed, announced that the assault had been postponed to the next day, and returned to his tents.

The failure of the third mine was not the only important event of this eventful day. Firuz Jang, the commander-in-chief of the besieging force, was wounded in two places, and, as it thus became necessary to fill his place, the emperor's third son, Muhammad A'zam, was appointed to the command. At the same time Aurangzib issued a proclamation formally annexing to the empire the kingdom of Golconda. Its issue may seem to have been premature, seeing that the capital had not yet fallen, and that Abul Hasan still had troops of his own in the field besides his allies, the Marathas, but it was not in fact so, for the ultimate fate both of the fortress and of the kingdom was assured, and it was by no means too early for arrangements for the better administration of districts in which anarchy prevailed, all semblance of civil administration being of necessity wanting. The latest addition to the empire was styled *Daru-l-jihad-i-Haidarabad*, or Haidarabad, the seat of war. Mughal officers were appointed to collect the revenue and administer justice. The consideration which Hinduism had enjoyed in the Deccan for more than three centuries was changed to persecution, and Hindu temples in Haidarabad, now the headquarters of the Mughal administrators, were overthrown, a rigid system of police being inaugurated for the prevention of unlawful rites and unlawful amusements.

About this time Saff Shikan Khan was accused of collusion with the besieged and was thrown into prison, his property being confiscated. It was, however, very soon discovered that the accusation was entirely false, his accusers being some of his fellow-countrymen and co-religionists (he was a Persian and a *Shiah*) whose religious susceptibilities he had offended by an unguarded expression intended to convey to them his conviction that the siege ought to be prosecuted at all costs. Aurangzib had little regard for *Shiah* susceptibilities, and much for an officer whose opinions coincided with his own on the great question of the moment. Saff Shikan Khan was accordingly released from prison, and was placed in command of the artillery.

Those of Abul Hasan's *amirs* who still remained faithful to him now began to weary of the apparently interminable siege. They understood, too, by this time, that Aurangzib's determination was unalterable and must sooner or later attain its object. They began to forsake their master and join the emperor, and the deserters were, as on the former occasion, honoured with titles and commands. Abul Hasan was seriously alarmed at the extent of the defection, and in his panic was foolish enough to arrest and imprison Shaikh Minhaj, who was said to be wavering, and to confiscate his property. The action alienated the affection of the remnant that was left, and in a short time the only officers of any importance remaining in Golconda were Abdur Razzaq Lari and Abdullah Khan Pani, the Afghan. The loyalty of the latter was not proof against temptation, as will be seen, but Abdur Razzaq rose superior to all temptation. He was offered the command of six thousand horse, with high rank in the imperial army, but treated the offer with contempt. He produced the emperor's letter in which it was contained before the troops under his immediate command, and, after acquainting them with its contents, tore it up before them with gestures so contemptuous that the historian shrinks from describing them. Aurangzib, on hearing of the manner in which his message had been received, openly abused "the accursed Lari" for an obstinate fool, but nevertheless expressed in private the greatest admiration for his loyalty; as well he might, for of all who were engaged on either side in this siege Abdur Razzaq commands the most respect, whether for his incorruptible loyalty or for his indomitable valour.

By this time the ditch had again been filled up with sandbags and with the corpses of men and beasts, and assaults, none of which was successful, were frequent. But Aurangzib had now a surer means of effecting his purpose. Abdullah Khan Pani had already been won over, and all that remained to be done was to concoct a plan in the execution of which his assistance would be of service. Towards the end of the month Zi-Qa'dah, A. H. 1098 (October A. D. 1687), the siege having lasted for eight months, Ruhu-'llah Khan, employing as his agent a fellow-tribesman, possibly a kinsman, of Abdullah Khan, arranged with Abdullah that his post at the wicket gate should be insufficiently guarded on the night chosen for the assault, and that the alarm should not be given until the escalading party had effected an entry. The escalade was successfully carried out by Ruhu-'llah Khan,

Mukhtar Khan, Ranmast Khan, Saff Shikan Khan, and Jan Nisar Khan guided by Abdullah Khan in person. Muhammad A'zam, the commander-in-chief of the besieging army, was waiting, with the main body of his forces, at the gate nearest to the wicket gate, which was to be opened from within by the escalading party. But by the time that the latter had reached the main gate Abdur Razzaq Khan Lari, to whom the news that the Mughals were entering the fort had been conveyed, arrived on the scene. Aroused suddenly from his sleep the gallant soldier had no time to arm himself or to assemble his men. Seizing a naked sword in one hand and a shield in the other, he mounted a bare-backed horse, and, calling on all who were true to their salt to follow him, threw himself headlong upon the Mughals. His followers numbered no more than twelve, and with these he attacked all the force that the besiegers could bring into the field. The small but gallant band were soon separated one from another, but Abdur Razzaq threw himself into the midst of the emperor's troops and fought until he fell, covered with wounds from head to foot. The description of his valour given by the historian Khafi Khan, then serving in the Mughal army, will bear quotation :—" Like a drop of water flowing into the sea, or like a mote of the sunbeam pressing onward to assail the sun, he rushed upon the army, and with valour and bravery beyond mortal comprehension, fought with all the power of valiant manhood, shouting the while, 'My life, while it lasts, is an offering to my master, Abul Hasan.' At each moment he advanced a step farther forward amongst thousands who struck at him with their swords, until it might be said, so severe were his wounds, that he was fighting with his own blood. From the crown of his head to the sole of his foot he was covered with countless wounds, each one of which appeared to be mortal. But, since his hour had not arrived, he fell not until the gate of the citadel was reached, but gave way slowly, still fighting. He received twelve wounds in the face, so that the skin of his forehead fell as a veil over his eyes and nose, and when it was afterwards raised it was found that one of his eyes had been destroyed by a sword-cut, while the wounds on his body were in number like the stars of heaven. His horse, too, smitten with countless wounds, at last stood trembling, when Abdur Razzaq, his strength being now spent, dropped the reins and allowed it to bear him whither it would. It wandered to a garden near the citadel, known as *Nagina Bagh*, and there stood under a cocoanut palm, where Razzaq threw himself down. On the morning of the next day some of Husaini Beg's men, who chanced to be passing, saw him and identified him. Moved with generous pity for so valiant a foe they raised him, half-dead, on to a bed, and conveyed him with his horse and arms to his house, and his family and servants busied themselves in attending to his wounds. I have placed on record this account of a fraction of his valour. What more I have to say regarding the loyalty of this most valiant hero will, please God, be related hereafter."

In the behaviour of Abul Hasan, when he received the news that the Mughals had at length effected an entrance into the fortress, there was nothing to recall the craven flight from Haidarabad to Golconda. He first betook himself to his harem, where he was assiduous in calming the fears aroused by the news that the rule of the Qutb Shahi kings was over. Then, having bidden farewell to the ladies, he arrayed himself in his robes of state and repaired to his throne-room, the *diwan-i-khass*, where he took his seat, for the last time, upon his throne, and awaited the arrival of his unbidden guests. When his usual meal-time arrived, he commanded food to be brought. The meal had no sooner been ordered than Ruhu-'llah Khan, Mukhtar Khan, and their companions arrived. They saluted the last Qutb Shah in the usual form, and he, "abating not one jot of his kingly dignity," replied "*wa'alaikum as-salam.*" The king and the Mughal officers remained in converse till the morning, discoursing principally, it appears, on indifferent matters. The Mughal historian has nothing but praise for the carriage, behaviour, and dignified stoicism of the defeated monarch. When the meal which had been ordered was laid, the king invited the imperial officers to join him, an invitation which some accepted while others held aloof. Among the latter was Ruhu-'llah Khan, who was unable to contain his astonishment at the king's possessing any appetite for food at such a time. To him the king replied with quiet dignity that he trusted in God who had given him day by day his daily bread, that he was accustomed to eat at the hour at which this meal was served and that he saw no reason to forgo the enjoyment of the gifts of his Creator.

After his meal Abul Hasan arrayed himself in his jewels and mounted his horse, and was then conducted to the gate where Muhammad A'zam was waiting, in a small pavilion prepared for the purpose, to receive him. The king, removing his necklace of pearls, presented it to the prince who, after accepting it, received him kindly and did his best to console him in his affliction. He then conducted Abul Hasan to the emperor, who received him graciously, and treated him with due honour. The fallen king was shortly afterwards sent to Daulatabad, where he remained as a state prisoner, and was allowed every indulgence till his death.

The discovery of the wounded hero of the defence, Abdur Razzaq Khan Lari, by some of Husaini Beg's men, has already been mentioned. From his house, whither he had first been taken, he was carried to Ruhu-'llah Khan, with whom Saff Shikan Khan happened to be at the time. The brutal Saff Shikan Khan proposed that "the accursed Lari" should at once be beheaded, and that his head should be exposed over one of the gates of the fortress. Ruhu-'llah Khan had the grace to rebuke his ungenerous colleague, and saved the life of the captive, reporting the capture to the emperor, by whose orders two surgeons, a European and a Hindu, were appointed to have charge of him. The faithful servant's loyalty to his master moved the unwilling admiration of the conqueror, who remarked, with good reason, that if Abul Hasan had had one more servant like Abdur Razzaq, the capture of Golconda would have been a more difficult undertaking than it had proved to be. The remark was evidently levelled at the traitor Abdullah Khan Pani, but it is far from improbable that Aurangzib wished it to be laid to heart by his own officers, for there were few, if any, among them who merited the trust that Abul Hasan had been able to repose in Abdur Razzaq.

The two surgeons examined their patient and counted in his body nearly seventy wounds, besides which, they said, there were wounds over other wounds, which could not be counted. One of his eyes was destroyed, and though the other had not actually been injured it was feared that it would be impossible to save its sight. After thirteen days the wounded man was able to utter a few indistinct words. As soon as the emperor heard that he was able to speak he sent him a message to say that he was forgiven, and that if he would send for his eldest son,

Abdul Qadir, and such other of his sons as might be fit for service, they would be honoured with commands. The message also conveyed to Abdur Razzaq himself the offer of a command, which the wounded man respectfully declined. He had, he said, little hope of life, and even if he lived his shattered body could be of little service to the emperor, apart from the consideration that he regarded the short span of life still remaining to him as due to his master, Abul Hasan, for whom he would cheerfully undergo again all that he had suffered. Aurangzib, on receiving Abdur Razzaq's reply, displayed some petulance, but his displeasure was of short duration, and gave way to sincere admiration of the sufferer's inflexible devotion. Abdur Razzaq's scruples were at length overcome, and after his recovery, which, considering the condition of the healing art in those days, was little less than miraculous, he entered the emperor's service, having first obtained his old master's permission to do so, and all his personal property, except a small portion of it which had fallen into the hands of plunderers, was restored to him.

The spoils of Golconda were enormous, and the imperial treasury was enriched to the extent of 61,51,000 golden *huns*, Rs. 2,00,53,000, a large quantity of jewels and plate and 1,15,13,00,000 copper dams.

Thus, after eight months' duration, ended the siege of Golconda, and thus Aurangzib at length plucked the fruit for the ripening of which he had so long waited. Making his religion a pretext for his designs, he had, in contravention of that religion, sent into captivity two fellow-Muslim sovereigns, destroying the last vestige of rivalry to his authority. The Mughal empire had now well nigh reached its utmost extent, and though as yet perhaps the signs of that fearfully rapid decay which led to its disintegration in the course of the next century were barely apparent, they were none the less present. The Marathas were as yet far from the zenith of their power, but were already a thorn in the side of the emperor, whose bigotry fanned their patriotism and whose ceaseless warfare inured them to arms and hardship. The forerunners of those ambitious and turbulent *amirs* who became virtually independent rulers of the provinces which Aurangzib's enfeebled successors dared not withhold from them, and in whose hands the great Mughal himself, before another century had passed, became a puppet, were, indeed, serving the old *padishah* with indifferent loyalty and moderated zeal, but the end was not far off, and when in 1707 the last of the house of Timur who commands our respect, died, worn out with warfare, the vast empire which he ruled was already in danger of falling to pieces with its own weight. Whether the integrity of the empire could have been maintained despite the degeneracy of the later descendents of the house of Timur is very doubtful, but there is no doubt that the maintenance of the kingdoms of Bijapur and Golconda as states in subordinate alliance with the empire would have been the most effective check to its enemies, the Marathas.

CHAPTER XII.

THE CAPITAL OF THE DECCAN.

The city of Haidarabad lies among the trees on the south bank of the Musi river, a city, " the like of which for beauty and cleanliness, is not to be found in the whole of Hindustan, east, west, south or north. Its compass is near five leagues, and its bazars, unlike those of other cities of India, are laid out on a fixed plan and are spacious and clean, and through them run water channels beside which grow shady trees."

Firishta's description of Haidarabad is somewhat highly coloured, but the situation of the city is undeniably beautiful. Of its aspect from the hill on which the Falaknuma Palace now stands, the *Kuh-i-Tur*, or Mount Sinai, of Qutb Shahi days, Colonel Meadows Taylor writes: " From one favourite point of view of mine the city lies stretched before you, the graceful Char Minar or gate* of the four minarets in its centre; the gigantic Mecca mosque standing out nobly; while the large tank lies at your feet, and the bold rock of the fort of Golconda rises in the distance. From hence, a rising sun gradually lighting up every object in the clear morning air, and the glowing, glittering landscape terminating in the tender blue of the distance, (the scene) is inexpressibly beautiful."

The city owes none of its interest to antiquity, for it is little more than three centuries old. In 1591 Muhammad Quli Qutb Shah, the fifth king of the Qutb Shahi dynasty of Golconda, grew weary of his fortress capital, which was then so overcrowded with habitations as to be both unhealthy and unpleasant as a place of residence. While hunting one day on the south bank of the river Musi he was attracted by the fresh and green appearance of the site on which the city of Haidarabad now stands, about six miles from the fortress of Golconda, and selected it as the cite of his new capital. He called his city at first Bhagnagar, after a favourite Hindu mistress, Bhag Mati, to whom he was much devoted, but, in later years, after her death, he grew ashamed of the infatuation which had led him to name his capital after a light o' love, and in an access of piety re-named it Haidarabad, or the city of Ali, the Lion of God; but the name of Bhágnagar is not yet forgotten.

* The Char Minar building is not, however, a gate.

The first work taken in hand was the laying out of four bazars, at the entrance of each of which a great arch was erected on the principal road, the space within the arches being designated the *Charkaman*, or "four arches," which name it still retains. The arches are large, plain Pathan arches covered with stucco, possessing neither beauty or interest.

To the south of this space was erected the Char Minar, already mentioned, which is to this day the most conspicuous object in the city of Haidarabad, and is represented as such on the obverse of the modern Haidarabad rupee. The Char Minar is a large building, square in plan, having an arch in each of its faces and a lofty decagonal minaret at each of its angles. The minarets are surmounted by small domes with gilt terminals, and each is surrounded by three galleries, two single and one double, of the typical Qutb Shahi pattern. The parapet of the building is adorned with panels of lattice work, in great variety of design, and below it runs a small arcade. Next comes an ornamental cornice, and below this again a larger arcade, and another ornamental cornice. The Char Minar was originally designed as a college, or the central hall of a college, but now does duty as a central police station for the city.

One of the earliest buildings to be taken in hand by a devout Muhammadan sovereign founding a new city in the *jami masjid*, or principal mosque, where all the inhabitants may meet for the general Friday prayers. This was founded in A.H. 1006 (A.D. 1597-98) as a Persian inscription over the gateway informs us. Most visitors to Haidarabad, misled by inaccurate guides and guide-books, consider the huge mosque now known as the Mecca *masjid*, undoubtedly the finest mosque in the city, to be the *jami masjid*, but this is not so. The far less pretentious building, with a somewhat mean entrance opening on the eastern side of the main street of the city, a short distance to the north of the Char Minar, was built as the *jami masjid*, and has remained so since it was founded, in spite of the superior size and magnificence of the Mecca *masjid*.

The next work to be undertaken was the throwing of a bridge over the river Musi, to connect the new city on its south bank with the old fortress capital of Golconda. This bridge still exists, and is known as the old bridge. It is the westernmost of the four bridges which now span the river between Haidarabad and its northern suburbs, and is carried on twenty-three pointed arches. Over it runs the old high road from the north-western gate of the city, through the suburb of Karwan to the principal gate of Golconda. The building of the bridge was followed by the building of a hospital and public baths, and the king's architects then set to work to design the royal palace, which was built on some open ground to the east of the Char Minar, probably the site now occupied by the Nizam's palace known as the *Purani Haveli*, though the present palace, despite its name, is not that built by Muhammad Quli Qutb Shah. An ornamental cistern called the *Gulzar Hauz*, or "cistern of the rose garden," was constructed at the same time. This cistern still exists in the centre of the *Char kaman*, but there is little in its surroundings that recalls a rose garden. The *Dad Mahall*, or hall of justice, a building which was unfortunately destroyed by fire early in the eighteenth century, when Ibrahim Khan was *subahdar* of the Deccan, was also built at the same time. Another building of the same date which cannot now be traced was the *Nadi Mahall*, or river palace. From the description given of it it probably occupied part of the ground on which the palace of the Nawab Salar Jang now stands. Gardens were laid out, other public buildings were constructed, and the nobles of the kingdom were encouraged to build palaces for themselves in the new city, which, however, remained destitute of one of the most important features of an eastern capital of those days, for it was not enclosed by walls, the present walls not having been built until after the kingdom of Golconda had fallen into the hands of the Mughals. It was for this reason that the later Qutb Shahi kings, while preferring Muhammad Quli's city as a place of residence, invariably took refuge in Sultan Quli's old fortress on the slightest indication of trouble.

Muhammad Quli Qutb Shah died in 1612, immediately after his new city had been further adorned by a large tank on its eastern side. This was the work of his prime minister, Mir Jumla, after whom it is named. It is now much silted up, and adds nothing either to the beauty or the salubrity of Haidarabad.

Muhammad Quli left no son, and was succeeded by his nephew Muhammad Quth Shah, who had married Muhammad Quli's daughter,

Hayat Bakhsh Begam. Muhammad still further beautified the city by laying out gardens; but his principal work was the foundation of the magnificent Mecca *masjid*, one of the finest mosques in India. An interesting legend is connected with its foundation. Muhammad Qutb Shah resolved that the foundation stone of the mosque which he intended to build to the honour of God should be laid by none but a person of the highest sanctity, and the test which he proposed was sufficiently severe. He called upon all the doctors of religion at his court to select one of their number, or any other person, who, since coming to years of discretion, had never omitted the recital of the midnight prayers, one of the most wearisome of the observances of Islam, and an exercise which is not enjoined as a duty, but is regarded rather as a work of supererogation. Nobody who fulfilled this test could be found, and at length the king came forward and swore that he had never omitted the observance of this office. He then raised a selected stone, shouldered it, and laid it in its place. His example was followed by the nobles and learned men of his court, and the building of the Mecca *masjid* proceeded, but only for a short time. A soothsayer predicted that the completion of the mosque would be the signal for the downfall of the Qutb Shahi dynasty, and the work which had been undertaken under such auspicious conditions languished and finally ceased. The prediction, as will be seen, was falsified, for, so far from the completion of the mosque being the signal for the downfall of the dynasty, the downfall of the dynasty was the signal for the completion of the mosque.

Muhammad Qutb Shah had some idea of rivalling his predecessor as the founder of a city, as is indicated by a mosque and some inchoate buildings about four miles to the east of Haidarabad. The projected city was surrounded by a parapet and a ditch, of which traces still exist, and one historian tells us that Sultannagar, as the new city was called, was intended to rival Golconda. This can hardly have been the case, for its site possesses no natural advantages. It is far inferior to that of Golconda as a military position, and in no way superior to that of Haidarabad in respect of salubrity, beauty, or convenience. Muhammad Qutb Shah either repented of his project or died before his city could be completed, for it was never inhabited, and its very name is now forgotten. The passer-by who inquires what the buildings are is informed that they are "an old fort," and if he should be sufficiently curious to seek for more definite information the answer will be repeated. It is probable that the nobles who had been induced or compelled by Muhammad Quli to build for themselves palaces in Haidarabad set their faces against his successor's attempt to provide a third capital for his kingdom.

Muhammad Qutb Shah died in 1626 and was succeeded by his son Abdullah Qutb Shah, during whose reign the hand of the Mughal began to fall heavily on the kingdom of Golconda. Mir Muhammad Said, entitled Mir Jumla, was prime minister during the early years of Abdullah's reign, and it was rumoured that he was on terms of intimacy with the queen mother, Hayat Bakhsh Begam, a masterful lady who managed both her young son and his kingdom, and never forgot that she was the daughter of a king, the wife of a king, and the mother of a king. Mir Jumla was appointed to the command in the Karnatak, and there won much credit for himself and much territory for his master, but his success was his undoing in Golconda, for Abdullah Qutb Shah feared that the conqueror of so much territory might aspire to the throne, and Mir Jumla's reputed *liaison* with Abdullah's mother, who had a hereditary claim to the throne, only served to intensify the king's apprehension. Abdullah began to betray his suspicions in his treatment of his minister and Mir Jumla wrote secretly to Aurangzib, who at that time dwelt in Aurangabad as his father's viceroy for the Mughal provinces in the Deccan, offering him his services. The offer was accepted and Mir Jumla was privately informed that he had been made a commander of 5,000 horse, and his son, Muhammad Amir, a commander of 2,000 horse in the imperial service. At the proper time Aurangzib summoned his two new officers to his presence, and sent orders to Abdullah Qutb Shah to place no obstacles in the way of their joining him. It is doubtful whether these orders ever reached Abdullah Qutb Shah, but, however this may have been, he received information of the communications between his officers and Aurangzib, and confiscated Mir Jumla's property and confined Muhammad Amir in Golconda. This was regarded by Aurangzib as an act of defiance, and in 1656 he set forth for Haidarabad to punish Abdullah. Abdullah, in order to appease his powerful enemy, sent Muhammad Amir and his mother to Aurangzib's camp, but, in order to retain his hold over Mir Jumla's family, still refused to deliver their property to them. Aurangzib accordingly pressed on, and, as he neared Haidarabad, Abdullah fled to Golconda with his ladies, leaving five or six thousand horse and twelve thousand foot to defend the capital, whence he had been unable to remove the valuable furniture of his palace. The next morning he sent an envoy, Muhammad Nasir, to Aurangzib with a box of jewels, in the hope that this offering would induce the invader to retire, but before Muhammad Nasir could reach Aurangzib, the Mughal troops had encountered the force left in Haidarabad by Abdullah, had compelled it to flee for refuge to Golconda, and had plundered the city of Haidarabad. Hakim Nizam-ud-din was then sent by Abdullah to Aurangzib with two chests of jewels, two elephants with trappings of silver, and four horses with trappings of gold. These were shortly followed by eleven elephants, sixty horses, and the rest of Muhammad Amin's property, but Aurangzib had not come to Haidarabad with the sole object of recovering his new servant's property, and he now advanced to Golconda and, after examining the fortifications, opened a regular siege. Some fighting took place in which Abdullah's troops were worsted and the siege was pressed on more vigorously. Abdullah now became seriously alarmed, and sent his mother, Hayat Bakhsh Begam, to intercede with Aurangzib. The royal lady fell at the prince's feet and covered them with her hair, besought him to pardon the offences of her son, offered him a crore of rupees as an indemnity, and also promised Abdullah Qutb Shah's second daughter in marriage to Muhammad Sultan, Aurangzib's eldest son, who was in his father's camp. Peace was now concluded on these conditions, coupled with the proviso that Muhammad Sultan, who was married at once to Abdullah's daughter, should be formally recognized as heir to the kingdom of Golconda, and Aurangzib left for Bijapur, capturing on his way the fortresses of Kaliani and Bidar. The Deccan was now unexpectedly relieved of the disturbing presence of Aurangzib, who hastened back to Hindustan on receiving the news of the emperor's illness in order that he might take his part in the contest for the throne. The temporary respite afforded by Aurangzib's return to Hindustan did not deceive Abdullah Qutb Shah, who perceived that his dynasty was tottering to its fall and that when his determined enemy was seated on the throne of Delhi he would again turn his attention to the two remaining kingdoms of the Deccan. Abdullah placed upon his seal and his coinage the pathetic legend :—

ختم بالخیر والسعادة

" It has come to a good and auspicious conclusion."

The motto is usually referred to his prescience of the fall of Golconda, but it appears probable that he was comforting himself with the idea that the kingdom would fall into the hands of the Mughals by peaceful succession, and not by conquest. This hope was not destined to be fulfilled, for Muhammad Sultan predeceased Abdullah.

When Abdullah Qutb Shah died in 1672 without a male heir the competitors for the kingdom were his two surviving sons-in-law, Sayyid Mir Ahmad and Abul Hasan. The choice fell on the latter, who, besides being Abdullah's son-in-law, was descended from the royal family, and Sayyid Mir Ahmad was imprisoned and put to death.

Nothing noteworthy occurred during Abul Hasan's reign until near its conclusion. The king, who had been a *darvish*, now gave himself up to sensual pleasures, and left the affairs of the kingdom in the hands of two Brahmans, Madanna and Venkanna, who governed the country in accordance with Hindu principles and went so far as to insult the religion of Islam and its professors. Reports of the manner in which the administration of Golconda was conducted reached the ears of Aurangzib and confirmed him in his intention of extinguishing the Qutb Shahi dynasty. How this was effected is described elsewhere. Golconda fell in 1687, Abul Hasan was taken and sent to Daulatabad, where he ended his days in captivity twelve years later, and Haidarabad became the headquarters of a province of the empire of Delhi.

Aurangzib, as we have seen, found the great mosque of Haidarabad incomplete when he captured Golconda, and one of his first acts was to complete it. It was finished in A.H. 1104 (A.D. 1692) as is recorded over its principal gateway. The mosque is a huge rectangular building of stone, standing in a spacious courtyard. Its façade is composed of five simple Pathan arches, the central arch being slightly larger than the rest, and above the arches runs a deep cornice, above which the building is completed by a range of ornamental *kanguras* or crenellations. At either end of the façade and adjoining the building stands a squat minaret, surrounded at the level of the parapet of the mosque by a gallery, immediately above which each minaret terminates in a dome. This mosque, though its minarets have the galleries which are characteristic of Qutb Shahi architecture, is distinguished from most other buildings in that style by being of stone undisfigured by stucco or by any of the tawdry and paltry decoration to which stucco so readily lends itself. Next to the Char Minar it is the most conspicuous object in Haidarabad. In the courtyard before the mosque are the tombs of the later Nizams of Haidarabad. It is commonly believed that this mosque is called the Mecca *masjid* owing to its design having been copied from that of a mosque at Mecca, but this is not the case. It has been called the Mecca *masjid* because, like the holy places of Mecca, it is said to never to be empty of worshippers.

After the annexation of the kingdom of Golconda by Aurangzib succeeding *subahdars* attempted to administer the new province of Haidarabad, but were unable to keep in check the plunderers who wasted the country and devoured the substance of its people. The first was Jan Sipar Khan, and the next his son Rustam Dil Khan, who was followed by Muzaffar Khan. Then came Yusuf Khan, more successful than the others, who died and was succeeded by Ibrahim Khan, during whose term of office the *Dad Mahall*, one of the finest buildings of the Qutb Shahi kings, was burnt down without an effort being made to save it. Mubariz Khan, who was appointed in the place of Ibrahim Khan, was originally on friendly terms with the great Asaf Jah Nizam-ul-Mulk, one of the most powerful nobles of the empire, who, in 1723, held the governorship of the province of Malwa; but when the *amirs* in power at Delhi intrigued to overthrow Asaf Jah they succeeded in detaching Mubariz Khan from his interest by promising to him, in the event of his overthrowing their enemy, the viceroyalty of the Deccan, which was well known to be the object of Asaf Jah's ambition. Mubariz Khan accordingly marched northwards from Haidarabad to meet Asaf Jah, who endeavoured to dissuade him from an appeal to arms, but failing in his negotiations met him at Shakarkhelda in Berar, where he defeated and slew him in October 1724. By this victory Asaf Jah became ruler of the Deccan, and scarcely acknowledged even a nominal dependence on Delhi. His descendants succeeded him and the present ruler of Haidarabad, Mir Sir Mahbub Ali Khan Bahadur, is the ninth of his line to occupy the *masnad* of Haidarabad.

The most remarkable work in the neighbourhood of Haidarabad is the Husain Sagar, an artificial lake with a circumference of nearly eleven miles, which lies immediately to the south of the British cantonment of Secunderabad and between it and the city. This lake is older than Haidarabad, having been constructed by Ibrahim Qutb Shah, who died in 1580, the father of Muhammad Quli Qutb Shah, who founded Haidarabad. The Mir Jumla tank which lies under the western wall of Haidarabad, has already been mentioned. This tank, which was probably at one time an imposing sheet of water and by the margin of which Kam Bakhsh, the youngest son of Aurangzib, encamped when he was attempting to assert in the Deccan his independence of his brother Bahadur Shah, who had succeeded to the imperial throne, is now silted up and is little more than an expanse of malodorous mud.

Yet a third artificial lake calls for notice. This is the Mir Alam lake, the surroundings of which are even more picturesque than those of the Husain Sagar. This lake was formed about a hundred years ago under the orders of Abul Qasim Mir Alam, minister of the State for English affairs, and founder of the fortunes of the Salar Jang family in Haidarabad, by closing with a dam a valley to the west of the city which runs down in a north-westerly direction towards the river Musi. This dam, which is the work of French engineers, is a wonderful piece of masonry. Its outline follows the arc of a circle with the convex side towards the water, and the dam is composed of a series of horizontal arches the extrados of each of which resists the pressure of the water. What would be the feet of the arches, were they upright, form buttresses which strengthen the whole structure. The branches of the lake run up into the small valleys of the hills which enclose its catchment area, and the scenery is picturesque in the extreme.

On a hill to the east of the city stands the tomb of the Nizam's famous French officer Raymond, whose corps was disbanded in 1798 at the instance of Lord Wellesley. The tomb is a simple and massive obelisk without any inscription other than the monogram J. R. and stands on a high plinth on the summit of the hill. Immediately to the west of it and on the same plinth is a shrine which contains the adventurer's *viscera*. Monsieur Raymond is developing by degrees into a saint under the title of Musa Rahmu, and his memory is honoured by an annual *urus* or festival at his tomb, on the occasion of which a bottle of French brandy and a cock are presented as acceptable offerings to his *manes*. His profession of the Christian religion is nevertheless indicated by a series of large crosses, painted in red around the plinth. The festival of Musa Rahmu is an interesting study in hero-worship and the development of popular religion.

To the south of Haidarabad stands a high hill already mentioned as that from which Colonel Meadows Taylor obtained his favourite view of the city and the surrounding country. This is now occupied by Falaknuma Castle, a modern palace built by the late Sir Vikar-ul-Umara, formerly the Nizam's minister, from whom it was purchased some twelve years ago by the present Nizam. The exterior of the building possesses no architectural merit, but it is beautifully situated and its marble entrance hall and staircase are extremely handsome. The Nizam does not occupy this, the finest of his palaces, but places it at the disposal of guests whom he desires to honour. Its most distinguished occupants have been the present Prince and Princess of Wales.

CHAPTER XIII.

THE SECOND MARATHA WAR IN THE DECCAN.

I.—ASSAYE.

EARLY in the year 1803 the great Maratha chiefs of Central India were seriously alarmed by an event which directly threatened their independence. Baji Rao Peshwa, driven from his capital by the rebel Jaswant Rao Holkar, was a fugitive in British territory, a rival set up by the rebel occupied his place, and there was no prospect of a restoration but by the help of British bayonets. The price of that help was heavy, being no less than the sacrifice of independence and the acceptance of the position of a feudatory of the East India Company, but the fugitive had no choice but to pay it. Accordingly, on the last day of 1802, he signed the treaty of Bassein, whereby he surrendered his independence as the price of assistance, and in May, 1803, he was reinstated on the *masnad* at Poona, while Holkar retired to Malwa. Meanwhile Daulat Rao Sindhya and Raghuji Bhonsla had been in communication regarding the action to be taken by them as a protest against the treaty of Bassein, for they contested the right of the Peshwa to conclude such a treaty without consulting the other members of the Maratha confederacy. Sindhya was at Burhanpur, and, though he endeavoured to conceal his preparations, his attitude was so threatening that he was called upon by the Governor-General, Lord Wellesley, to declare his intentions; to which demand he replied that he would answer after he had met Raghuji Bhonsla. Shortly after this Sindhya and Bhonsla joined forces and advanced southwards into the Nizam's dominions. By this time Major-General Arthur Wellesley, who had been detached from the Madras army with 8,000 infantry and 1,700 cavalry, and Colonel Stevenson with the Haidarabad Subsidiary Force, were ready to act against the allies, who had failed to induce Holkar to join them. In July Wellesley was encamped in the neighbourhood of Ahmadnagar, the old capital of the Nizam Shahi dynasty, Stevenson being on the Godavari; and by the beginning of August the allies had advanced to Malkapur in Berar. General Wellesley, who had full power as agent to the Governor-General, his brother, demanded from Sindhya and Bhonsla a statement of their intentions, and received the reply that they wished for peace but desired to discuss some details of the treaty of Bassein. Wellesley replied that if they wished for peace they should return to their own territories. This they declined to do, and the British Resident, Colonel Collins, was dismissed from the camp at Malkapur on August 3rd with their refusal, which was tantamount to a declaration of war.

On August 8, Wellesley stormed the town of Ahmadnagar and three days later the fort surrendered. The opening scene of the second Maratha war was thus described by a Maratha chief residing in the British camp, in a letter to his friends at Poona:—"The English are a strange people, and their General is a wonderful man. They came here in the morning, looked at the Pettah wall, walked over it, killed all the garrison, and then turned in to breakfast. Who can resist such men as these?" From this graphic account of the assault on Ahmadnagar it must not be inferred that the city was captured without loss to the British. The 78th Highlanders alone lost two officers and twelve men killed and one officer and five men wounded. The army lost in all 140 men Of the two officers of the 78th killed one was Captain Thomas Mackenzie-Humberston, heir male, after his brother Lord Seaforth, of the great house of Kintail. On August 29 Wellesley advanced as far as Aurangabad, the allies being encamped at Jalna, and on his approach they advanced in a south-easterly direction, thus threatening his communications with the south, whence he received his supplies. To prevent the plunder of the country and to cover his communications Wellesley marched to the south bank of the Godavari: the enemy then retired to the north and Stevenson occupied Jalna. On September 21, the Maratha army was encamped at Bhokardan, and Wellesley and Stevenson met at Badnapur and arranged to march against the enemy by separate routes and attack him in concert. On the 23rd Wellesley reached the village of Nalniya where he was about to encamp when he received information that the enemy was encamped on the Kailna river within six miles of him. "With great prudence and decision, founded on a remarkable discernment of the character of his enemy, he instantly resolved on attacking them without waiting for Colonel Stevenson. Had General Wellesley hesitated, the enemy's infantry would have moved off, their horse would probably have been encouraged to attack his baggage and annoy his camp, the service must have been prolonged and by one day's delay or hesitation, a new character might have been given to the war."

Leaving his baggage in Nalniya, Wellesley advanced with his force against the enemy, riding in advance with the cavalry to reconnoitre. On reaching some rising ground he saw the whole of the Maratha army drawn up in line along the Kailna. The enemy had over 50,000 men, of whom more than 30,000 were horse and 10,500 were Sindhya's regular infantry, with 128 guns. On the right of the line were Sindhya's irregular cavalry, the centre was occupied by Bhonsla's irregular troops, and on the left were Sindhya's regular infantry, a fine body of troops dressed, armed, and accoutred like the Company's sepoys and trained by European officers: the infantry were formed in 17 battalions drawn up in three brigades. Alison thus describes the appearance of the Maratha army:—"The sight was enough to appal the stoutest heart: thirty thousand horse, in one magnificent mass, crowded the right; a dense army of infantry, powerfully supported by artillery, formed the centre and left; the gunners were beside their pieces, and a hundred pieces of cannon, in front of the line, stood ready to vomit forth death upon the assailants. Wellesley paused for a moment, impressed but not daunted by the sight.......But feeling at once that retreat in presence of so prodigious a force of cavalry was impossible, and that the most audacious course was, in such circumstances, the most prudent, he ordered an immediate attack."

To meet this army Wellesley could bring into the field no more than 4,700 men, of whom about 1,500 were Europeans, and 26 guns. The corps which had the honour of serving in the action were H. M.'s 19th Light Dragoons, 74th Highlanders, and 78th Highlanders (Ross-shire Buffs), the 4th, 5th, and 7th Madras Native Cavalry, detachments of Madras and Bombay Artillery, the first battalions of the 2nd, 4th, 8th and 10th, and both battalions of the 12th Madras Native Infantry.* The 1-2nd Native Infantry guarded the baggage at Nalniya and the 1-12th appears to have been on rearguard duty.

*These regiments are now represented as follows:—the 1-2nd by the 62nd Punjabis, the 1-4th by the 64th Pioneers, the 1-12th by the 83rd Wallajahbad Light Infantry and the 2-12th, by the 84th Punjabis. The first battalions of the 8th, and 10th, were the late 8th and 10th Regiments of Madras Infantry.

As General Wellesley approached the enemy for the purpose of reconnoitring their position they opened a cannonade, the first gun of which, fired at 1-20 P.M., killed one of his escort. He was now in front of the enemy's right, but resolved to attack their left, as an attack on their right could only have resulted in the dispersal of the irregular cavalry, and the enemy could not be effectually defeated until the regular infantry and the guns were routed and captured. He therefore ordered his force to march towards the enemy's left flank while the staff were employed in searching for a ford by which the Kailna could be crossed. An unguarded ford was found beyond the enemy's left flank, near the fort of Pimpalgaon, and the troops, who had suffered some loss from the enemy's artillery fire during their flank march across his front, effected the passage of the river. The Marathas now for the first time perceived Wellesley's design, and changed position so that their right rested on the Kailna, where their left had formerly been, while their left was withdrawn to the village of Assaye on the Juah, which was strongly held by infantry and artillery, the first line extending across the ground between the two rivers. Wellesley, after the passage of the river, drew up his troops in three lines nearly parallel to and about 500 yards distant from the enemy's position. In the first line were the picquets, four twelve-pounders, the 1-8th and 1-10th Native Infantry, and the 78th Highlanders; in the second which extended beyond the right flank of the first, were the 74th Highlanders and the 2-12th and 1-4th Native Infantry; and in the third, which again extended beyond the right flank of the second, were the 4th Native Cavalry, the 19th Light Dragoons, and the 5th and 7th Native Cavalry. The picquets, on the right of the first line, were named as the battalion of direction, and Wellesley, at 2-45 P.M., ordered the infantry to advance as quickly as possible and charge with the bayonet. It was discovered shortly afterwards that the picquets were not advancing as directed, and that the guns could not proceed owing to casualties among the bullocks. To correct the alignment it was necessary to halt the first line, which had hitherto been partly protected by a depression in the ground but had now reached a ridge. The second line moved up and the troops, halted on the rising ground, offered a mark for the enemy's artillery. The 74th Highlanders, who were on the right of the line, suffered most severely from a fire of grape and round shot, and were immediately afterwards charged by a large body of Maratha horse, led by Sindhya in person. The British Cavalry were then ordered forward, and the 19th Light Dragoons, accompanied by the 4th Native Cavalry "passed through the broken but invincible 74th, whose very wounded joined in cheering them as they went on, cut in and routed the horse and dashed on at the infantry and guns. Never did cavalry perform better service or contribute more to the success of a battle." Meanwhile Wellesley had ridden up to one of the native corps in the first line, and cheered them on. The second order to advance was received with loud cheers, and the three battalions of the first line, followed by the 1-4th, advanced in quick time upon the enemy with great steadiness and determination.

The 78th Highlanders, on coming within 150 yards of the enemy's first line, withdrew their advanced centre sergeant and prepared to charge. The battalion opposed to them fired a volley, and the 78th ported arms and advanced at the double, whereupon the enemy's infantry opposed to them broke and fled. The 78th pushed on and fired, and, coming to the charge, overtook and bayoneted some of the enemy, doing great execution among the gunners, who stood stoutly to their guns, and at about the same time the 1-10th Native Infantry closed with the enemy in gallant style. The 78th Highlanders now halted to complete their files and restore order.

After the defeat of the enemy's first line the British troops found his second line, which had not changed front with the first, unbroken. It lay nearly at right angles to the position of the first, following the line of the river Juah. Wellesley now had to change front to the right, the pivot being the 74th Highlanders, near the village of Assaye. The 78th Highlanders were on the extreme left of the line, and were consequently the last to reach their new position, on attaining which they found their left threatened by a body of the enemy's best cavalry, while a galling fire of grape and round shot harassed them from their right and from the rear, where several of the enemy's gunners who had at first feigned death, had repossessed themselves of the guns of the first line, and were turning them on the rear of the British army. They stood their ground with great steadiness, awaiting orders, until the British Cavalry came up and drove off the Maratha horse, which were threatening their left. The 78th Highlanders and the 7th Native Cavalry now moved to the rear and charged the guns of the enemy's first line, which were once again in action. This was a most arduous task, and the 78th had frequently to change their front and attack successive bodies of the enemy. Some of the enemy's light troops, which had been engaged in plundering, now appeared on the field, but fled at the approach of the Mysore horse. The second line of the Marathas now began to retire, at first in good order. One brigade was charged by the 19th Light Dragoons, at the head of whom Colonel Maxwell was killed. The retreat of the enemy soon became a rout, and they were forced into the Juah at the point of the bayonet and charged by the cavalry as they reached the opposite bank. The enemy's cavalry hovered about for some time, but the battle had been decided by the utter defeat of the infantry, and at about half-past four the firing ceased and the Marathas blew up their tumbrils and fled. The British Cavalry, owing to the part they had played in the battle, were unable to pursue, and the Marathas, after plundering their own dead, their camp, and their bazar, retreated along the Juah for about ten miles and halted, but no sooner did they move again than the retreat became a disorderly flight. They descended the Ajanta Ghat into Khandesh and made for Burhanpur, where they were described as having no artillery nor any body of men that looked like a battalion, while the roads were strewn with wounded and dying men. Seven stand of colours and 98 guns, besides a few recovered from the Juah river, where they were abandoned, fell into the hands of the victors. The victory was hardly won, the British force having more than one-third of its number either killed or wounded. Of the three British corps engaged the 74th Highlanders suffered most severely, having been exposed to the heavy artillery fire of the enemy's left. The 78th Highlanders, who half a century later won the title of the Saviours of India, suffered less severely, but the 19th Light Dragoons lost their Colonel and many officers and men.

The loss of the enemy was very heavy. One thousand two hundred were found dead on the field, and the whole neighbourhood was covered with their wounded. Yadav Rao Bhashkar, Sindhya's minister, and the chief instigator of the war, was severely wounded and died a few days afterwards, and Colonel Dorsan, the principal French officer in Sindhya's service, was killed. Raghuji Bhonsla, ever a coward, fled at the commencement of the action, and Sindhya did not tarry long. The irregular cavalry behaved disgracefully, but the credit of the Maratha troops was to some extent redeemed by the obstinate valour of the artillery and most of the regular infantry.

Such was the battle of Assaye, a feat of arms which deserves to be remembered for all time.

II.—Argaum.

After the battle of Assaye Sindhya and Raghuji Bhonsla fled across the Narbada, pursued at first by Stevenson. As they turned westward General Wellesley halted to the south of the Ajanta Ghat to prevent a descent on Poona while Stevenson, under Wellesley's orders, abandoned the pursuit and marched against Burhanpur, which he captured, and then against Asirgarh, which fortress he reduced by October 21. The confederates, on receiving intelligence of Stevenson's movements, prepared to follow him, in order to protect Burhanpur and Asirgarh, but Wellesley marched northwards and descended the Ajanta Ghat, whereupon Sindhya halted while Raghuji Bhonsla, who had left him, marched southwards. Wellesley then again withdrew to Aurangabad, in order to cover Haidarabad, and Raghuji Bhonsla retraced his steps towards his own dominions. Wellesley followed him and descended the *ghat* at Rajura with the object of supporting and covering Stevenson. Meanwhile Sindhya had made overtures of peace, and had succeeded in obtaining for himself an armistice on the condition that he should occupy a position 20 *kos* to the east of Ellichpur and forage still further to the eastward. The armistice did not include Raghuji Bhonsla, who had made no overtures.

Raghuji Bhonsla's army was encamped by this time at Argaon (Argaum), a village near Akot in Berar, under the command of his brother, Vyankaji Bhonsla, and Sindhya, disregarding the terms of the armistice, had his cavalry within five miles of the position. By November 28 Stevenson was within a short distance of the Maratha armies and halted in order to allow Wellesley to come up. Sindhya's agents tried to dissuade Wellesley from attacking the confederates, but he explained that no armistice had been granted to Bhonsla, and that the armistice which had been granted to Sindhya was at an end as its terms had been broken, and he added that he would "certainly attack the enemies of the Company wherever he should find them."

On November 28 Wellesley joined Stevenson at Hatti Andora, and on the following day marched towards the enemy and selected Pathardi as the site of his camp. As the troops approached Pathardi, bodies of Maratha cavalry appeared in their front, and the Mysore cavalry were sent against them. Wellesley led out the infantry picquets to support the Mysore cavalry and to take up the ground for the encampment, and, as he advanced, he saw the armies of the confederates, a long line of infantry, cavalry, and artillery, drawn up on the plain of Argaon, about six miles from Pathardi. The day was now far advanced, but Wellesley determined to attack at once. The Maratha armies, though nearly as numerous as at Assaye, were neither so well disciplined nor so well appointed, and their artillery consisted of no more than thirty-eight guns. Their position was thus described by Wellesley in his despatch to his brother, the Governor-General:—

"The enemy's infantry and guns were in the left of their centre, with a body of cavalry on their left. Sindhya's army; consisting of one very heavy body of cavalry, was on the right, having upon its right a body of Pindaris and other light troops. Their line extended above five miles, having in their rear the village and extensive gardens and enclosures of Argaum, and in their front a plain, which, however, was much cut by water courses, etc."

The troops engaged at Argaon were H. M.'s 19th Light Dragoons. 74th Highlanders, 78th Highlanders, (Ross-shire Buffs), and 94th Foot, the Company's Artillery, the 3rd, 4th, 5th, 6th, and 7th Madras Native Cavalry, and the 1-2nd, 2-2nd, 1-3rd, 1-4th, 1-6th, 2-7th, 1-8th, 2-9th, 1-10th, 1-11th, and 2-12th Madras Native Infantry.* The infantry were drawn up in one line with the 78th on the right, having the 74th on its immediate left, and the 94th on the extreme left of the line. The cavalry were formed in a second line, the regular cavalry being on the right and the Mughal and Mysore horse on the left. The right of the line was somewhat thrown forward, in order that the first blow might be struck at the enemy's left.

*Of these regiments the 1-3rd are represented by the 63rd Palamcottah Light Infantry, the 1-6th by the 66th Punjabis, and the 1-11th by the 81st Pioneers.

As the lines were forming at a distance of about 1,200 yards from the enemy the latter opened a cannonade, which did no actual damage, but threw nearly three entire battalions of Native Infantry, which had behaved admirably under a much heavier cannonade at Assaye, into confusion. They took refuge in a village, behind which the cavalry were halted in column prior to deployment, leaving the Highlanders and the artillery alone in the field on the right. Fortunately Wellesley was close at hand, and was able to rally these battalions, but much valuable time was wasted. When the line had been formed, the troops advanced in perfect order, the march of the 78th being directed against a battery of nine guns on the enemy's left. As this battery was approached a body of about 800 infantry, supposed to have been Persians, but more probably Arabs, which had been sheltered behind it, charged with the apparent intention of breaking through the interval between the 74th and the 78th. These two regiments, however, closed the interval and pressed on with ported arms to meet the enemy. They were unfortunately prevented from closing with the bayonet by a deep muddy *nala* but they maintained a steady fire until the attacking force, which displayed the most obstinate courage, was entirely destroyed. Sindhya's cavalry charged the 1-6th Native Infantry on the left of the line, next to the 94th, but were repulsed, and the Maratha army then broke and fled in confusion, leaving the whole of their artillery and ammunition in the hands of the victors. The British Cavalry pursued them for several miles, destroying great numbers and capturing many elephants and camels, and much baggage, and the Mughal and Mysore cavalry continued the pursuit, doing the enemy much damage. Wellesley wrote that had there been one hour's more daylight not a man of the enemy would have escaped, and the delay caused by the unaccountable panic of some of his best native infantry was a great disappointment to him. As it was the Marathas were completely demoralised. Vithal Pant, who commanded Bhonsla's cavalry, was killed, and Gopal Bhau, who commanded Sindhya's cavalry, was wounded.

Although the enemy offered a less obstinate resistance than at Assaye, the troops had an arduous task to perform. They were under arms and Wellesley was in the saddle from 6 A.M., till midnight, the cavalry continuing the pursuit by moonlight. The British losses were not heavy. They amounted to 15 rank and file killed and 9 officers and 15 rank and file wounded among the British, and 31 rank and file killed, 148 wounded, and 5 missing among the native troops. Of the two Highland Regiments engaged, Wellesley wrote in his despatch: "The 74th and 78th Regiments had a particular opportunity of distinguishing themselves, and have deserved and received my thanks." The Mughal cavalry under Salabat Khan and the Mysore cavalry under Bisnappa Pandit were also mentioned as having distinguished themselves. In a demi-official letter, dated the 6th December 1803, addressed to Colonel Close, the Resident of Poona, Wellesley said: "Our late victory was grand; it has made a great impression throughout the country. Indeed between the great destruction there dealt out and the consequent desertion of troops, the enemy have but few troops left, and I anxiously hope that they will come within reach to allow me to give them a parting blow with our cavalry only."

After this signal victory Wellesley marched towards Gawilgarh, a fortress in the Satpuras to the north-east of Ellichpur, held for Raghuji Bhonsla.

III.—Gawilgarh.

General Wellesley's objective after the victory of Argaon was the hill fort of Gawilgarh, held for Raghuji Bhonsla by the Rajput, Beni Singh. Marching from Pathardi through Akot and then along the foot of the Satpuras, Wellesley reached Ellichpur on December 5, and halted there to make his preparations for storming the fortress and to establish a hospital for his wounded. On the 7th Wellesley's and Stevenson's division marched from Ellichpur, the former towards Deogaon below the southern face of the fort, and the latter by a track about thirty miles in length, through the hills, to the village of Labada, situated immediately to the north of the fort, and on the same level, the Chikalda plateau, on which Labada was situate, being joined to the Gawilgarh hill by a *col.* The fort itself is thus described by Wellesley: "The fort of Gawilgarh is situated in a range of mountains between the sources of the rivers Purna and Tapti. It stands on a lofty mountain in this range, and consists of one complete inner fort, which fronts to the south, where the rock is most steep; and an outer fort, which covers the inner to the north-west and north. This outer fort has a third wall, which cover the approach to it from the north by the village of Labada. All these walls are strongly built and fortified by ramparts and towers."

From the 7th to the 12th of December, Stevenson's division underwent great hardships, dragging the heavy ordnance and stores by hand over mountains and through ravines by roads which the troops themselves made for the occasion. On the 12th Stevenson established himself at Labada, and on that night erected two batteries opposite to the north face of the outer fort, where the principal assault was to be made. On the same night Wellesley's division erected a battery on a hill under the southern gate, the Fath Darwaza, but this battery was of little use except to distract the enemy's attention from the attack on the north face, for the heavy iron guns could not be moved to the top of the hill and the brass guns produced but little effect.

On the morning of December 13 all the batteries opened fire on the fort, and by the night of the 14th the breaches in the northern face were practicable, and all arrangements had been made for storming the place. The storming party consisted of the flank companies of His Majesty's 94th Regiment and of the Native Corps in Stevenson's division, and was commanded by Lieutenant-Colonel Kenny, of the 11th Madras Native Infantry. It was supported by the battalion companies of the 94th and Lieutenant-Colonel Halyburton's Brigade, Lieutenant-Colonel Macleane's Brigade being in reserve; and the attack was made at 10 A.M. At the same time Wellesley made two attacks from the south. One attack was directed against the southern gate: the attacking party consisting of the 74th Highlanders, five companies of the 78th Highlanders, and the 1-8th Madras Native Infantry, under the command of Lieutenant-Colonel Wallace, of the 74th, and the objective of the other was the north-western gate, the attacking party consisting of the remaining five companies of the 78th Highlanders and the 1-10th Madras Native Infantry, under the command of Lieutenant-Colonel Chalmers.

The fort was strongly garrisoned by Rajputs, and by a great part of Beni Singh's regular infantry, which had escaped from the battle of Argaon, and the garrison was commanded by Beni Singh.

The principal attack, as has been said, was Stevenson's attack on the north face, Wellesley's two attacks from the south being designed merely to distract the enemy's attention, unless it should be found possible to blow in the gates. Neither of the gates was blown in, but Chalmers's column was able to perform useful service, for it arrived at the north-western gate at the same time as a detachment sent forward by Stevenson, who had effected an entrance into the outer fort, to establish communication with Chalmers, and in time to intercept considerable numbers of the enemy who were flying from that detachment through the gate. Chalmers was thus enabled not only to enter the outer fort without difficulty, and thus join forces with Stevenson for the attack on the northern face of the inner fort, but also to destroy large numbers of the fleeing enemy.

The next task of the besiegers was to effect an entrance into the inner fort, the wall of which had not been breached, and some ineffectual attempts were made to force an entrance by the Delhi Gate which is the strongest gate in the fort, and is exceedingly well provided with flank defences, on the Indian system of fortification. A place was then found where it was possible to escalade the wall, and Captain Campbell, with the light company of the 94th, fixed the ladders, escaladed the wall, and opened the Delhi Gate to the storming party. After a brief resistance the fort was in the possession of the besiegers, but the slaughter of the enemy was very great, especially at the gates. The bodies of the *qalahdar* and Beni Singh were found amidst a heap of slain inside the Delhi Gate. Some of the Rajputs, including these two men, attempted to perform the rite of *jauhar* before sallying out to meet the besiegers, but fortunately the work was clumsily done, for of twelve or fourteen women only three were found to be dead, some of the others being wounded. The survivors were treated with respect and were well cared for.

The British losses were very small, considering the nature of the operation. Among the British troops three officers were wounded, of whom two, Lieutenant-Colonel Kenny, of the 11th Native Infatry, and Lieutenant Young, of the 2-7th Native Infantry, died, and five rank-and-file were killed and 59 wounded. The casualties among the native troops were eight killed and 51 wounded.

General Sir Jasper Nicolls in his diary praises the personal bravery of Beni Singh and the *qalahdar*, but adds that they did not seem to have been able to frame any regular plan for the defence of the inner wall, or to have infused much of their own spirit into their sepoys. It is indeed evident, from the insignificance of the besiegers' losses, that the victories of Assaye and Argaon had cowed the troops of the Marathas and that the defence of the fort was far from being resolute. The difficulties with which the attacking force had to contend arose principally from the nature of the country. Stevenson's arduous march through the hills has already been mentioned. Of this feat Wellesley wrote, "the troops in his division went through a series of laborious services, such as I never before witnessed, with the utmost cheerfulness and perseverance." Wellesley's own division was less severely tried, but the erection of a battery on the hill under the southern gate must have entailed much heavy labour, and their operations on December 15 must have been most exhausting, for the approaches to the fort from the south are exceedingly difficult.

Two days after the fall of Gawilgarh a treaty was signed at Deogaon, Wellesley's headquarters, by which Raghuji Bhonsla agreed to withdraw from the plains of Berar to the east of the river Wardha, retaining, however, the fortresses of Gawilgarh and Narnala, and the hill tract in which they are situate. This treaty, which was described by the Governor-General in a private letter to his brother as "wise, honourable, and glorious," was followed by a treaty of peace with Sindhya signed on December 30, 1803. These two treaties brought the war in the Deccan to an honourable conclusion.

APPENDIX.

DYNASTIC LISTS.

(1)—The Yadavas of Deogir.

A.D.

1187 (1) Bhillama I.

1191 (2) Jaitrapala I, son of (1).

1210 (3) Singhana, son of (2),
Jaitrapala II, son of (3),

1247 (4) Krishna, son of Jaitrapala II.

1260 (5) Mahadeo, son of Jaitrapala II.

1271 (6) Ramchandra or Ramdeo, son of (4).

1309 (7) Shankar, son of (6).

(8) Harpal, son-in-law of (6), put to death in 1318.

(2)—The Kakatiyas of Warangal.

(1) Tribhuvanamalla Betmaraja.

1150 (2) Prodaraja or Prolaraja, son of (1).

1163 (3) Prataparudradeva I, son of (2).

(4) Mahadeo.

1231 (5) Ganpati, son of (4).

1257 (6) Rudrammadevi, wife of (5).

1294 (7) Prataparudradeva II, grandson of (5).

1325 (8) Krishna (? Kanhayya.)

(3)—The Hoysalas of Dvaravatipura or Dhorasamudra.

1048 (1) Vinayaditya.

(2) Ereyanga, son of (1).

1103 (3) Ballala I, son of (2).

1117 (4) Tribhuvanamalla Vishnuvardhana, son of (2).

1159 (5) Tribhuvanamalla Nrisimha I, son of (4).

1173 (6) Tribhuvanamalla Vira Ballala II, son of (5).

1224 (7) Nrisimha II, son of (6).

1234 (8) Vira Someshvara, son of (7).

1254 (9) Vira Nrisimha III, son of (8).

1292 (10) Vira Ballala III, son of (9).

(4)—The Khaljis of Delhi.

A.D.

1290 (1) Jalal-ud-din Firuz Shah II.
1296 (2) Rukn-ud-din Ibrahim Shah I, son of (1).
1296 (3) Ala-ud-din Muhammad Shah I, nephew of (1).
1316 (4) Shahab-ud-din Umar Shah, son of (3).
1316 (5) Qutb-ud-din Mubarak Shah I, son of (3).
1320 (6) Nasir-ud-din Khusrav Shah, slave of (5).

(5)—The Tughlaqs of Delhi.

1320 (1) Ghiyas-ud-din Tughlaq Shah I.
1325 (2) Muhammad II bin Tughlaq, son of (1).
1351 (3) Firuz Shah III, nephew of (1).
1388 (4) Tughlaq Shah II, grandson of (3).
1389 (5) Abubakr Shah, grandson of (3).
1389 (6) Muhammad Shah III, son of (3).
1394 (7) Sikandar Shah I, son of (6).
1394 (8) Mahmud Shah II, son of (6).
1395 (9) Nusrat Shah, grandson of (3).
1399 Mahmud restored.
1412 (10) Daulat Khan Lodi.

(6)—First Dynasty of Vijayanagar.

(1) Sangama I.
1339 (2) Harihara I, son of (1).
1354 (3) Bukka I, son of (1).
1379 (4) Harihara II, son of (2).
1406 (5) Bukka II, son of (4).
1408 (6) Devaraya I, son of (4).
1413 (7) Vira Vijaya, son of (6).
1424 (8) Devaraya II, son of (7).
1453 (9) Mallikarjuna, son of (8).
1470 (10) Virupaksha I, son of (8).
1479 (11) Rajashekhara, son of (9).
1483 (12) Virupaksha II, son of (9).

(7)—Second Dynasty of Vijayanagar.

A. D.

1455? (1) Timma.

(2) Ishvara.

1473 (3) Narasa or Nrisimha, son of (2).

(4) Vira Nrisimha.

1508 (5) Krishnaraya, son of (3).

1530 (6) Venkataraya.

1542 (7) Sadashivaraya, slain at Talikota, A. D. 1565.

(8)—The Bahmanis of Gulbarga and Bidar

1347 (1) Ala-ud-din Bahman Shah I.

1358 (2) Muhammad Shah I, son of (1).

1375 (3) Mujahid Shah, son of (2).

1378 (4) Daud Shah, son of (1).

1378 (5) Muhammad* Shah II, grandson of (1).

1397 (6) Ghiyas-ud-din Shah, son of (5).

1397 (7) Shams-ud-din Shah, son of (5).

1397 (8) Firuz Shah, grandson of (1).

1422 (9) Ahmad Shah Wali I, grandson of (1).

1435 (10) Ala-ud-din Ahmad Shah II, son of (9).

1458 (11) Humayun Shah (Zalim), son of (10).

1461 (12) Nizam Shah, son of (11).

1463 (13) Muhammad Shah III, (Lashkari) son of (11).

1482 (14) Mahmud Shah, son of (13).

1518 (15) Ahmad Shah III, son of (14).

1529 (16) Ala-ud-din Shah III, son of (14).

1523 (17) Wali-ullah Shah, son of (14).

1525 (18) Kalimullah Shah, son or brother of (14), died A.D. 1526 or 1527.

(9)—Kings of Gujarat.

1396 (1) Muzaffar Shah I.

1411 (2) Ahmad Shah I, grandson of (1).

1442 (3) Muhammad Karim Shah, son of (2).

1451 (4) Qutb-ud-din Shah, son of (3)

1459 (5) Daud Shah, son of (2).

*Wrongly styled Mahmud by Firishta.

A.D.

1459 (6) Mahmud Shah I, Baigarah, son of (3).

1511 (7) Muzaffar Shah II, son of (6).

1526 (8) Sikandar Shah, son of (7).

1526 (9) Nasir Khan Mahmud II, son of (7).

1526 (10) Bahadur Shah, son of (7).

1536 (11) Miran Muhammad Shah Faruqi of Khandesh, grandson of (7).

1537 (12) Mahmud Shah III, bin Latif, grandson of (7).

1553 (13) Ahmad Shah II.

1561 (14) Muzaffar Shah III, Habib, son of (12), surrendered to Akbar in 1572.

(10)—The Khaljis of Malwa.

1436 (1) Mahmud Shah I, Khalji.

1475 (2) Ghiyas Shah, son of (1).

1500 (3) Nasir Shah, son of (2).

1510 (4) Mahmud Shah II, son of (3), Malwa annexed by Gujarat, 1530.

(11)—The Faruqi Kings of Khandesh.

1370 (1) Malik Raja.

1399 (2) Nasir Khan.

1437 (3) Miran Adil Khan I.

1441 (4) Miran Mubarak I.

1457 (5) Adil Khan II.

1503 (6) Daud Khan.

1510 (7) Adil Khan III.

1520 (8) Miran Muhammad Shah I.

1535 (9) Miran Mubarak II.

1566 (10) Miran Muhammad II.

1576 (11) Raja Ali Khan.

1596 (12) Bahadur Shah.

(12)—The Adil Shahi Kings of Bijapur.

1490 (1) Yusuf Adil Shah.

1510 (2) Ismail Adil Shah, son of (1).

1534 (3) Mallu Adil Shah, son of (2).

A.D.

1534 (4) Ibrahim Adil Shah I, son of (2).
1557 (5) Ali Adil Shah I, son of (4).
1580 (6) Ibrahim Adil Shah II, son of (5).
1628 (7) Muhammad Adil Shah, son of (6).
1656 (8) Ali Adil Shah II, son of (7).
1672 (9) Sikandar Adil Shah. Bijapur taken by Aurangzib 1686

(13)—The Nizam Shahi Kings of Ahmadnagar.

1490 (1) Ahmad Nizam Shah.
1518 (2) Burhan Nizam Shah I, son of (1).
1554 (3) Husain Nizam Shah I, son of (2).
1565 (4) Murtaza Nizam Shah I, son of (3).
1586 (5) Husain Nizam Shah II, son of (4).
1589 (6) Ismail Nizam Shah, cousin of (5).
1590 (7) Burhan Nizam Shah II, father of (6).
1594 (8) Ibrahim Nizam Shah, son of (7).
1595 (9) Ahmad Nizam Shah II, usurper.
1595 (10) Bahadur Nizam Shah, son of (8).
1603 (11) Murtaza Nizam Shah II, grandson of (2).
1630 (12) Husain Nizam Shah III, son of (11), taken prisoner 1633.

(14)—The Qutb Shahi Kings of Golconda.

1512 (1) Sultan Quli Qutb Shah.
1543 (2) Jamshid Qutb Shah, son of (1).
1550 (3) Subhan Quli Qutb Shah, son of (2).
1550 (4) Ibrahim Qutb Shah, son of (1).
1580 (5) Muhammad Quli Qutb Shah, son of (4).
1612 (6) Muhammad Qutb Shah, nephew of (5).
1626 (7) Abdullah Qutb Shah, son of (6).
1672 (8) Abul Hasan Qutb Shah, son-in-law of (7), sent into captivity 1687.

(15)—The Imad Shahi Kings of Berar.

1490 (1) Fathullah Imad Shah.
1504 (2) Ala-ud-din Imad Shah, son of (1).

A.D.

1529 (3) Darya Imad Shah, son of (2).

1560 (4) Burhan Imad Shah, son of (3). Tufal Khan usurped the throne and Berar was annexed by Ahmadnagar in 1572.

(16)—The Barid Shahi Kings of Bidar.

1487 (1) Qasim Barid.

1504 (2) Amir Ali Barid, son of (1).

1542 (3) Ali Barid Shah, son of (2).

1579 (4) Ibrahim Barid Shah, son of (3).

1586 (5) Qasim Barid Shah II, son of (4).

1589 (6) Amir Barid Shah, cousin of (5).

1601 (7) Mirza Ali Barid Shah, cousin of (6).

1609 (8) Ali Barid Shah II, imprisoned in Bijapur, 1619

(17)—Emperors of Delhi, of the House of Timur.

1525 (1) Babar.

1530 (2) Humayun, son of (1), Interregnum.

(2) Humayun restored.

1556 (3) Akbar, son of (2).

1605 (4) Jahangir, son of (3).

1628 (5) Shahjahan, son of (4).

1658 (6) Aurangzib Alamgir, son of (5).

1707 (7) Shah Alam Bahadur Shah, son of (6).

1712 (8) Jahandar Shah, son of (7).

1712 (9) Farrukhsiyar, nephew of (8).

1719 (10) Rafi-ud-darajat, cousin of (9).

1719 (11) Rafi-ud-daulah, brother of (10).

1720 (12) Muhammad Shah, cousin of (11).

1748 (13) Ahmad Shah, son of (12).

1754 (14) Alamgir II, son of (8).

1759 (15) Shah Alam II, son of (14).

1806 (16) Akbar II, son of (15).

1820 (17) Bahadur Shah, son of (16). Died at Rangoon, November 7, 1862.

(18)—The Nizams of Haidarabad.

A.D.		
1724	(1)	Chin Qilij Khan, Asaf Jah, Nizam-ul-Mulk.
1748	(2)	Nasir Jang, son of (1).
1750	(3)	Muzaffar Jang, grandson of (1).
1751	(4)	Salabat Jang, son of (1).
1763	(5)	Nizam Ali, Asaf Jah, son of (1).
1803	(6)	Sikandar Jah, son of (5).
1829	(7)	Nasir-ud-daulah, son of (6).
1857	(8)	Afzal-ud-daulah, son of (7).
1869	(9)	Mir Sir Mahbub Ali Khan, G.C.B., G.C.S.I., Asaf Jah, Nizam-ul-Mulk.

Pioneer Press, No. 1231.—16·10·07.